Patterns
of Architecture

Architectural Design
November/December 2009

Guest-edited by Mark Garcia

IN THIS ISSUE
Main Section

OFFICE POLITICS
Alejandro Zaera-Polo of Foreign Office Architects explores the political and cultural opportunities of sophisticated patterning techniques on the building envelope, which usurp traditional and contemporary iconography in their ability to bridge the local and the global. P 18

PATTERNING PARAMETRICALLY
Patrik Schumacher of Zaha Hadid Architects advocates the application of surface pattern design in parametric architecture as a significant means of architectural articulation, providing the exterior surface with various levels of differentiation and correlation. P 28

THE PATTERN ENGINEER
In an exclusive interview with Mark Garcia,
Hanif Kara of Adams Kara Taylor extols the many applications of patterns in structural engineering, from the micro to the meta. P 66

SYLVAN STUDIES
Jayne Merkel describes how Hopkins Architects have provided Yale University's pioneering School of Forestry and Environmental Studies with a living laboratory of energy-efficient design. P 118+

WILEY
wiley.com

Architectural Design

Vol 79, No 6 (November/December 2009)
ISSN 0003-8504

Profile No 202
ISBN 978-0470 699591

Editorial Offices
John Wiley & Sons
International House
Ealing Broadway Centre
London W5 5DB

T: +44 (0)20 8326 3800

Editor
Helen Castle

Regular columnists: Valentina Croci, David
Littlefield, Jayne Merkel, Will McLean, Neil
Spiller, Michael Weinstock and Ken Yeang

Freelance Managing Editor
Caroline Ellerby

Production Editor
Elizabeth Gongde

Design and Prepress
Artmedia, London

Printed in Italy by Conti Tipocolor

Sponsorship/advertising
Faith Pidduck/Wayne Frost
T: +44 (0)1243 770254
E: fpidduck@wiley.co.uk

Front cover: AD Parametric patterned spaces:
AD logotype transformed into a series of illusory,
emergent patterns. Cover concept by Mark
Garcia. Designed by Chrysostomos
Tsimourdagkas, PhD Candidate, Department of
Architecture, Royal College of Art, London. ©
2009 Chrysostomos Tsimourdagkas. Back cover:
© German Aerospace Center (DLR) Global
landcover facility (GLCF)

Editorial Board

Subscribe to AD

AD is published bimonthly and is available to
purchase on both a subscription basis and as
individual volumes at the following prices.

PRICES
Individual copies: £22.99/$45.00
Mailing fees may apply

ANNUAL SUBSCRIPTION RATES
Student: UK£70/US$110 print only
Individual: UK £110/US$170 print only
Institutional: UK£180/US$335 print or online
Institutional: UK£198/US$369 combined print
and online

Subscription Offices UK
John Wiley & Sons Ltd
Journals Administration Department
1 Oldlands Way, Bognor Regis
West Sussex, PO22 9SA
T: +44 (0)1243 843272
F: +44 (0)1243 843232
E: cs-journals@wiley.co.uk

[ISSN: 0003-8504]

Prices are for six issues and include postage
and handling charges. Periodicals postage
paid at Jamaica, NY 11431. Air freight and
mailing in the USA by Publications Expediting
Services Inc, 200 Meacham Avenue, Elmont,
NY 11003.
Individual rate subscriptions must be paid by
personal cheque or credit card. Individual rate
subscriptions may not be resold or used as
library copies.

All prices are subject to change
without notice.

Postmaster
Send address changes to 3 Publications
Expediting Services, 200 Meacham Avenue,
Elmont, NY 11003

RIGHTS AND PERMISSIONS
Requests to the Publisher should be
addressed to:
Permissions Department
John Wiley & Sons Ltd
The Atrium
Southern Gate
Chichester
West Sussex PO19 8SQ
England

F: +44 (0)1243 770620
E: permreq@wiley.co.uk

CONTENTS

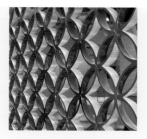

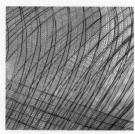

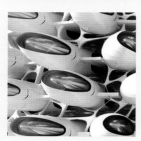

Editorial

Helen Castle

In this issue, guest-editor Mark Garcia captures the *Zeitgeist*. He not only asserts the significant place that patterns now have in contemporary architecture – whether it is in terms of iconography, formalism, urban pattern recognition, landscape design, structural engineering or interior design – but also their newfound integrity. For many centuries, architects have had an ambivalent relationship with pattern. Patterns have smacked of the imitative: with the speculative builder or mason supposedly 'unknowingly' copying decorative detailing from pattern books. They have also hinted of the profligate and the extraneous, suggesting an excessive application of surface ornament more characteristic of the vernacular builder than the trained architect. For the architectural profession, which is all too wary of the need to retain its position as designers of the tectonic and the tectonic alone, patterns can also occupy a place far too close to the decorative – the domain of the interior decorator rather than the architect. In everyday life, pattern has also taken on derogatory overtones. References to 'patterned

carpets' or 'patterned wallpaper' in someone's home all too easily implying unbridled decoration and taste.

Patterns' newfound integrity in architecture can be explained to some degree by the fundamental role that they play in computer science, artificial intelligence and biology, as a series or sequence of repeated elements. This has made architects realise that patterns are not just skin deep, a matter of decoration, but are intrinsic to the natural and the man-made world. The shift in discussion is from the notion of pattern-making alone to pattern recognition. The recognition of particular urban patterns, for instance, is an essential analytical tool for urban designers or for landscape architects for whom work has to be site specific. It is also just as important for architects and engineers seeking a biomimetic approach, learning from the patterns evident in biological systems. The elevation of patterns from their previously lowly position in architectural culture, enabled by their recognition in the natural and computer sciences, has also allowed a new take on pattern-making to emerge. This is most apparent here with Patrik Schumacher of Zaha Hadid Architects espousing the application of surface pattern design in parametric architecture as a significant means of architectural articulation, and Alejandro Zaera-Polo of Foreign Office Architects exploring the possibilities of patterns as a new type of iconography that can build new bridges by transcending the local and the global. For it seems the act of pattern recognition has liberated architecture from one of its demons, so that it is able to put some of its self-imposed reservations about patterns behind it and start to realise the significance and possibilities of pattern-making in design. ∆

Text © 2009 John Wiley & Sons Ltd. Images: p 4 © Steve Gorton; p 5 © NASA, ESA, and E Peng (Peking University, Beijing)

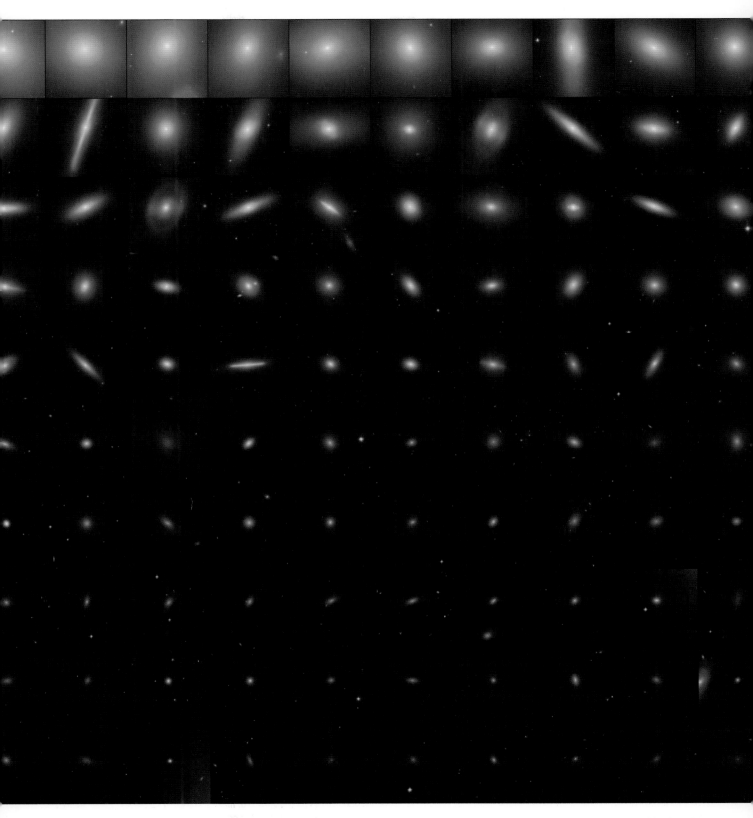

Hubble ACS image of 100 Virgo cluster galaxies. Patterns of galaxies/galaxies of patterns: ubiquitous and universal natural patterns stretch on into infinity.

5

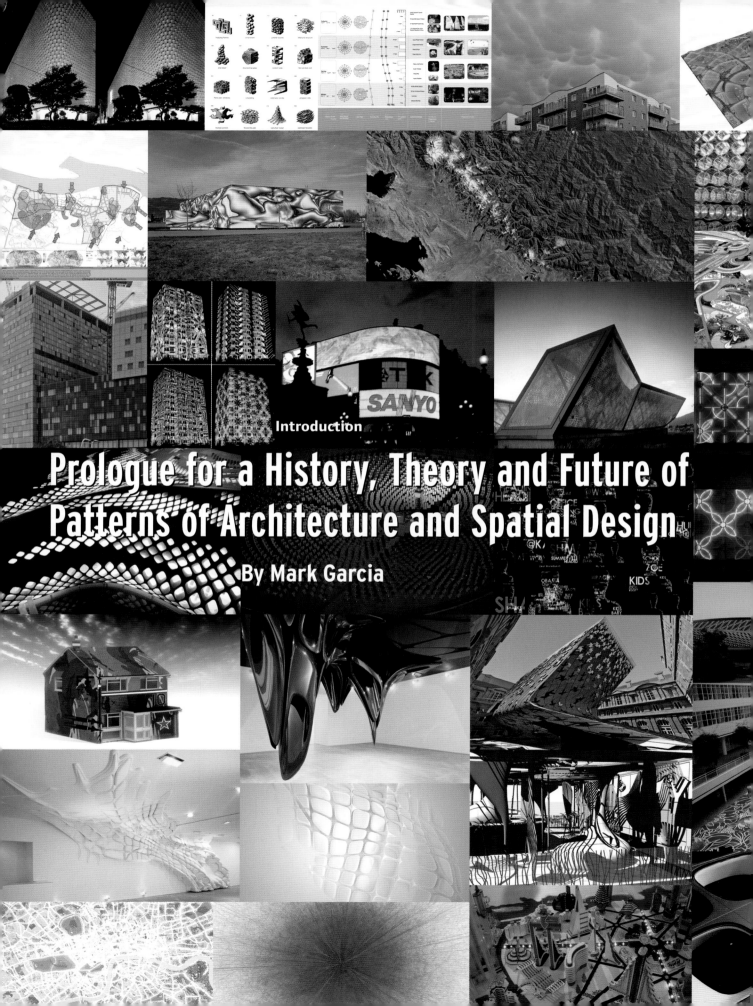

Introduction

Prologue for a History, Theory and Future of Patterns of Architecture and Spatial Design

By Mark Garcia

Left to right:

Top row: UNStudio, Seoul department store, 2007; François Blanciak, Patterned Siteless Architectures, 2008; Ken Yeang, Public Plaza, Macau, 2008; Rare breast-pattern Mammatucumulus clouds over Stepney, London, 14 July 2009; Centre for Advanced Spatial Analysis (CASA), Virtual London pattern of air pollution in central London, 2007; Amanda Levete Architects, Central Embassy, Bangkok, Thailand, 2009; Ken Yeang, Green Square, Sydney, 2008.

Second row: Ken Yeang, Huanan City, Guangzhou, China, 2008; Dietrich | Untertrifaller Architekten, Walch's Event Catering, Lustenau, Austria, 2000; German Aerospace Agency, Satellite multispectral photograph of Bolivia; Jun Aoki, Louis Vuitton store, Tokyo, 2002; Gemma Douglas (Department of Architecture, Royal College of Art), UKHO, 2008; Amanda Levete Architects, Central Embassy, Bangkok, Thailand, 2009.

Third row: HOK, Royal London Hospital, Whitechapel, 2009; The same Modernist building projected with different patterns to mark the opening of the third Luminale festival in Frankfurt am Main, 2006; Hypermedia- and trans-architectures have shifted patterned architectures into a virtual, digital realm where rapidly changing, interactive screens and projections are transforming architecture and urban/public spaces into spatial pattern-machines/factories; Daly Genik, Art Center College of Design South Campus Building, Pasadena, California, 2004; Astrid Krogh, Danish Parliament Building, 2008; Nigel Coates, Structural 'Henna' pattern for the Finger City building in Mixtacity, Thames Gateway, 2008.

Fourth row: Reiser + Umemoto, Terminal 3, Shenzhen Airport, China, 2008; The Solar One farm near Barstow, California; Alex Dragulescu and Judith Donath (MIT Sociable Media Group), Lexigraphs I, 2008; Astrid Krogh, Danish Parliament Building, 2008; Daniel Libeskind, The Spiral: Extension to the Victoria & Albert Museum, London, 1996.

Fifth row: FAT, Camouflage House, 1996; Zaha Hadid Architects, Stalactites installation, Sonnabend and ROVE Galleries, New York, 2008; Zaha Hadid Architects, Louvre Museum extension, Paris, 2007; Zaha Hadid Architects, Zaragoza Bridge Pavilion, 2008; Zaha Hadid Architects, Port House, Antwerp, 2009.

Sixth row: Zaha Hadid Architects, Kartal Pendik installation, Sonnabend and ROVE Galleries, New York, 2008; Zaha Hadid Architects, Kartal Pendik, Istanbul, Turkey, 2007; SMC Alsop, Dubai Creek Ferry Terminal, 2009; Michael Lin, Floor of Tulips in Atrium City Hall, The Hague, 2002; SANAA, Dior store, Toyko, 2003; Toyo Ito, Todd's Store, Tokyo, 2004; Klein Dytham Architecture, Central East Tokyo, Nihonbashi, Tokyo, 2004

Seventh row: Simon Elvins, Silent London, 2005; Neil Banas, Rosette, 2008; Bodyz Isek Kingelez, Ville de Sete. Detail of the Afro-futurist critical regionalist patterns on the model of this African city in AD 3009; Reiser + Umemoto, Terminal 3, Shenzhen Airport, China, 2008; Marina Appolonio, 'Spazio ad Attivazione Cinetica', Hesse, Germany, 2007; Michal Slowinski (Department of Architecture, Royal College of Art), 3-D pattern of the Internet and its connectivity in Battersea, London, 2008.

Images (left to right). Top row: © Christian Richters; © François Blanciak; © Ken Yeang; © Mark Garcia; © Centre for Advanced Spatial Analysis, University College London and Environmental Research Group at Kings College London; © Amanda Levete Architects; © Ken Yeang. Second row: © Ken Yeang; © Ignacio Martinez; © German Aerospace Center (DLR)/Global Landcover Facility (GLCF); © Mark Garcia; © Gemma Douglas; © Amanda Levete Architects. Third Row: © Mark Garcia; © Ann Dedert/epa/Corbis); © Mark Garcia; © Nic Lehoux; © Astrid Krogh; © Nigel Coates. Fourth row: © Reiser + Umemoto; © Grafton Marshall Smith/Corbis; © The Sociable Media Group, MIT Media Lab; © Astrid Krogh; © Studio Daniel Libeskind, photo courtesy of Miller Hare. Fifth row: © Fashion Architecture Taste (FAT) Ltd; © Isa Wipfli; © Zaha Hadid Architects. Sixth row: © Isa Wipfli; © Zaha Hadid Architects; © Alsop Architects; © Photo Yvonne Eeuwes, courtesy Stroom, The Hague; © Mark Garcia; © Klein Dytham architecture. Seventh row: © Simon Elvins (original data collected by DEFRA - Department for Environment, Food and Rural Affairs); © Neil Banas, neilbanas.com; © Mark Garcia; © Reiser + Umemoto; © Frank Rupenhorst/dpa/Corbis; © Michal Slowinski.

It is not unreasonable to regard patterns as a fundamental ontological reality ... as we apply our intelligence, and the extension of our intelligence called technology, to understanding the powerful patterns in our world (for example, human intelligence), we can re-create – and extend! – these patterns in other substrates ... It's through the emergent powers of the pattern that we transcend ... The power of patterns to endure goes beyond explicitly self-replicating systems, such as organisms and self-replicating technology. It is the persistence and power of patterns that support life and intelligence. The pattern is far more important than the material stuff that constitutes it.
Ray Kurzweil, *The Singularity is Near*, 2005, p 478[1]

Hervé Graumann, Vanite 2, 2003
Defamiliarisation and deconstruction of representation, reference, sign and meaning through 3-D spatial pattern.

Paradoxically, the most original and significant patterns in spatial design are now often the most inconspicuous. It is the invisible, immaterial, dynamic, intangible, conceptual and virtual patterns of space that constitute its future. Sufficiently, but not necessarily, dependent on the classical and traditional concept of patterns (as formal, material, ornamental and decorative), the most innovative are now the stealthier patterns of the contents, contexts and consequences of space on ourselves and our world. To understand the origins of this seeming aporia, we need to consider the histories and theories of patterns, and other, wider, multidisciplinary patterns research.

The etymology of 'pattern' is from the Latin *pater*, or *patronus*, meaning father, patron, god or master, from which is derived the notion of pattern as a model, example, matrix, stencil or mould. The contemporary concept of pattern is as a sequence, distribution, structure or progression, a series or frequency of a repeated/repeating unit, system or process of identical or similar elements. Synonyms and related concepts include habit, meme, template, motif, configuration, organisation, arrangement, figure, tessellation, system, process, sample, duplicate, convention and texture. This multiplicity of meanings points to the manifold roles of pattern in the creation, reproduction, evolution and processes of space.

It is therefore unsurprising that humans have evolved so that the bulk of our brain activity is now constituted by trillions of (often unintentional, unconscious) pattern-perception and recognition tasks. Some patterns can be perceived in the mind's eye (as with forms of synaesthesia and Asperger's or Savant syndromes), or directly hallucinated, for example in the case of psychedelics or in psychological, neurological or optical disorders. Certain kinds of pattern cause powerful physiological effects such as stress, nausea, vomiting of blood and convulsions, as

in the medical condition known as 'pattern-induced epilepsy'. And compulsive, neurotic and paranoid spatialised pattern recognition defines the psychotic condition of apophenia (the experience of seeing patterns or connections in random or meaningless data).

The intuitive, unintentional, autopoietic recognition and production of patterns (and of their meaning/s) is also part of creative processes.[2] That the perception, recognition or design of a spatialised pattern can be the basis of new knowledge and understanding is a fundamental principle of information design/visualisation and in graphic, interaction and systems design. As information architect and designer Richard Saul Wurman explains: 'I can see patterns when I understand things. I see the world as visual patterns of connectivity. I think pattern recognition is a fundamental part of a creative mind ... I see everything as patterns.'[3] But the most compelling reason for an urgent reappraisal of contemporary and future spatial design patterns is that new technologies are accelerating and expanding the kinds of spatial pattern that can be designed. It is timely, then, to consider the possibilities for rethinking ourselves in relation to the impacts of the technological shifts in the design of our spatial patterns.

Patterns in Spatial Design
Patterns are a fundamental feature of spatial design (interior, architectural, urban and landscape). The physical world and our bodies act as constraints (productive and malignant) on the patterns we design, build and use, and the patterns emerging from the interactions between these multiple systems are produced at a number of different dimensional, temporal and scalar levels, including the spectrum of natural and man-made patterns. As process (method, technique) and as product (object, material form), patterns, like typologies and

programmes, are also repeated and human-imposed spatial design solutions, concepts and effects. Each theory, design and space has its own unique identity patterns that record and fingerprint index the different kinds of spatial patterns that constitute its histories and forms of habitus and territorialisation. This is partly why and how pattern can also become, or be made to be, logo, brand, icon and place. But what kinds of space and place can patterns be designed to make? As the histories and theories of spatial patterns design research suggest, it is new technologies that are most significantly changing and centralising the roles of patterns in the futures of space and place design.

The History of Spatial Patterns

Despite their abstract appearance, even early, Neolithic patterns are thought to be symbolic, diagrammatic and apotropaic. The apotropaic function of patterns (designed to avert evil spirits by engaging them in the unravelling of an impossibly, complex design) signals also the pleasures of pattern remaking and unmaking, as with cryptography, puzzles, jigsaws, riddles and enigmas.[4] The first significant theoretical reference to spatial patterns in the Western tradition was in Plato's *Timaeus*, in which he described the world as filled with patterns of closely packed atom-like solids and geometric forms. Pattern has always been the DNA, or diagram, of style. Pattern as style, detail, ornament, decoration, adornment, embellishment and structure was (in the Western/European tradition) deeply influenced by religion,

Frank Gehry, Guggenheim Museum, Bilbao, Spain, 1997
Titanium cladding of the museum envelope, acquiring patterns of use, atmosphere, climate and time.

geometry and maths as well as the arts, design and crafts. The concepts and theories through which spatial pattern was theorised include *order, hierarchy, organisation, system, scale, proportion, symmetry, balance, complexity, beauty, unity, function, decorum, representation, symbol, joint, nature, expression, imagination and creativity*. Other pattern-related concepts (such as harmony, rhythm, narrative and colour) were influenced by other disciplines in the mechanical and liberal arts. Patrick Healy has documented the range of these,[5] but for Paul Emmons the dominant historical meta-patterns of space were alternately ladders/steps, chains, trees, vortices, concentric circles and orbits.[6]

Aside from applied styling, ornament and decoration, designing and building geometrical and trompe l'oeil optical pattern illusions was practised (from ancient Greece and Rome to the present) by many artists and architects. These patternings were produced for symbolic, theological and philosophical purposes and to enhance (or distort) the meanings, affects and aesthetics of perspective space. They are perhaps the earliest form of non-representational and conceptual virtual spaces. Vitruvius approved of realistic trompe l'oeil optical pattern illusions,[7] and their otherworldly spatial affects (through impossible forms, moiré, interference, parallax, Doppler and other such effects, can be found in many premodern designed spaces like the Mezquita (Great Mosque) of Córdoba (AD 784). Patterns are also fundamental to Islamic architecture because of the central metaphysical concept of *Nizam*, or pattern, a key aesthetic, epistemological and ontological category in Islamic philosophy[8] where wisdom (*tawhid*) consists of recognising and understanding 'patterns within patterns'.[9]

From the emergence of architectural 'pattern books' (at least as early as the 15th century in Europe) to the present, designed patterns have become ever more important to the production of space. Their significance began to accelerate in the late 17th, 18th and 19th centuries with the rise of global capitalism, the Industrial Revolution, and the imperial/colonial and Enlightenment/scientific projects, becoming increasingly aesthetically diverse, materially sophisticated and mechanically and functionally precise. Theorists, architects and designers including Karl Friedrich Schinkel, Johann Joachim Winckelman, John Ruskin, Karl Gottlieb Wilhelm Bötticher, Gottfried Semper, Alöis Reigl, Christopher Dresser and Louis Sullivan, wrote treatises on pattern, and world trade exploded mass-produced patterns around the planet. In the first period of significant taxonomic and morphological research and theorising of patterns, the 18th- and 19th-century pattern theorists (influenced by Darwin and Linnaeus)[10] attempted to find ways of generating sublimely infinite and evolving, biological types of variable (aperiodic) patterns from the simplest of elements.[11]

The 20th century was the first in which designed and made patterns were reclassified as 'art'.[12] The Modern period also produced psychological theorisations of pattern with the founding of the Gestalt (German for 'pattern') school of psychology in 1912. And it was also during this warring period that multivalent Surrealist morphing patterns, camouflage and the use of pattern design for security,

Patterns of ourselves and our identities develop as an integrated system across our bodies, in our spaces and beyond.

A Ndebele home in Botshabelo, South Africa. Ndebele patterns are communicative advertisements, and spatial and design practices, that diagram shifting personal, group, place and other social and auto/biographical narratives.

A Tibetan Buddhist *Kalachakra* (wheel of time) sand mandala. Created by a team of lamas, the sand mandala pattern is also a diagram of a world pattern, a cosmogram, and of a Buddhist divine palace. Mandala patterns have been used to structure Asian cities and buildings from the time of the Buddha to the present.

Yayoi Kusama, *Gleaming Lights of the Soul*, Liverpool Biennial, 2008
Japanese artist Kusama lives with a psychological condition in which she literally sees patterns (dots, flowers and nets) in environments everywhere.

**The Mezquita (Great Mosque),
Córdoba, Spain, AD 784**
Perspectival illusions, after effects,
interference and Doppler-type
effects emerge when visitors walk
around Córdoba's Mezquita.

Suleymaniye Mosque, Istanbul, Turkey, 1550–57
The pattern of individual prayer spaces on the carpet.

**Jakob Prandtauer, Benedictine
Abbey, Melk, Austria, 1702–36**
A late-Baroque spiral staircase
articulated with a tromp l'oeil
moulding pattern.

privacy, dematerialisation and disguise/disarticulation in space was popularised.[13] The stereotyping of Modernism as dogmatically antipattern and against decoration and ornament is inaccurate, as numerous examples attest.[14] Aside from the kitsch mass-production of patterns, Modernist patterns were notable for their associations with Fordism, Taylorism and 'scientific management' (and then later with artificial intelligence, cybernetics, computing, complexity sciences and information theory). In the 1930s they can be found in the work (and particularly the urban plans) of Le Corbusier, the Smithsons (urban pattern layers), Kevin Lynch (city types), DG Emmerich (knot road-patterns), Christopher Tunnard and Boris Pushkarev (city 'scatter patterns'), the Metabolists (particularly Fumihiko Maki's serialist concept of the 'field')[15] and Buckminster Fuller's geodesic, building energies and structural patterns. However, aside from Fuller, the most significant role for patterns in spatial design theory came in 1977 with the publication of Christopher Alexander's book *A Pattern Language*.[16] Alexander's 'pattern language' consisted of 253 spatial patterns, which were summarised as diagrams. Examples include 'carnival', 'old people everywhere', 'dancing in the streets', 'beer hall', 'sleeping in public', 'gradual stiffening', 'something roughly in the middle', 'things from your life' and 'small services without red tape'. Alexander's work influenced, among others, that of Bill Hillier and Julienne Hanson on sociospatial patterns and the subsequent work on 'space syntax' in the 1970s and 1980s, but also, intriguingly, the work of the Sims games designer Will Wright and Italian urbanist Paula Vigano from the 1990s. Since Alexander, many new kinds of patterns, such as fractals, have emerged.[17] However, these have not yet been fully integrated into a coherent history or theorisation of this field.

In the 1980s and 1990s, Postmodernist patterns predominated, and especially those of Robert Venturi,[18] Rem Koolhaas, Stan Allen and Sanford Kwinter (fields), along with historicist, folding, sprawl, cross-programming, high-density/proximity, non-places and other Deconstructivist and high-tech patterns. In 1992, Henri Lefebvre's last book *Rhythmanalysis: Space, Time and Everyday Life* was published.[19] Because Lefebvre's keystone concept of 'rhythm' is identical to 'pattern', it stands (together with Gilles Deleuze and Félix Guattari's notions of 'difference and repetition') among the decade's most important theories of pattern in space. Postmodernist patterns opposed the hygienic, white, rectilinear, legible, navigable, functional, light, rational and transparent ones of Modernism with the fragmented, decentred, warped, heterogeneous, disembodying, delirious, disorientating, formless, chaotic and illusory ones that reflected the fragile contemporary subject and the now more problematic spaces of social and everyday life.

Spatial Patterns of the Present

While Herzog & de Meuron, Jean Nouvel, Venturi Scott Brown, OMA, Zaha Hadid, UNStudio, ONL, MVRDV and Will Alsop have been at the forefront of the spatial pattern design revolution, a number of other organisations (including Future Systems, ALA, Klein Dytham, Reiser + Umemoto, Lab Architecture Studio, Sauerbruch Hutton, LAB[AU], NOX, Daniel Libeskind, FAT, MAKE, Hild Und K, Jüergen Mayer, David Adjaye, ETH Zurich, the MIT SENSEable City Lab, MIT Sociable Media Group, Aranda/Lasch, Popularchitecture and P-A-T-T-E-R-N-S) are also now entering the field. Recent books, journals and exhibitions are also indicative of the patterned turn in spatial design. In 2004, *OASE Ornament* (NAI Publishers) was closely followed, in 2006, by Michael Kubo and Farshid Moussavi's *The Function of Ornament* (2006), Reiser + Umemoto's *Atlas of Novel Tectonics* and Princeton's 306090 *Decoration* (2006). Cecil Balmond released *Element*, a manifesto for patterns in engineering, in 2007,[20] and Birkhauser published *Patterns in Architecture, Art and Design* (2007) and *Pattern (Context Architecture)* (2009).[21] The group exhibition 'Pattern Theory' at MKG127 (Toronto) in 2007, and the Harvard Graduate School of Design 'Patterns: Cases in Synthetic Intelligence Exhibition' in 2008 were also portents in a sample that does not even include many recent pattern compendia and style/swatch catalogues, and sociocultural, geographical, anthropological and ethnographic books on the subject.[22]

This rash of books, shows, designs and designers is evidence of spatial patterns as a whole reorienting towards greater, more high-tech and conceptual, dynamic, virtual, intangible, immaterial and invisible functions, effects and types. It is only new technologies that have allowed design to expand the range of types and the accuracy with which we are now able to visualise, diagram and realise these other, stealthier, more inconspicuous new patterns of designed space. Only now can patterns enhance cultural, social, programmatic *and* environmental, material and structural performance in a single pattern design system. Design has only recently, through new digital design and diagramming techniques, been able to incorporate these stealthier, more inconspicuous new patterns into viable spatial designs.[23] This novel ability to recognise, use and continuously re/design space with these innovative patterns is driving a revolutionary type of more accurately patterned and intelligent spatial designs that goes beyond the old notion of pattern which can include, but also exceed and extend, its historical and limited scope as purely style, ornament and decoration.

Reiser + Umemoto, Terminal 3, Shenzhen Airport, China, 2008
Exterior view and close-up. The parametrically patterned 'dragon's skin' envelope here creates moving internal 4-D 'cloud dapple' light patterns.

Marcin Mostafa, Natalia Paszkowska and Wojciech Kakowski, Polish Pavilion, World Expo, Shanghai, 2010
above: Macroscale Polish lace pattern: a critical regionalist supergraphic superimposition of a national pattern.

Matthew Richie, Benjamin Aranda and Chris Lasch, The Evening Line, Venice Architecture Biennale, 2008
right: A fractal multiscalar 4–D pattern as an evolving, dynamic environment.

Today's spatial design pattern morphologies are mainly digital/parametric or Postmodern reworkings of ancient patterns (like waves) or new ones (like DNA) found or simulated with new and emerging visualisation and design technologies. Among these we find patterns of *soap bubbles, Fibonacci series, hydrological and vascular systems, protein folds, cellular automata, attractors, force fields, Sierpinski cubes, skins, moirés, knots, messes, fractals, networks, swarms/flocks, atoms and molecular structures (including crystals and quasi-crystals), fluid and gas/smoke/meteorological forms and dynamics, architextiles,*[24] *viruses and micro-organisms, blobs, Voronoi cells, Lindenmeyer systems, light, fire, landscapes/geology/geography, rhizomes and various hybrids and permutations of these.*

In many of these designs, the crucial innovation is either technologically enabled patterns and/or patterns as fields, membranes, complex surfaces, deep structures or formless ambient environments and affective atmospheres.[25] The most technically sophisticated are designed using genetic algorithms, and parametrically with software programs such as Grasshopper, Generative Components, Processing and L-Systems. More broadly, the most interesting spatial applications of these new pattern-recognition and application technologies are in the management of urban defence, logistics, transport, resources, services, commodities and crowds, and in disaster control and global communications. This consilience of mathematics, computing and the arts is driving other, high-tech breeds of pattern to create critical new intelligent and high-performance spatial patterns. Some of the most encouraging examples are those being used in socially, politically and culturally engaged interactive architectures (such as those by ONL, Jason Bruges, Electroland, Diller Scofidio + Renfro, ETH Zurich and, particularly, the MIT SENSEable City Lab and the Sociable Media Group).[26] Other examples include developments in new aperiodic, fractal and quasi-crystalline structures as well as spaces in which spatial patterns research is cross-fertilising with the fine arts (Neo-geo, world art/critical-regionalism, Op Art), sciences, technology, anthropology, ethnography, and cultural and media studies.

While spatial designers have managed to assimilate the most salient multidisciplinary patterns research of the past decade or so, there is still much to achieve. With new research into optical illusions and effects, materials advances, progress in computing and other visualisation technologies we can now further expand the ranges of pattern we design to include more critical intangible, immaterial, dynamic, invisible, virtual and conceptual and spaces.[27] But spatial design is lagging behind the spatial patterns revolutions in other disciplines (marketing, advertising, security, defence, retail, finance

left: Hypermedia and transarchitectures projects have shifted patterned architectures into a virtual, digital realm where rapidly changing, interactive screens and projections are transforming architecture and urban/public spaces into spatial pattern-machines/factories.

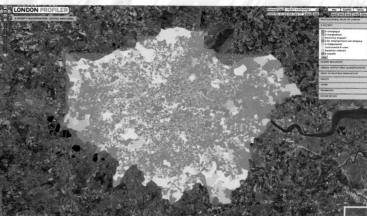

Centre for Advanced Spatial Analysis (CASA), E-Society London, 2009
above: 'E-enabledness', Internet connectivity and other such related digital, virtual and computational indicators now form some of the most powerful urban patterns.

MIT Sociable Media Group, Loom 2, MIT Media Lab, 2001
left: Loom 2 is a pattern of emotions in digital media space – a 'landscape/topography' of the mood of social relations in a newsgroup diagrammed as a pattern of 'angry' words and punctuation.

and government) in which national or international scales of research have been undertaken. These have harnessed massive supercomputing, data-collection and mining, and artificial intelligence systems to find, create, synthesise, design and redesign spatial patterns to a breadth, depth, accuracy and detail that is largely non-existent in the spatial design disciplines. These projects use pattern-recognition software to monitor, predict and profile our spatialised desire, psychological, emotional and other preference, consumption and activity patterns. The panopticon is no longer the diagram of a physical space and materials; it is the government-controlled and corporate-traded pattern of the network of our personal real-time, planetary-wide monitoring patterns. Whether of these kinds of problematically pathological patterns or otherwise, spatial designers seem largely unable and unwilling to address this crucial aspect of spatial patterns research.

Christian Nold, Greenwich Emotion Map, 2005–06
Patterns of emotional responses of inhabitants.

The Future of Spatial Patterns Design

... we're getting a restricted view of actual patterns. And the restricted view says that people do things deliberately, in concert ... where in truth there are actual patterns that emanate from beyond people. And they're certainly not directed at any one of us, you know; they're much broader, and they work through us.

Phillip K Dick (1974) in Preface to *The Father Thing*, 2001, p 1[28]

The histories, theories and recent multidisciplinary research in this field indicates that spatial patterns design research needs to further combine visual, tangible, ornamental, decorative, structural, material and formal patterns with those that are simultaneously patterned in multicritical, consilient, research-based, interactive, ephemeral, informed, multidisciplinary and technologically innovative ways. This will then yield more valuable and significant multidimensional, multiscalar, multivariate, performative and meaningful kinds of spatial patterns. These will include *high-resolution and accurate, real-time dynamic patterns* and how they relate to patterns of the *personal, historical, social, cultural, political, psychological, economic, ecological, ethical and aesthetic patterns of space.* They might be *relations, information, networks, genealogies, theories, communications, preferences, desires, power, memories, potentials, participation, transactions, flows, inhabitation, identity, ideas, laws, emotions, atmospheres, sensations, events, activities, lifestyles, behaviours, pathologies, injustices, organisms, energies, resources, meanings, rarities, lost, endangered and other re/distributions of the contents, contexts and consequences of space and its possible futures.* Only then (to apply Yale University architectural theorist Daniel Barber's argument)[29] will the most ameliorative, significant and innovative spatial pattern designs of the future meet Guattari's injunction for the bridging of his 'three ecologies': the patterns of the personal/psychological, the interpersonal/social and the natural/environmental.[30] These stealthier, new multicritical, multidisciplinary spaces of the future will pattern the future in ways that will extend the existing patterns of spatial design in previously unimaginable ways.

The Patterns of Architecture

This issue of *AD* has been designed to provide a representative cross section of the patterns of patterns in spatial design and of the ways in which spatial design is addressing these other, new kinds of pattern.[31] The contributors were chosen for their specific expertise or positions in the field and represent academia, industry and commerce, theory and research, design and practising/professional designers. Together, Mark Taylor (interior design), Brian McGrath and Victoria Marshall (urban design), Simon Swaffield (landscape design), Hanif Kara (engineering), Helmut Pottmann (mathematics and geometry), Julian Vincent (biology and biomimetics) and Patricia Rodemann (the psychology of pattern design) investigate patterns across the broad spectrum of spatial design disciplines. Architect-academics Patrik Schumacher (parametric patterns), Alejandro Zaera-Polo (the politics of patterns), Achim Menges and Michael Hensel (high-performance patterns), Theodore Spyropoulos (cybernetics, robotics and artificial intelligence patterns) and Mike Silver (software, programming and CAM, and production patterns) examine the topic from the more particular perspectives of spatial patterns design practices, processes and technologies. The overall pattern of the issue offers both negative critical insights and positive projective, predictive, conjectural and speculative proposals that together show there is a deep connection between evolving ourselves and the evolving patterns of spatial design. Loos was wrong: a new kind of ornament, through pattern, is not impossible,[32] for through this new kind of future spatial pattern design, a different future is being patterned in the present. Like Kengo Kuma, we can now see 'that completely new patterns can be generated. They will be entirely different from any pattern we have seen so far, and generate entirely different spaces and architectures ... pattern making holds the greatest promise for the next generation.'[33] △

With thanks to Charo Garcia, Nigel Coates and to Helen Castle and Caroline Ellerby at Wiley, the best editorial team I could wish for.

Notes
1. Ray Kurzweil, *The Singularity is Near*, Gerald Duckworth & Co (London), 2005, p 478.
2. Some creativity researchers, like David Bohm in his *On Creativity* (Routledge, London), 2004, define creativity in terms of patterns.
3. RS Wurman, 'Seeing the World as Visual Patterns of Connectivity', in G Schuller (ed), *Designing Universal Knowledge,* Lars Muller (Basel), 2009, p 105.
4. DK Washburn and DW Crowe, 'The role of pattern in culture', *Symmetries of Culture: Theory and Practice of Plane Pattern Analysis,* University of Washington Press, 2004.
5. P Healy, 'Ornament Now?', *OASE 65 Ornament*, NAI Publishers (Rotterdam), 2004, pp 40–2.
6. P Emmons, 'Embodying networks: bubble diagrams and the image of modern organicism', *The Journal of Architecture*, Vol 11, No 4, 2006.
7. E Gombrich, *The Sense of Order*, Phaidon (New York), 2006, p 34.
8. See S Akkach in his *Cosmology and Architecture in Premodern Islam,* State University of New York Press (New York), 2006.
9. See Keith Critchlow, 'The use of geometry in Islamic lands', *AD Islam and Architecture*, Vol 74, No 5, Nov/Dec 2004, pp 71–7.
10. For example, P Dominique Douat's *Méthode pour faire une infinité de desseins différents avec des carreaux mi-partis de deux couleurs par une Ligne diagonale, ou observations*, Paris, 1722, or the later work of Wolfgang von Wersin.
11. There is still no meta-taxonomy or multidisciplinary classification of pattern morphologies. Nor is there much coherence between existing and partial pattern taxonomies, and there is no discipline of 'patternology' or 'patternetics'.
12. Gombrich, op cit, p 59.
13. This includes the razzle-dazzle pattern principle invented primarily for use on warships.
14. This was a polemic of the exhibition 'Ornament and Abstraction' at the Fondacion Beyeler Markus Brüderlin in 2002. Examples include Mies van der Rohe's choices of luxurious patterned materials, Le Corbusier's patterned commercial wallpapers for Salubra (1931–2) and the tiles of many Frank Lloyd Wright houses.
15. See his references to pattern in his *Investigations in Collective Form*, Washington University Press (St Louis, MO), 1964.

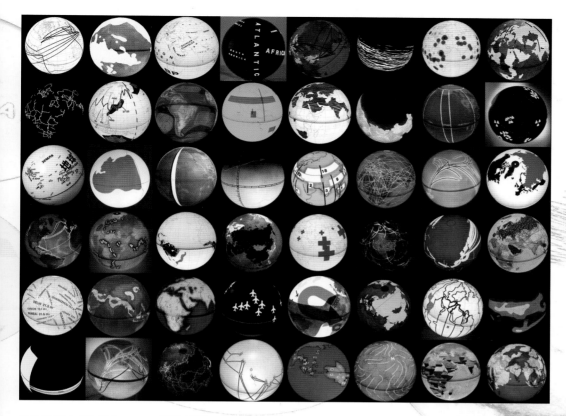

Ingo Günther, World Processor, 1988–2009
Ongoing project to map global patterns showing various international patterns (including CO_2 emissions, energy consumption, population distribution and refugee currents).

16. Christopher Alexander, *A Pattern Language*, Oxford University Press (New York),1977.

17. M Batty and P Longley, *Fractal City*, Academic Press (San Diego, CA), 1994.

18. R Venturi, 'Diversity, relevance and representation in historicism, or Plus ça change … plus a plea for pattern all over architecture with a postscript on my mother's house', *Architectural Record*, June 1982, pp 114–19.

19 Henri Lefebvre, *Rhythmanalysis: Space, Time and Everyday Life, Éléments de rythmanalyse*, Éditions Syllepse (Paris), 1992.

20. Cecil Balmond, *Element*, Prestel Verlag (New York), 2007. See also Cecil Balmond, *Informal*, Prestel (New York), 2002; Cecil Balmond, 'Survival Patterns', *306090 Models*, 2007; and Cecil Balmond, 'Cross Catalytic Arhcitectures: In Conversation', *306090 Element*, 2007.

21. A Gleiniger, G Vrachliotis and A Belting et al (eds), *Pattern (Context Architecture)*, Birkhauser (Basel), 2009; and P Schmidt, A Tietenberg and R Wollheim (eds), *Patterns in Design, Art and Architecture*, Birkhauser (Basel), 2005.

22. For example, B Massumi, *Parables for the Virtual: Movement, Affect, Sensation*, Duke University Press (Durham, NC), 2002; S Bell, *Landscape: Pattern, Perception and Process*, Taylor & Francis (London),1999; M Conforti, *Field, Form and Fate: Patterns in Mind, Psyche and Nature*, Spring Journal (Woodstock, CT), 1999; N Thrift, *Patterned Ground: Entanglements of Nature and Culture*, Reaktion (London), 2004; DK Washburn and DW Crowe, *Symmetries of Culture: Theory and Practice of Plane Pattern Analysis, Streets and Patterns: The Structure of Urban Geometry*, Washington University Press (Seattle, WA),1988; S Marshall and S Routledge, *Streets and Patterns: The Structure of Urban Geometry*, Spon Press (London), 2004.

23. Recent examples include Simon Heijden's Lightweeds (2006), ADA by ETH Zurich (2002), various MIT SENSEable City projects, hypermedia and transarchitectures projects including TransPorts (2000), Hyperbody (2003) and Digital Pavilion Korea (2006) by ONL, media facades by realities:united, and Tom Kovac's Visualising the Virtual Concourse (2008).

24. M Garcia, *AD Architextiles*, Vol 76, No 6, Nov/Dec 2006.

25.This debate can be traced back to Robert E Somol and Sarah Whiting's article 'Notes around the Doppler effects and other moods of Modernism', in Michael Osman, Adam Ruedig, Matthew Seidel and Lisa Tilney (eds), *Mining Autonomy, Perspecta*, 33, 2002, pp 72–7; Brian Massumi's article 'Sensing the virtual, building the insensible', in *AD Hypersurface Architecture*, 133, 1998, pp 16–25; and Daniel A Barber's analysis of these in his essay 'Militant architecture: destabilising architecture's disciplinarity', in J Hill and J Rendell et al (eds), *Critical Architecture*, Routledge (London), 2007.

26. See M Garcia, 'Otherwise engaged: socially interactive space', *AD 4Dsocial: Interactive Design Environments*, Vol 77, No 4, July/Aug 2007.

27. For example M3Architecture's Creative Learning Centre, Brisbane (2007) and SO-AD's Moiré House (2008).

28. Phillip K Dick [1974], in Preface to *The Father Thing*, Gollancz (London), 2001, p 1.

29. Barber, op cit.

30. Félix Guattari, *The Three Ecologies*, Athlone Press (New Brunswick, NJ), 2000.

31. Some will not be new inventions, but discoveries, as with the case of Daniel Tammet, the Aspergers savant who sees and makes complex mathematical calculations with patterns of numbers and numerical systems, experienced as forms and animated pattern landscapes in his mind. See D Tammet, *Born on a Blue Day*, Hodder & Stoughton, 2007.

32. A Loos, 'Ornament und Verbrechen', *Trotzdem: 1900–1930*, G Prachner (Vienna), 1982 [1931], pp 86–7.

33. A De Looz, 'Smart looks: Kengo Kuma on decoration', *306090 Decoration*, 2006, p 47.

Patterns, Fabrics, Prototypes, Tessellations

New technologies have enabled architects to develop sophisticated patterning techniques. This is epitomised by the expressive possibilities now available to the building envelope: smooth geometries, tessellation, material textures and layers, such as solar shading. For **Alejandro Zaera-Polo** of Foreign Office Architects, though, patterns have cultural and political possibilities far beyond mere decoration, enabling new practices to address in the urban context some of the crucial problems posed by globalisation: bridging the dichotomy between tabula rasa and contextualism, and the articulation between the local and global.

Patterns and fabrics have recently enjoyed a powerful return. Since groups such as Team X, the Dutch Structuralists and Japanese Metabolists attempted to correct the excessive focus on the object practised by classical Modernists by promoting the use of a serial, modular construction of the architectural project to enable flexibility and represent a democratic, bottom-up approach, patterns have been largely absent from architectural debate.

The climate of progressive politics in which the 1960s debate was framed meant that the investigation of patterns and fabrics became a promising opportunity, on both an urban and constructive scale, in the face of the exploration of formal autonomy that characterised Modernism. But the flexibility and openness of such proposals was limited to the addition and subtraction of, and replacement with, identical parts. Thus the possibility of addressing diverse needs within the structure was also limited. The Structuralist experiment was also severely restricted in its ability to produce an image of a whole. Some variations to the Structuralist approach were developed to introduce variation in the pattern: the reintroduction of 'wholeness', or monumentality, was often seen in the work of Louis Kahn or the Metabolists. And from the engineering fields, Le Ricolais and Nervi explored the possibility of topologically deforming patterns in order to accommodate the differential behaviours of structures.

However, these experiments to differentiate fabrics or to provide them with legibility could not prevent the general crisis of Modernism and the emergence of Postmodernism as a response to the exponential proliferation of difference produced by the postwar economic, geopolitical and social order. Postmodernism abandoned the project of consistency embedded in the late-Modernist experimentations and delved into the exploration of autonomy on the levels of language, material consistency and part-to-whole relationship. The only remains of consistency were within the more historicist varieties of Postmodernism committed to the preservation of urban fabrics, fenestration and ornamentation patterns. If Modernism explored the autonomy of the object from the field, Postmodernism explored further the autonomy between the parts and the whole as an index of a seemingly fragmented and hybridised culture, giving expression to the collapse of the Modern project and its ambitions of consistency and collective redemption. Techniques such as collage and montage were prioritised as compositional devices against the characteristic patterned modularity of the Structuralist revision of Modernism, and the topological deformations with which informalism tried to inject new energy into the modern project.

It was not until the mid-1990s that the discourse on the generic resurfaced, propelled primarily by the theoretical work of Rem Koolhaas as well as his work on generic space and the architectural effects of globalisation. This opened the field to a range of explorations by a generation of younger architects aimed at overcoming the opposition between the generic and complexity as structuring and compositional devices, to investigate new technologies and sensibilities. Theorised under the labels of 'Intensive Coherence', 'Folding Architecture' and so on, these experimentations returned to the subjects of pattern as the material organisations suitable to embody the new forms of the generic.

FOA, Institute of Legal Medicine, Madrid, 2006
The surface of the building is composed of two spherical surfaces and a torus. The tiling is made with tangent elliptical shields that form a varying rainscreen that incorporates the circular windows as another element of the envelope's pattern.

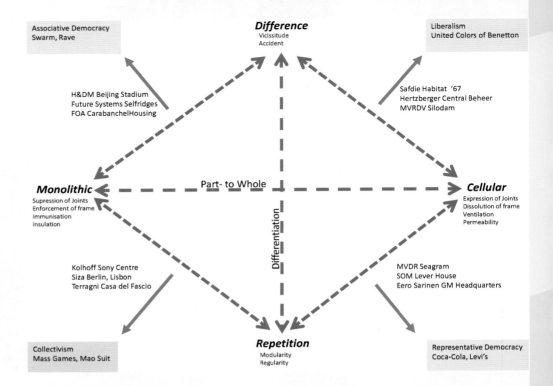

Difference
Vicissitude
Accident

Associative Democracy
Swarm, Rave

Liberalism
United Colors of Benetton

H&DM Beijing Stadium
Future Systems Selfridges
FOA CarabanchelHousing

Safdie Habitat '67
Hertzberger Central Beheer
MVRDV Silodam

Monolithic
Supression of Joints
Enforcement of frame
Immunisation
Insulation

Part- to Whole

Cellular
Expression of Joints
Dissolution of frame
Ventilation
Permeability

Differentiation

Kolhoff Sony Centre
Siza Berlin, Lisbon
Terragni Casa del Fascio

MVDR Seagram
SOM Lever House
Eero Sarinen GM Headquarters

Collectivism
Mass Games, Mao Suit

Repetition
Modularity
Regularity

Representative Democracy
Coca-Cola, Levi's

FOA, Institute of Legal Medicine, Madrid, 2006
The building envelope's tessellations.

Pattern Domains: Urban Fabrics and Envelopes

If the current interest in patterns is likely to be an effect of the cultural necessity to embody complexity through consistency rather than through contradiction, this tendency has been reinforced by the availability of new technologies that enabled architectural practices – such as Foreign Office Architects (FOA), Greg Lynn FORM, Reiser + Umemoto, OMA and UNStudio – to develop increasingly sophisticated patterns on different scales of operation. These enhanced capacities of the material practices to deal with patterns have been applied primarily into two domains: the production of urban fabrics (from Peter Eisenman's master plan for Rebstock Park (2001) to MVRDV's 'datascapes', and the design of envelopes such as in the work of Herzog & de Meuron and FOA.

One of the possibilities that artificial intelligence (AI) has made available is the ability to model fields that were not previously visible and for this reason had not yet entered into the instrumental realm of material practices. Linking directly quantitative analysis with a graphic output, and the consistency and exactness that the calculating engines introduce in this process, has enabled new practices to address some of the crucial problems posed by globalisation: namely, the dichotomy between tabula rasa and contextualism, and the articulation between local and global. This has become particularly evident in the design of urban fabrics. If Postmodernists resorted to the reproduction of urban patterns of the historic city and its typologies (historicists) or dissolving pattern in an inconsistent collection of objects

(Deconstructivists), the new experiments on urban fabrics are testing the possibility of constructing urban consistency without having to resort necessarily to the literal – or critical – reproduction of the material structures of the pre-existing city.

These new technologies have expanded the limits of urban context to include other dimensions of space and time. The same applies to the articulation between the parts and the whole within architectural artefacts. The dichotomy between bottom-up and top-down formal genesis has been put into crisis by artificial intelligence, which allows the modelling, with great precision, of the traits of a material mediation, rather than relying on an idealist worldview where the whole is built as the accretion of parts and where the part is a mere subdivision of the whole.

Having virtually disappeared from the technical arsenal of interesting architecture for two decades, the geometrical structure of the project – *tracé regulateur* – has regained relevance and become a common place of architectural experimentation. If the presence of a regulating mesh in the Structuralist approach seemed to throw into question the system's capacity for integration and flexibility, the new possibilities of operating directly in a vectorial space enable us to retain internal and external consistencies without resorting to a rigid grid or reference system.

Pattern Politics: Difference/Repetition and Single/Multiple

One of the fields of contemporary architectural research where the investigation on patterns has been more intense is the subject of the building envelope. Compared with other domains of contemporary building technology, the building envelope is probably the most unitised, and therefore the geometry of the tessellation is crucial to determine its various performances: environmental, iconographic or

FOA, Ravensbourne College of Design
and Communication, Greenwich,
London, due for completion 2010
North elevation view. The pattern of the
facade relates to the size of the windows.

expressive. The building envelope is also the architectural element that is more directly linked to the representational functions of the building. As the traditional articulations of the building envelope, such as cornices, corners and fenestration patterns, become technically redundant, the envelope's own physicality, its fabrication and materiality, its geometry and tessellation have taken over the representational roles that were previously trusted to architectural language and iconographies. The current proliferation of alternative political practices, such as trends, movements and other 'affect-driven'[1] political forms, runs parallel to the development of envelopes that resist primitive models of 'faciality',[2] no longer structured on the oppositions between front and back, private and public, or roof and wall, rendering the hierarchies of interface between building elements more complex.

The politics of rhetoric, symbolic reasoning and representation are giving way to a new breed of 'object-oriented' politics,[3] invested in modes of production and exchange and primarily implemented through the production of affects, an uncoded, prelinguistic form of identity capable of transcending the propositional logic of more traditional political rhetoric. The envelope, as the primary site of architectural expression, has become engaged in the production of surfacial effects, both as an environmental and a security device, and as the vehicle that will produce the building's facialisation, make it human, turn it into a political entity.[4] There is a new politics of faciality at play that affects the envelope as the locus of political expression.

The renewed relevance of the subject of patterns as a critical expressive device in contemporary architecture stems from these changes in the nature of contemporary politics. Beyond the solution to environmental concerns, there are questions of representation that the patterns of the envelope need to address now.

The renewed relevance of the subject of patterns as a critical expressive device in contemporary architecture stems from these changes in the nature of contemporary politics. Beyond the solution to environmental concerns, there are questions of representation that the patterns of the envelope need to address now. One such challenge is the production of identities for an increasingly inconsistent and mobile community while insulating and immunising its population against the abrasive global

atmosphere. Another is the representation of the emerging heterarchical orders that increasingly construct their power by both producing and using diversity, while simultaneously trying to produce consistency.

Frank Gehry's Guggenheim Museum in Bilbao (1997), Future Systems' Selfridges department store in Birmingham (2003), OMA's Seattle Public Library (2004) and Casa da Musica in Porto (2005), or Herzog & de Meuron's Prada Tokyo (2003) are notable examples of a tendency towards a multidirectional, differential faciality that resists linguistic coding, orientation and other traditional forms of representation to engage in the production of new expressions and political affects.

The demise of the primitive figures of building faciality has found resonance in the availability of technical possibilities (such as glass silk-screening technology and CAM manufacturing) which have enabled architects to play not only with smooth geometries, tessellation patterns and material textures, but also with a wide repertory of layers that can also perform technical functions (such as solar shading and visual occlusion). The introduction of certain cladding and roofing technologies, such as curtain wall systems, silicon joints and plastic waterproofing membranes, has eliminated the need for cornices, corners, pediments and window reveals. The difference between the roof and the wall has disappeared, as have many other traditional articulations of the building envelope.

These conventional figures of the building envelope are being replaced by more nuanced interfacial embodiments in which different layers of performance are played out against each other to produce a wide range of complex effects. The decoupling of the patterns of visual, thermal and atmospheric permeability has opened unprecedented possibilities for a molecular facialisation of the envelope by dissolving or intensifying the joints at will through the phasing and dephasing of these layers.

There seems also to be a tendency towards polygonal tessellations in contemporary envelopes – including PTW's Beijing Water Cube (2007), Future Systems' Selfridges department store and FOA's Ravensbourne College of Design and Communication in Greenwich, London (due for completion in 2010) – that oppose the Cartesian grid division of the late Modern screens. This tendency is first made possible by the release of the envelope from structural and environmental control functions.

Polygonal geometries have additional performances: for example, a hexagonal tiling has less joint length than a rectangular tile of the same area. If the contemporary envelope has more stringent requirements in terms of insulation and security performance, a polygonal tessellation will provide a smaller joint length per surface unit than rectangular grids, so this tendency may even be driven by a contemporary desire for sealed, immunising atmospheres.[5] But it is certainly enhanced by a faciality that is no longer structured in planar, vertical and discrete faces, as some of these envelopes explore differential geometries of the surface: the construction of bubble envelopes is not possible using a Cartesian tessellation.

OMA, CCTV Building, Beijing, China, 2009
The differential structural performance of the envelope has been made visible to produce a differentiated patterning of the surface.

Gehry's fish-like skins are an index of these tendencies: the staggering of the joints, originally driven by the constructive purpose of waterproofing the membrane by overlapping the tiles, becomes a characteristic pattern that breaks the continuity of the joints and enhances the three-dimensional, dynamic affect of the skin. The proliferation of diagrids and non-orthogonal tessellation patterns – OMA's Seattle Public Library (2004) and CCTV building (2009), Herzog & de Meuron's Prada Tokyo (2003) and Beijing National Stadium (Bird's Nest, 2008), Foster's Swiss Re (2004) and Hearst (2006) towers in London and New York, respectively – display a general tendency towards the incorporation of the structure in the skin, producing anti-gravitational, uprooted, unstable and differentiated affects.

The differential faciality that we find in some of the quoted examples here explores the expression of a sort of politics that moves away from the ideal, modular democratic organisation based on indifference, independence and interchangeability: if modularity was typically a quality of a democratic system that prioritises the part over the whole, some of the emerging envelope geometries seem to be exploring modular differentiation as a political effect and developing alternative forms of tessellation capable of addressing emerging political forms.[6]

The modular grid, indifferent to the relative weight of individuals or politically active subgroups, embodied the ideals of democratic equality and liberal individualism

and a preference for non-hierarchical organisations in which individuals are equal and will submit to the will of majority. However, emerging social structures characteristic of globalised societies and their heterogeneous populations tend to produce trans-scalar entities, from subindividual to transnational. In these emerging social assemblages, individuals, groups and other agents are primarily defined by relations of exteriority.[7] The allometric modularities and variable repetitions that emerge as almost generic traits of contemporary envelopes are probably more adequate to express a collective purpose within 'weighted' models of democracy (either those committed to the exercise of civil liberties or those that are driven by a hierarchical bureaucratic and authoritarian regime overlaid on to apparent democratic protocols).

The convergence towards those types of affect by both political structures with a multicultural tradition in the aftermath of 9/11 (such as Chirac's French law on secularity and conspicuous religious symbols in schools, and Trevor Phillips' 'Britishness') and states with an authoritarian background aiming to become integrative without losing their consistency, is remarkable. The question is whether the differentiated facialities and tessellations of the envelope seen emerging, for example in the Beijing Olympic projects, are genuine devices to allow the envelope to relate to a larger variety of concerns – environmental, social, economic and so on – or a strategy to step up the immunization levels while representing an ideally differentiated public. Do they inflect in response to multiple agencies and incorporate specificities rather than resorting to the production of spectacular embodiments of global capitalism and authoritarian bureaucracies?

FOA, John Lewis Building, Highcross retail and cinema complex, Leicester, 2008
Double facade patterns. A pattern created from an upholstery design from the tenant, to provide different degrees of transparency, was silk-screened on both layers of the facade to produce certain effects of transparency and translucency depending on the position of the observer in respect to the envelope.

As the politics of affect bypass the rational filter of political dialectic to appeal directly to physical sensation, the construction of an effective frame of reference within the discipline for discussing expression becomes critical. One can no longer sustain the ideological assumption that a more regular or a more differentiated pattern, one more permeable or more closed, is better at expressing a certain society and the production of transformative effects. The political accuracy of a certain envelope needs to be judged in respect to very concrete assemblages. The most acknowledged envelopes among the iconic Beijing Olympics projects are probably those in which the architects have succeeded in creating a plausible alibi for the differentiated pattern wrapped around the massive unarticulated volume of the buildings, where a resonance between literal performance and affect has been achieved. This is where a new discipline of the envelope becomes politically operative as an act of resistance that does not get caught in the negative project of the critical tradition or in the use of architecture as a mere representation of politics.

FOA's Pattern Politics

Probably as a result of its engagement with commercially driven projects, FOA has been investigating the problem of the envelope for a number of years. As a result it now has a body of project-based research on the problem of the envelope's tessellation. Considering the projects that have been engaged in this investigation, it is interesting to trace the tendencies present in the envelope's patterns, performing as environmental and expressive devices. The hypothesis of this analysis is that the four tendencies are towards the monolithic, differentiated, frameless and rootless,

and that these are representative of, and consistent with, the primary political affects of the work.

Firstly, there is a general propensity in the work towards envelopes that express a monolithic quality that foregrounds the perception of the object as a whole rather than as a composition of parts. In several cases, the massing of the envelope is predetermined by the nature of the programme or the project's site previous to FOA's involvement: the Spanish Pavilion for Aichi 2005 in Japan, Ravensbourne College of Design and Communication, the Trinity EC3 office complex in London (2006) or the Highcross retail and cinema complex in Leicester (2008) are exemplary of this tendency. The atomisation of the face, the seamlessness, the bias towards a body without organs which expresses changes of intensity rather than figures of organisation are some of the qualities these projects share. As a result, the buildings produce affects of effacement, liquefaction, de-striation.

A second trait that we can identify across all the projects is a deliberate attempt to produce differentiated patterns. In the Spanish Pavilion for Aichi 2005, the pattern is differentiated automatically by the particular geometrical quality of the six deformed hexagons, with no other purpose than to represent a differentiated colour field that, despite its contingent appearance, is governed by the geometrical laws of the parts. The Ravensbourne College of Design and Communication is the only project where we can see a pierced fenestration: the geometry of the pattern enables perforations of different sizes in respect to the specific needs of the interiors. The differentiated fenestration pattern is then projected into the structure of the tessellation pattern. Here, the differentiation is produced locally in respect to programmatic factors.

In the Affordable Housing in Carabanchel, Madrid (2007), the difference engine is located also in the contingent action of the inhabitants to set their own preferences in respect to daylight, shading and views, changing over time as those conditions change, as a direct register of the collective's desires; like in a swarm, the part and the whole are seamlessly related in performance and expression. And in the Leicester Highcross retail and cinema complex the differentiation

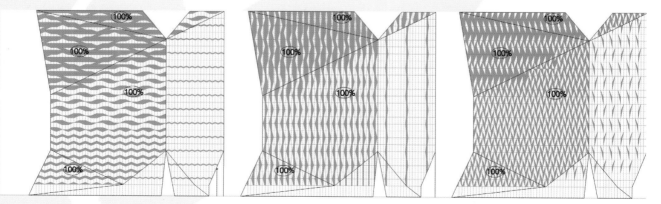

FOA, Building 1, Trinity EC3 office complex, London, 2006
Tests of solar-shading patterns. The cumulative exposure of the facade to solar radiation was measured locally and transformed into a different percentage of coverage for a silk-screened pattern, producing a palette of eight different tiles that can approximate the recommended G-values for every zone of the facade.

FOA, Spanish Pavilion, Aichi Universal Exhibition, Japan, 2005
right: Tessellation. Six different hexagonal ceramic tiles, colour-coded with a hue of yellow and red tones, form a system that automatically produces a contingent pattern of colour.

FOA, Ravensbourne College of Design and Communication, Greenwich, London, due for completion 2010
opposite: Correlation between windows and facade tessellation. The tiles are coded depending on their position in respect to the centre of the polar array of tiles that surrounds every perforation. The colour-coding of the tiles changes according to the size of the window, forming a varying pattern.

is embedded in the silk-screened pattern that covers the John Lewis department store's glass facade and the optimisation of the stainless tiling of the cinema block, but most importantly it is produced by the movement of the spectator around the building causing a flickering moiré effect, together with the changing reflections on the mirrored surfaces.

In the Iconic Towers in Dubai (2004) and the Trinity EC3 office complex, the differentiation of the pattern is local and generated by the differential solar exposure of the specific surfaces interacting with the facade tessellation. In the Institute of Legal Medicine in Madrid (2006), the circle-packing geometry is differentiated to adjust to the basic geometry formed by two spheres and a torus. Whether the differentiation is driven by the functional performances of the envelope in relation to varying parameters such as solar exposure, views and so on, or whether the differentiation is applied as a global order to the envelope, or it is related to the joints and joining patterns, details or the localised functional performances, the work displays a tendency towards differentiated patterns.

The envelope patterns in these projects present a tendency to merge the frame and the infill, the whole and the parts, which is particularly distinctive in comparison with other contemporary experiments in tessellation: the

Barcelona Coastal Park and Auditoria (2002), the Spanish Pavilion and the Ravensbourne College of Design and Communication present repeatedly an edge to the envelope that is directly conformed by the geometry of the tiles rather than by a cornice or a corner, or any other framing structure. The exploitation of an integral correspondence between parts and whole is one of the constants that appears repeatedly through the work, projecting the buildings as open, frameless, incomplete entities.

Finally, the analysis of the envelope's patterns displays a proneness towards polygonal tessellations and packing structures, a trope that we can see in most of these projects. From all the cases listed, the Leicester Highcross retail and cinema complex, the Affordable Housing in Carabanchel and the Trinity EC3 office complex retain the more conventional orthogonal grid as an organising structure for the envelope's construction. However, the orthogonal grid is usually disguised by introducing an overlapped pattern or a 3-D manipulation of the surface. The conceptual argument behind this approach could be addressed by different hypotheses, but one of its most direct effects is the suspension of gravity as the primary organising force behind the envelope tessellation. The envelope becomes, by virtue of this configuration, a hovering, rootless object that presents itself as a skin rather than as a topographic construction. The case of the Barcelona Coastal Park and Auditoria is interesting here as it is not an envelope proper, but a topography where the gliding of tiles in respect of each other produces an 'effect' of instability that communicates a similar 'affect' of rootlessness.

Analysing the work under this scope underlines the emergence of a series of affects in the patterns of envelopes that are to a degree independent of both the programmes and the technologies used in their design. These characteristics may be seen as the 'atmosphere' of the work. However, to take things a step further, these atmospheric qualities are a basic index of a political stance or the work previous to translation into a political vocabulary. In fact monolithicness, differentiation, framelessness and rootlessness are concepts with a strong political baggage. ∆

Notes

1. Following Deleuze, 'affects' are 'pre-personal intensities' that are transmitted by empathy between material organisations rather than through codes, signs or conventional forms of representation. Gilles Deleuze, 'Percepts, concepts, affects', in Gilles Deleuze, Félix Guattari, Janis A Tomlinson and Hugh Tomlinson (eds), *What is Philosophy?*, Columbia University Press (New York), 1996. As Nigel Thrift has pointedly noted, contemporary politics are progressively less reliant on representation and proposition and more dependent on the production of affects. See Nigel Thrift, *Non-Representational Theory: Space, Politics, Affect*, Routledge (London), 2007.
2. I adopt the term proposed by Deleuze to address the theorisation of systems of expression or representation. See Gilles Deleuze and Félix Guattari, 'Year Zero: Faciality', in *A Thousand Plateaus: Capitalism and Schizophrenia,* University of Minnesota Press (Minneapolis, MN), 1987.
3. The term is borrowed from Rodney Brooks, a pioneer of behaviourist AI, who has promoted the idea of a 'physically grounded artificial intelligence' from the field of robotics as an alternative to centrally structured coded wholes based on symbolic reasoning. Brooks argued that interacting with the physical world is far more difficult than symbolically reasoning about it. Rodney Brooks, 'Elephants don't play chess', and 'Intelligence without representation', *Cambrian Intelligence: The Early History of the New AI*, MIT Press (Cambridge, MA), 1999. See also his 'The relationship between matter and life', *Nature* 409, 2001, pp 409–11.
4. The idea of extending a human, political dimension to things or sub-human entities is very much the project that Bruno Latour explores in his proposition of a Dingpolitik. This is the term coined by Latour to address the politics resulting from the crisis of objectivity triggered by the collapse of Modernity and the search for a new model of objectivity in which politics become intrinsic to the object, its sciences and nature at large. Bruno Latour and Peter Weibel, 'Introduction', *Making Things Public. Atmospheres of Democracy*, exhibition catalogue, MIT Press (Cambridge, MA), 2005.
5. 'Immunisation', 'insulation' and 'ventilation' are some of the terms coined by Peter Sloterdijk to describe the artificial diversification of the atmosphere within the capsular society. The human island, the capsule and the greenhouse are the prototypical devices for a new generation of buildings committed to this diversification of the atmosphere. Peter Sloterdijk, *ESFERAS III. Espumas. Esferología plural*, Siruela (Madrid), 2006.
6. Richard Sennett's definition of associative democracy, (see 'Democratic spaces', in *Hunch No 9*, Berlage Institute (Rotterdam), 2005); Latour's Actor-Network Theory (*Reassembling the Social: An Introduction to Actor-Network-Theory*, Oxford University Press (Oxford), 2007); and Sloterdijk's foams (op cit) coincide to describe emerging social structures as organisations where the articulation between individual and society, part and whole, is drawn by influences and attachments across positions, agencies and scales that transcend both the individuality of the part and the integrity of the whole.
7. Manuel DeLanda has applied Deleuze's theory of assemblages to describe these emerging forms of social and political organisation. Assemblages are non-essentialist, historically contingent, actual entities (not instances of ideal forms) and non-totalising (not seamless totalities, but collections of heterogeneous components). Manuel DeLanda, *A New Philosophy of Society*, Continuum International Publishing Group (New York), 2006.

Parametric

For
Patrik
Schumacher
of Zaha Hadid
Architects, articulation is
the central core competency of
architecture; and designed patterns
provide one of the most potent devices for
architectural articulation. Schumacher ushers in a
new era of parametric architecture in which pattern
becomes an innovative and powerful register of articulation,
providing amplification of surface difference and correlation, ultimately
resulting in dynamic, high-performance ornamentation.

Patterns

Zaha Hadid Architects, Louis Vuitton Store, Macau, China, 2007
The slight distortion in the cubic volume is visually amplified by means of the correlated pattern.

LOUIS VUITTON

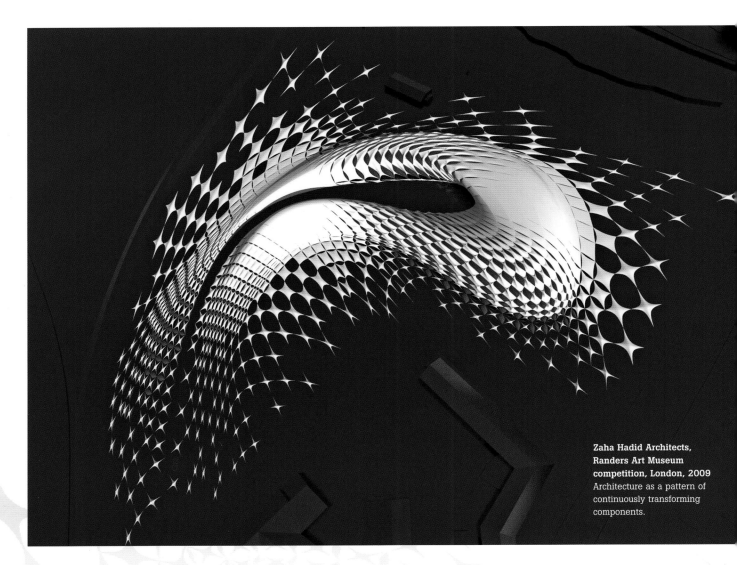

Patterns are explored here in the narrow sense of designed patterns that spread across all sorts of surfaces, including architectural surfaces.[1] They have been covering architectural surfaces since time immemorial, in the same way that they have been spread all over man-made objects. The human body was perhaps the first surface to receive designed patterns. Architectural patterns thus have a broad and deep lineage, and one should not expect them to have any well-defined, unitary function. As patterns evolve they acquire new functions and lose their prior functions, or new functions are superimposed upon older ones. Patterns might serve purposes of decorative enhancement, feature accentuation, camouflaging, totemic identification, semiotic differentiation, or any combination of these.

There are two general terms from traditional architectural theory that cover the different practices referred to here: 'ornament' and 'decoration'. To oppose ornament or decoration to function would be a fallacy. In classical architectural theory, decoration was the complementary term for a fundamental distinction and was considered within an overall tripartite division of architecture's teachings: distribution, construction and decoration, the three fundamental tasks of architectural design. This division of architectural knowledge was established in French architectural theory by Augustin-Charles d'Aviler in his *Cours d'architecture* (1691–93), a standard reference work throughout the whole of the 18th century. The triad of distribution, construction and decoration is also found in Jacques-François Blondel's opus magnum *Cours d'architecture* (1771–77), and Karl Friedrich Schinkel (1802) refers to it in his (unfinished) architectural treatise. According to Schinkel:

> The purposefulness of any building can be considered from three principal perspectives: purposefulness of spatial distribution or of the plan, purposefulness of construction or the joining of materials appropriate to the plan, purposefulness of ornament or decoration.[2]

Schinkel's conception, once more, shows that the later (modern) opposition between decoration and function is false.

In place of the classic triad referred to above, the distinction between 'organisation' and 'articulation' could instead represent the two central dimensions of the task of architectural design. The aspect of construction has been largely outsourced to the disciplines of building engineering. Organisation is concerned with the spatialisation of the social order via objective distances/proximities and via physical divisions/connections between domains. Articulation is concerned with the subjective comprehension of the spatialised social order. Articulation cannot be dispensed with; it involves the central core competency of architecture. Articulation contains the *differentia specifica* that demarcates architecture/design from all engineering disciplines. Articulation reckons with the fact that buildings function only via the user's active 'reading' of their spatial organisation. What things look like matters. At a certain level of social complexity, adequate spatial organisations can only become effective if their ordering operations can enlist the user's capacity to actively 'read' the urban/architectural environment. Only on the basis of articulate organisations will users be enabled to navigate, and collectively utilise, the built environment to its fullest potential. The reference problem for the task of articulation is orientation. Articulation should facilitate orientation by making the spatial organisation, and the social order within it, legible. Orientation also implies the steering of expectations about the social scenarios that might unfold within a space and about the conduct that is appropriate within that space.

The distinction of articulation versus organisation cannot be aligned with the distinction of form versus function: the two intersect each other. Both organisation and articulation have functional as well as formal aspects. Both organisational diagrams and strategies of articulation need to be selected on the basis of their social functionality, and both are dependent on the availability of a pertinent formal repertoire.

Architectural patterns are a potent device for architectural articulation. For instance, in classical architecture ornamental patterns (mouldings) often emphasise a building's ordering of symmetry axes. Typical ornamental motifs are also used to distinguish typical functions. Traditionally, the concepts of 'character' and 'expression' were deployed as mediating terms to explain how decoration is to be related to a building's purpose. These were taken from the theatre and were first introduced into architectural theory by Germain Boffrand in his *Livre d'architecture* of 1745:

Papua facial ornamentation and Chinese opera masks
Both the Papua facial treatments and the traditional Chinese opera masks work with the accentuating enhancement of facial features. Both sets of enhancements serve as mediums of distinction. In the case of the opera masks, there exists an elaborate system of typical characters.

Architecture … its component parts are so to speak brought to life by the different characters that it conveys to us. Through its composition a building expresses, as if in the theatre, that the scene is pastoral or tragic; that this is a temple or a palace, a public building destined for a particular purpose or a private house. By their planning, their structure and their decoration, all such buildings must proclaim their purpose to the beholder. If they fail to do so, they offend against expression and are not what they ought to be.[3]

It is noteworthy here that all three terms of the classical tripartite division – planning (distribution), structure (construction), decoration – are together involved in expressing the character of the building. Boffrand goes on:

If you are setting out to build a music room, or a salon in which to receive company, it must be cheerful in its planning, in its lighting, and in its manner of decoration. If you want a mausoleum, the building must be suited to its use, and the architecture and decoration must be serious and sad; for Nature makes us susceptible to all these impressions, and a unified impulse never fails to touch our feelings.[4]

The unified impulse that touches our feelings might be best translated into our contemporary language as the 'atmosphere' of a space. Jacques-François Blondel referred to 'imperceptible nuances' in connection with the concepts of character and expression:

> It is by the assistance of these imperceptible nuances that we are able to make a real distinction in the design of two buildings of the same genre but which nevertheless should announce themselves differently: preferring in one a style sublime, noble and elevated; in the other a character naïve, simple and true. Distinct particular expressions … that need to be felt … contribute more than one ordinarily imagines in assigning to each building the character that is proper to it.[5]

Ornamental patterns that convey atmospheric values are received semiconsciously. In fact, architectural articulation in general operates largely via patterns that are perceived in passing, in a mode of 'distraction'[6] rather than focused attention. The information processing that is relevant for the quick, intuitive orientation of users is largely unconscious. In this way articulated spaces achieve the behavioural priming appropriate for the respective social setting.

The concept of decoration does not carry the full intent and emphasis of what the agenda of articulation involves today. Architectural projects are now often confronted with unique briefs and institutional arrangements that require solutions of unprecedented novelty.

The concept of decoration does not carry the full intent and emphasis of what the agenda of articulation involves today. Architectural projects are now often confronted with unique briefs and institutional arrangements that require solutions of unprecedented novelty. Reliance on a handful of given character-types can no longer exhaust the task of articulation. Articulatory strategies have to be devised that order the visual field and guide the eye to recognise abstract configurations and the focal moments or key distinctions within them. However, the traditional concept of decoration did go beyond its current connotations of superficial and arbitrary beautification. As demonstrated above, decoration, in classical architectural theory, was linked to the twin concepts of character and expression. Decoration was seen as a necessary ingredient of architecture, as it was a necessary ingredient of all artefacts. A building without decoration was unfinished, unable to enter the social world, just as it was impossible to join society naked, or without sufficient behavioural decorum. Decoration, expressing the appropriate character of a space, was linked to propriety within a sophisticated system of social distinctions. Today spaces seem more neutral, encounters are less ritualised and decorum seems less conspicuous. But have these registers of social coding disappeared altogether?

The decorative patterning of surfaces was still taken for granted all the way through the 19th century until, suddenly, Modernism opted for the clean, white wall — in the footsteps of the clean, white shirt.

The decorative patterning of surfaces was still taken for granted all the way through the 19th century until, suddenly, Modernism opted for the clean, white wall – in the footsteps of the clean, white shirt. The first examples of unadorned, naked architecture were causing public scandals, most notoriously Adolph Loos' Haus am Michaelerplatz (1898) in Vienna. However, Loos soon won the argument. The re-evaluation of values was extreme: ornament signified backwardness. According to Loos, the evolution of culture is synonymous with the removal of ornament. His famous polemic compared ornamentation with the tattoos of criminals, and his reasoning goes as follows: 'Primitive men had to differentiate themselves by various colours; modern man needs his clothes as a mask. His individuality is so strong that it can no longer be expressed in terms of items of clothing.'[7]

Loos' allusion to modern individuality is pertinent here. However, the demise of traditional ornament does not imply the demise of articulation. The accelerating and intensifying fashion system bears witness against his account. The end of ornamentation is not synonymous with the end of design's expressive function, neither does it spell the end of the phenomenon of style, as Loos presumed, nor the final demise of surface patterning.

The modern denigration of overt ornament cannot be accounted for by the mere fact that industrialisation overtook handicraft production. It was only after nearly a hundred years of industrialisation, after the social revolutions that followed in the aftermath of the First World War, that the pure *Sachlichkeit* of 'White Modernism' succeeded. To be sure, this radical rejection of what had been taken for granted for thousands of years was a heroic act of iconoclasm fully consistent with the revolution and with the general emancipation of creative potentials that the Modern Movement delivered. The traditional orders and regimes of ornamentation stood in the way of unfettered design research. They had to go. Thus, if we now call for a vigorous return to the deployment of patterns in architecture and design, this does not imply that unadorned, Modernist architecture was a mistake. Equally, the fact that Modernism as a whole went into crisis also does not imply that it was a mistake – Modernism delivered a huge material step forward – but it does imply that it would be a mistake to continue the Modernist paradigm and to prolong its strictures against ornament/decoration. On the back of Modernism's achievements a new, more complex and versatile societal formation has evolved that poses new challenges for the task of architectural organisation and articulation. Today's 'White Minimalism' is indeed a historical mistake.

Modernist strictures against ornament/decoration were first challenged by Postmodernism. Although historical motifs were brought back in a mode of playful eclecticism, there was no engagement with systematic articulatory patterning. Notwithstanding Minimalism's historical fallacy, it was from within this movement that the return to patterns, and the attendant new embrace of ornament, was initiated during the 1990s. The seminal project in this respect was Herzog & de Meuron's 1993 Ricola Storage Building in Mulhouse-Brunstatt, France. The introduction of different surface effects, like different material textures, had already happened within the later phases of Modernism, but artificial, quasi-graphic techniques of surface treatment and surface patterning were now being deployed. These moves signal the enrichment of the formal repertoire of architecture, without falling back on traditional regimes of adornment and their meanings. Instead, new atmospheres with new associations and nuances could be projected and elaborated. However, from the vantage point of today, Minimalist pattern deployment had obvious limitations: the underlying spatial organisation of its compositions was exceedingly simple and the surfaces that received patterning were simple, flat planes. Patterns were repetitive and were applied like wallpaper.

In the meantime, the avant-garde that had followed on from Deconstructivism under the heading of 'folding in architecture'[8] was at first focusing only on (complex) geometry, progressing from faceted surfaces to smooth nurb surfaces. Towards the end of the 1990s, new possibilities of patterning were discovered by applying the technique of texture mapping on to warped nurb surfaces, and such effects were achieved on built projects by projecting video images on to curvilinear surfaces, or by embedding digital display systems within the surfaces. In 1998, *AD* published *Hypersurface Architecture*,[9] a whole programmatic issue dedicated to these new possibilities. Architectural patterning had arrived within the avant-garde movement that we now – both in retrospect and in anticipation of more exciting explorations to come – promote as the style of parametricism.[10]

The technique of texture mapping has since been replaced by scripting, and mapping only survives as an initial short cut to test or illustrate effects that are then to be implemented by scripts. Early examples of nurb surface articulations that were not just arbitrary mappings or projections emerged with the introduction of CNC milling. Bernard Cache and Greg Lynn both experimented with effects like heightened contour lines and tool paths, producing a contemporary translation of the idea of 'faktura' (the deliberate deployment of the visual traces of the manufacturing process). At the same time, the question of how nurb surfaces could be tessellated became an issue. The need for tessellation became an opportunity for articulation, and the difficulty of devising both feasible and elegant tessellations for double-curved surfaces was the occasion that brought parametric modelling and scripting to the fore.

The problem of fitting panels on to a complex surface has also been driving the development of Bentley Systems' GenerativeComponents (GC) associative and parametric modelling system with its central idea of populating a complex host surface with computationally self-adapting elements. The classical GC setup involves the design of an inherently variable component that is defined across a range of surface parameters. To ensure perfect fit, each instantiation is parametrically adapted to its unique position on the host surface. The result might be called a 'parametric pattern'. However, in this classical setup the curvature variation of the surface provides the dataset that drives the parametric adaptation of the component with the aim of keeping the pattern as even and homogeneous as possible. The aim is to maintain component identity by compensating for the underlying surface differentiation.

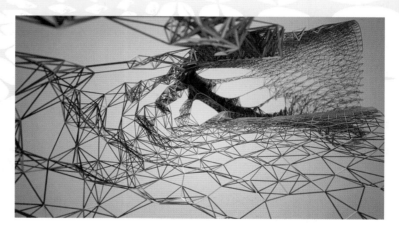

Krisztian Csemy, Jasmina Frincic and Jakub Klaska, Interiorities, Masterclass Zaha Hadid (tutors: Patrik Schumacher and Ali Rahim), University of Applied Arts, Vienna, 2009
This intensely differentiated spatial pattern is emerging from a network script that varies the networking rule according to the parameters of the different surface conditions. To further amplify the differentiation effect, the script also drives a colour differentiation (dark to light) in correlation with the stick length.

Parametricism transforms this technique of parametric pattern design into a new and powerful register of articulation. The crucial move that inaugurates 'parametricist patterning' is the move from adaptive compensation to the amplification of differences. The underlying surface variability is utilised as a dataset that can drive a much more radical pattern differentiation. The underlying surface differentiation is thus amplified and made much more conspicuous. This strong emphasis on conspicuous differentiation is one of the hallmarks of parametricism.

Differentiation might also be introduced wilfully, by 'painting' the surface with any pattern or image that then becomes the dataset to drive component differentiation. In the current phase of technique exploration and formal experimentation, this arbitrary play with differentiation might be tolerated. Ultimately, however, such an injection of differentiation should be rejected; it is 'ornamental' in a rather questionable sense. The differentiation of the surface should serve as a medium of articulation, and it can do so only if it is correlated with the geometric or functional aspects of the space the surface constructs. A strong emphasis on correlation is a second hallmark of parametricism. The articulation by means of correlative surface differentiation is free to take on any relevant dataset of the overall spatial construct within which the respective surface is situated. Significant correlates might include the underlying primary structure. The surface articulation might correspond to structural flow-lines or stress distribution.

Correlates might further include the apertures that are set into the surface. Patterns might accentuate apertures, a surface might be made to correlate with the furnishings within a space, and the expected pattern of occupation might also be utilised as a dataset driving a corresponding surface differentiation. A sophisticated setup should be able to cater for multiple datasets simultaneously.

Huang Yung-Chieh, Hang Jin and Wen-Kai Li, Parametric Urbanism, Architectural Association Design Research Lab (DRL) (tutors: Patrik Schumacher and Christos Passas), London, 2009
The patterning participates within a cascade of subsystem correlation: the facade pattern articulation correlates with the structural system which in turn correlates with both exterior shape and the shape-dependent interior voiding. The result is a deep relationality that serves orientation.

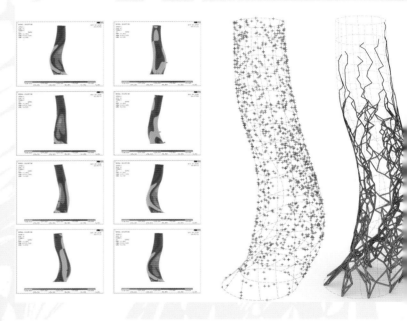

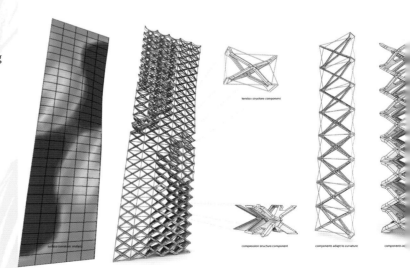

Zaha Hadid Architects, Civil Courts, Madrid, 2007
An environmentally adaptive facade. The facade component is modulated in adaptation to the gradually changing sunlight exposure. Opening size and the projection of the shading element vary accordingly. Although this is essentially a performative adaptation, the aesthetic effects of differentiation and accentuation are keen aspects for the parametricist designer.

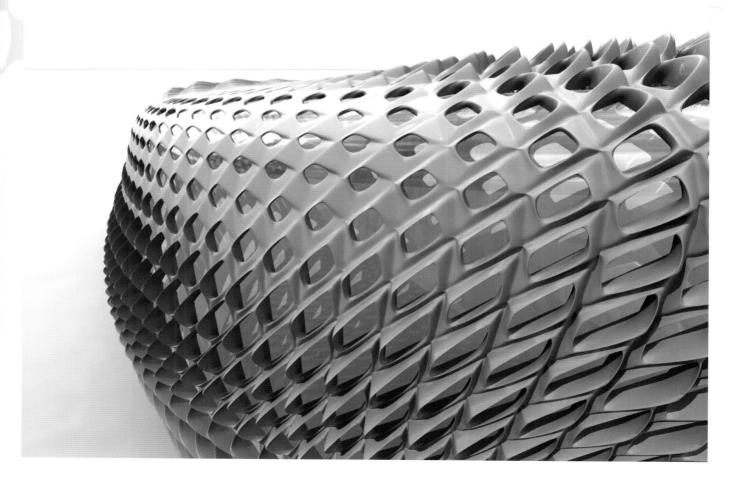

Another powerful opportunity is the adaptive differentiation of facades with respect to environmental parameters that vary widely according to the orientation of the surface. Here, functional and formal variation go hand in hand. The gradual variation of sunlight intensity on a curved surface translates into a gradient transformation of the component formation. Within parametricism, such functional exigencies are heightened into an artistic concept.

It is important to note that parametricism, as a style, constitutes an artistic agenda that embodies a will to form. Appearances matter, but they matter as part of performance. The ethos of this artistic agenda is one of articulation that stands against a mere formalism. Appearances are revealing an otherwise invisible performativity, or accentuate and make conspicuous what might otherwise get lost in an unarticulated visual chaos.

The following specific registers of surface articulation might be distinguished: relief, seaming, material, texture, colour, reflectivity and translucency. Potentially, all of these registers should be not only utilised but choreographed via correlating scripts. Surface relief is of particular interest here because it makes the surface sensitive to both changing light conditions and changing view angles.

In order to take the conditions described above into account, parametric design must extend its attention beyond the consideration of object parameters to include both

This head, hand-carved by a Maori craftsman, depicts traditional facial tattoos.

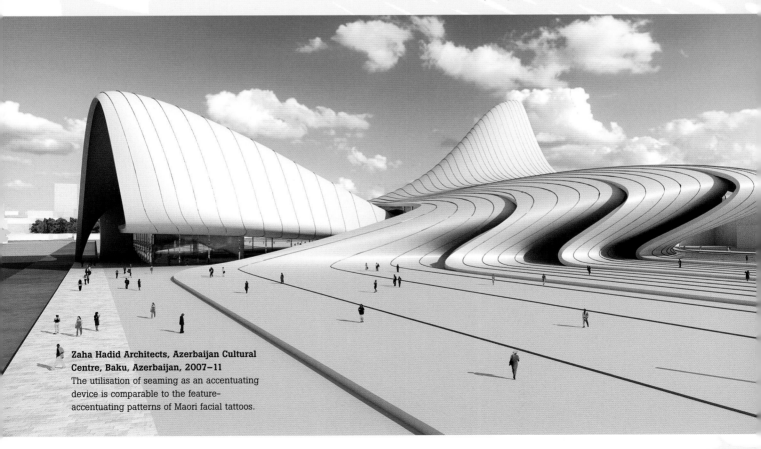

Zaha Hadid Architects, Azerbaijan Cultural Centre, Baku, Azerbaijan, 2007–11
The utilisation of seaming as an accentuating device is comparable to the feature-accentuating patterns of Maori facial tattoos.

Zaha Hadid Architects, Paris Philharmonie competition entry, 2007
Close-ups of models. The applied patterns follow and accentuate the changing direction of the surface. As the surface orientation shifts the relief pattern transforms.

Johannes Elias, Christoph Hermann,
Thomas Milly and Neger Niku, Simultaneity
and Latency, Masterclass Zaha Hadid
(tutors: Zaha Hadid and Patrik
Schumacher), University of Applied Arts,
Vienna, 2008
Variable light/shadow effects. The patterns
exploit variable lighting conditions (ambient
parameters) to achieve a strong differentiation
in the character of the respective surfaces.
The designs are ambient sensitive.

Peter Schamberger, Valencia
International Port Terminal,
Masterclass Zaha Hadid
(tutors: Zaha Hadid and
Patrik Schumacher),
University of Applied Arts,
Vienna, 2007

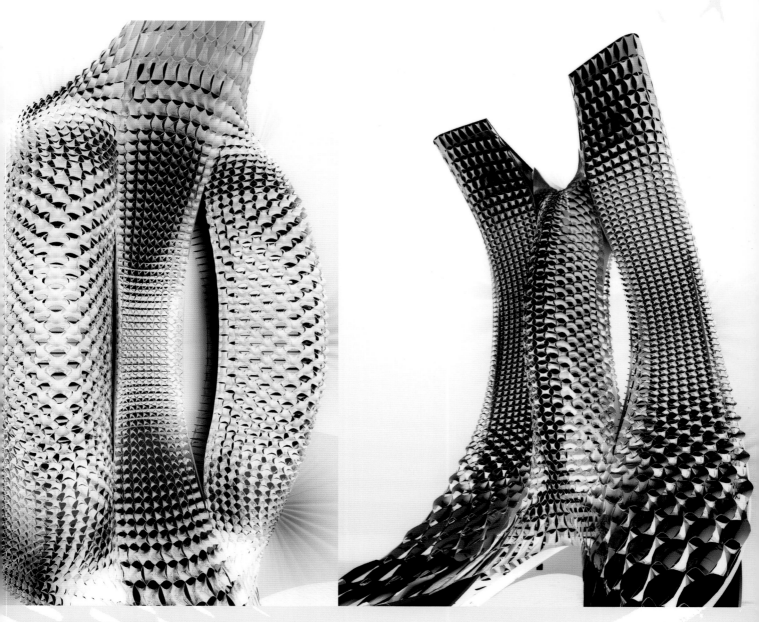

Maren Klasing, Martin Krcha, Manuel Froeschl and Konrad Hofmann, Compressed Complexity, Masterclass Zaha Hadid (tutors: Zaha Hadid and Patrik Schumacher), University of Applied Arts, Vienna, 2006
Accentuating deployment of facade relief. It is important to note that, in all instances presented, the pattern correlates and enhances the three-dimensional shape rather than constituting an arbitrary application. The relief exploits light/shadow effects.

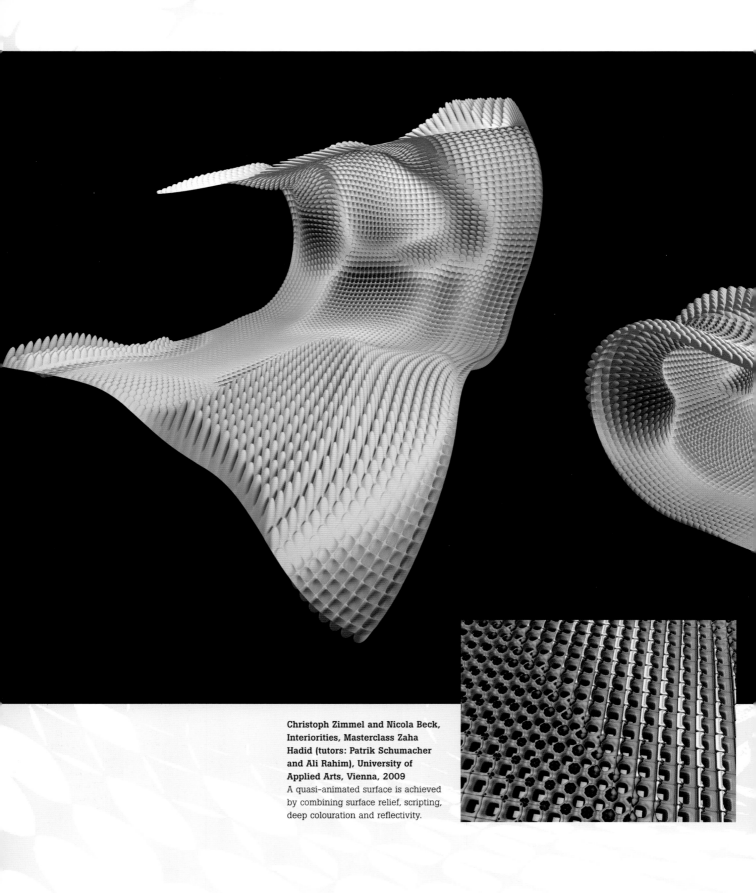

**Christoph Zimmel and Nicola Beck,
Interiorities, Masterclass Zaha
Hadid (tutors: Patrik Schumacher
and Ali Rahim), University of
Applied Arts, Vienna, 2009**
A quasi-animated surface is achieved
by combining surface relief, scripting,
deep colouration and reflectivity.

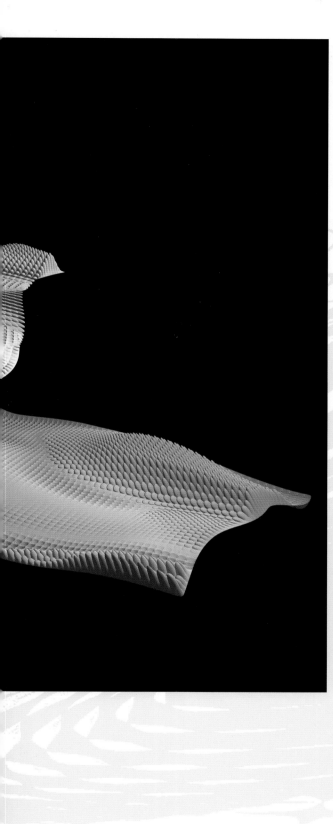

ambient and observer parameters. The systematic work with such parameters enhances the sense of animation that can be achieved with respect to the articulation of architectural surfaces. The manipulation of lighting conditions, and shifts in observer position might trigger dramatic shifts in the appearance and understanding of a surface or space. Patterns might be set up in such a way that key parameters become Gestalt sensitive, so that a small variation in a critical parameter – object, ambient or observer – triggers a surprising Gestalt switch. This design agenda has been referred to as 'parametric figuration'.[11] For architectural surface patterns to participate in this agenda a certain degree of surface depth is required. Parametric figuration is perhaps the most ambitious form of architectural articulation and to become really effective it would need to go beyond merely visual effects. The Gestalt switches would need to be correlated with the changing events scenarios that would benefit from a shift in understanding and orientation. Only at that stage would we be able to talk about dynamic, high-performance ornaments. ∆

Notes

1. Patterns in the more profound application of patterns of spatial organisation that structure urban and architectural space have been treated in the author's article 'Parametricism: A new global style for architecture and urban design', in Neil Leach (ed), *AD Digital Cities*, Vol 79, No 4, July/August 2009.
2. Karl Friedrich Schinkel, *Das Architektonische Lehrbuch*, Deutscher Kunstverlag (Munich/Berlin), 2001, p 22. The text from 1805 remained an unpublished fragment during Schinkel's time.
3. Germain Boffrand, *Book of Architecture Containing the General Principles of the Art*, Ashgate Publishing (Aldershot), 2003, pp 21–2; French original, *Livre d'architecture* (1745), excerpt in Harry Francis Malgrave (ed), *Architectural Theory*, Blackwell Publishing (Oxford), 2006, p 193.
4. Boffrand, op cit.
5. Jacques-Francois Blondel, *Course of Architecture*, 1771, excerpt in Malgrave, op cit, p 198. Blondel goes on to utilise the distinction of male versus female as an analogical character distinction applicable to buildings. The male character entails massiveness, firmness, grandeur, should be sparse in the detail of its ornament, show simplicity in general composition and feature projecting bodies that throw large shadows.
6. Walter Benjamin, 'The Work of Art in the Age of Mechanical Reproduction', in Walter Benjamin, *Illuminations: Essays and Reflections*, Schocken Books (New York), 1969.
7. Adolf Loos, *Sämtliche Schriften 1897–1930*, Herold Druck- und Verlagsgesellschaft (Vienna), 1962.
8. See Greg Lynn (ed), *AD Folding in Architecture*, Vol 63, No 3–4, 1993.
9. See Stephen Perrella (ed), *AD Hypersurface Architecture*, Vol 68, No 5–6, 1998.
10. Schumacher, op cit.
11. The author has been experimenting with the agenda of parametric figuration in various teaching arenas: Innsbruck University, the Architectural Association Design Research Lab (DRL), Yale University and the University of Applied Arts, Vienna.

RELENTLESS PATTERNS

THE IMMERSIVE INTERIOR

Ingo Maurer, Rose, Rose, on the Wall...,
Salone del Mobile, Milan, 2006

**What happens when patterns become all
pervasive? When pattern contagiously
corrupts and saturates adjacent objects,
artefacts and surfaces; blurring internal
and external environment and dissolving
any single point of perspective or static
conception of space. Mark Taylor
ruminates on the possibilities of relentless
patterning in interior space in both a
historic and a contemporary context.**

Writing in *Space, Time and Perversion* (1995) philosopher
Elizabeth Grosz poses the question as to whether architecture can
be rethought in terms of the outside, 'in terms of surfaces, in
terms of a certain flatness, in terms of dynamism and movement
rather than stasis or the sedentary.[1] Taking a Deleuzian line of
enquiry, Grosz argues the outside as that which is not 'inside'
architecture and its history. The intent is to open architecture
beyond traditional frameworks in order to suggest what its future
might be. One 'internal' history is through the architectural canon
of Vitruvius, Alberti, Laugier and so on, a lineage that Mark Wigley
in *White Walls: Designer Dresses* discusses through purity of form
and materials, and the privileging of 'whiteness'.[2] Taking clues
from Modernism's interest in geometries, planar colours and
Minimalism, shelter magazines and real-estate agents tend to extol
this paradigm as 'clean lines,' 'neutrality' and 'flowing spaces'.

Pattern or patterned surfaces, objects and fabrics are to some
extent outside this; they are placed, in the gendered binary
division of architecture, in the negative, often as a covering to
some truthful material beneath. Interest sparked by the Aesthetic
Movement's wallpaper designs by William Morris, Lewis Day,
Christopher Dresser, Charles Eastlake and Walter Crane has in
recent years been recast, reflecting a marked interest in more
decorative or ornamental surfaces of the kind extolled by Herzog &
de Meuron, Melbourne-based practice Lyons and others. But even
these uses of patternation operate within a refined and controlled
order, supporting a larger architectural intent.

At the other end of the scale are interiors where the same
repeating motif is placed over all interior surfaces including the
wall, bed hangings, curtains, cushions and coverings. Whether
using floriated or abstract motifs, the effect of objects imitating
other objects is that the environment becomes blurred and
confused, resulting in patterns being indistinct from the
object/surface and becoming active components of its identity. In
this saturated environment objects, artefacts and surface
coverings occupy particular spatiotemporal, or proxemic, positions.

One early example is found in Robert Adam's Etruscan Dressing Room (1775) at Osterley Park in Middlesex, where chair rails are both the same dimension and painted in the same manner as the room's dado. This doubling of the painted surface blurs and confuses the chair's relation to the wall, so that one might be mimicking the other. The pattern of one surface has in a sense corrupted the other, as if the chair and wall are contagious, or combined. Roger Caillois, when discussing the biological and epistemological problems of surface mimicry, suggests that 'properties of objects are contagious. They change, reverse, combine and corrupt each other if too great a proximity permits them to interact.'[3]

Karl Friedrich Schinkel's design for a boudoir at Schloss Charlottenhof in Potsdam, Germany (1824–30)

comprises a continuous fabric surface that flows across the ceiling, down walls and out into space. Fine timber stools, chairs and daybeds are upholstered with the same material, producing, according to Ben Pell, 'an intoxicating atmosphere for Friedrich Wilhelm IV and his guests'.[4] In this instance the room is, as Pell argues, a fully immersive environment constructed through the relentless repetition of the graphic.

Although both of these examples are composed of abstract motifs, floriated and vegetal images have infused interior domestic spaces. Some blur the real and artificial and dissimulate the environment through application of the same or similar patterns across several surfaces, fabrics and objects. For example, Catherine Beecher and Harriet Beecher Stowe's, *The American Woman's Home* (1869) contains a drawing entitled 'A window with plants and ward's case' that contains a number of plants symmetrically arranged around the

**Catherine E Beecher and Harriet Beecher Stowe,
A window with plants and ward's case, 1869**
This Illustration from the Beechers' *American
Woman's Home* blurs the relation between inside
and outside, fracturing the interior.

**Robert Adam, The Etruscan Dressing
Room at Osterley Park, 1775**
The painted chair rail and dado are of
similar width and pattern so that they
imitate and corrupt each other, confusing
the chair's relation to the wall.

window.[5] Structured in a manner to support the
geometry of the static window, this image tends to blur
the relation between inside and outside, while beginning
to fracture the interior.

A more poignant example is described by Lady Barker
in *The Bedroom and the Boudoir* (1878) wherein the real
and artificial blend into one. She states:

> I know a rural bedroom with a paper representing a
> trellis and Noisette roses climbing over it; the carpet
> is shades of green without any pattern, and has only
> a narrow border of Noisette roses; the bouquets,
> powdered on the chintzs, match, and outside the
> window a spreading bush of the same dear old-
> fashioned rose blooms three parts of the year.[6]

In this short description, Lady Barker establishes a direct connection
between the inside and outside. Noisette roses are the agent to a spatial
reading that establishes the interior room as an extension of landscape.
That is, this room breaks the traditional reading of interior architectural
space as discrete rooms conforming to a greater architectural whole. The
existing architecture is neither regarded as a structure/substrate for
surface ornamentation, nor as an ordering system to be enhanced with
decorative motifs. Lady Barker's room is disassociated from traditional
physical and spatial systems, and is constructed in relation to the
exterior vegetation, which is mimicked through a form of abstracted
representation. It is an intense experience engaging the senses and
producing an immersive intoxicating atmosphere for the woman in her
boudoir. As such it is in contrast to the way architecture is traditionally
conceived as a machinic structure with adjustable components, forming a
functional entity of discrete parts subject to processes of removal or addition.

Old Battersea House, Wandsworth, London, 1980–92
Pattern desires to be dispersed and to be within everything, offering a mimetic spatial experience.

At Old Battersea House, pattern is also lured into material space creating a fully immersive environment.

This outlaying of vegetal patterns across objects and surfaces alters our perception of space and conversely alters architectural space. The resultant spatiality mimics the garden, inasmuch as patterned surfaces/objects imitate each other, so that the relationship between pattern and environment is blurred and confused. The environment is no longer distinct from the object, but remains an active component of its identity. It is room becoming garden, becoming dynamic, disorientating; it is desire as production.

Michael Ostwald has, through the writing of Roger Caillois, opened the idea that mimicry is not limited to animals and insects, but extends to architecture. He points out how in Australian practice Lyons' Victoria University On-line Training Centre in St Albans, there is confusion between building and landscape, and the building's surface – a digital topography that appears to be 3-D until closely scrutinised. Taking this idea into the relentlessly patterned interior, a form of mimicry occurs which, in the case of Caillois' insects, might be to do with the 'distinctions and confusions' it produces between itself and the environment. However, it is also the ability to morphologically imitate so that 'the creature, the organism, is no longer the origin of the coordinates, but one point among others'.[7] We could therefore say that the disorder of spatial perception and the desire for similarity has a goal, which is to 'become assimilated into the environment.'[8]

Greg Natale Design, Gonano Apartment, Summer Hill, Sydney, 2002
The intense use of a repeating pattern by Australian designer Florence Broadhurst in a small bedroom replaces traditional static space with a dynamic shifting state.

This assimilation of patterns into space hides or releases clearly identified physical forms from their static role. Bedspreads resemble walls, resemble lamps, resemble cushions, resemble hangings, and resemble covers and upholstery. For example, in one bedroom of the restored 18th-century Old Battersea House in Wandsworth, London, a deep-blue ground with flower motif descends the wall, flowing out across the headboard and bedspread. A small picture frame bleeds into the corner, while several framed paintings float in space. Another bedroom has a fabric 'tented' ceiling with a white and pink floriated motif that extends down the walls. Curtains, bedspreads, drapes and four-poster bed canopy are also finished in the same material, offering a mimetic spatial experience.

While these examples evoke design from another era, Sydney-based Greg Natale Design has used a similar strategy with a repeating pattern by the Australian designer Florence Broadhurst. Here, the design surfaces walls, bed covering and pillows, and even announces its 'worth' as a framed print. At the same time a number of artists and designers are using other Broadhurst fabrics on bags and accessories, inviting the print to travel through seemingly unrelated cultural categories. More conscious of this ability to 'run riot', Marimekko, the Finnish textile and clothing design company, has launched a range of prints that are inextricably bound through media and imaging as much as through cultural association. These 'licensed' patterns link the interior to clothing and accessories as a collection, identifying the wearer with an unbounded 'couture' interior.

As the manner of their location and operation becomes increasingly sophisticated, the appearance of patterns is also changing. Digital technologies offer the possibility of cutting at different scales and on various materials. For example, Atelier Manferdini has unleashed a laser-cut pattern on to a metal tray, a dress, a pair of Nike AirScale running shoes and a building. Operating at different scales, and cut into the material, this pattern is freed from the constraints of conventional ordering devices, and begins to take over, not to create an immersive environment but to immerse itself within the environment.

New technologies offer the possibility of non-static motifs, or the regeneration of patterns through interactive technologies such as those employed by Ingo Maurer. His recent installation, Rose, Rose, on the Wall..., is a 'wallpaper' project composed of 900 circuit boards with around 10 per cent equipped with RGB LEDs set out in a rose pattern. Complete with flat plasma-screen fire, the colour and brightness of this domestic wallpaper can be adjusted and programmed according to mood, thereby changing the appearance of the repeating pattern.

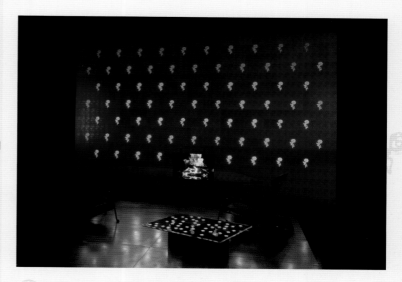

Ingo Maurer, Rose, Rose, on the Wall..., Salone del Mobile, Milan, 2006
Maurer's programmable 'domestic wallpaper' consists of 900 circuit boards, some equipped with RBG LEDs, set out in a rose pattern. Colour and brightness can be adjusted according to mood, offering a variable environment.

While this last project is static in location but variable in intensity, other patterns discussed above are lured into material space and desire to be dispersed everywhere, to be within everything, and even to be matter itself. We could say that under this conception objects and environment withdraw pushing back the constraints by which we realise space, so that it becomes a fully immersive environment. Although Caillois' psychasthenia is a response to the lure posed by space for the subject's identity, in the saturated interior the subject's (pattern) response is constructed in a similar manner. That is, the interior as a dissected and stratified entity is replaced by one of movement and shifting states, which for the occupants removes their traditional right to a 'perspectival point' and, to use Grosz's terms, forces the participant to 'abandon themselves to being spatially located by/as others'.[9] ⌀

Notes

1. Elizabeth Grosz, *Space, Time and Perversion*, Allen and Unwin (St Leonards), 1995, p 135.
2. Mark Wigley, *White Walls, Designer Dresses: The Fashioning of Modern Architecture*, MIT Press (Cambridge, MA), 1995.
3. I am indebted to Michael Ostwald for his discussion of Caillois and surface effects in his 'Seduction, subversion and predation: Surface characteristics', in Mark Taylor (ed), *AD Surface Consciousness*, Vol 73, No 2, 2003, pp. 75–80.
4. Ben Pell, 'Walldrobe/Wearpaper', in Emily Abruzzo and Jonathan D Soloman (eds), *Decoration*, 306090, Inc (New York), 2006, p 117.
5. Catherine E Beecher and Harriet Beecher Stowe, *The American Woman's Home: or Principles of Domestic Science; Being A Guide to the Formation and Maintenance of Economical, Healthful, Beautiful, and Christian Homes*, JB Ford and Company (New York), 1869.
6. Lady Barker, *The Bedroom and Boudoir*, Macmillan and Co (London), 1878, p 11. For a fuller discussion of this see Mark Taylor and Julieanna Preston, 'Interior bowers: Dormant wilderness in nineteenth century boudoirs', *IDEA Journal*, 2005, pp 75–83.
7. Roger Caillois, cited in Elizabeth Grosz, op cit, p 89.
8. Roger Caillois, 'Mimicry and legendary psychasthenia', in Claudine Frank (ed), *The Edge of Surrealism: A Roger Caillois Reader*, Duke University Press (Durham), 2003.
9. Elizabeth Grosz, op cit, p 90.

NEW PATTERNS IN URBAN DESIGN

Leven Betts Studio, Chicago Filter Park, Chicago, Illinois, 2003
Leven Betts Studio's Chicago Filter Park design confronts the negative impact of parking lot sprawl in cities and suburbs by recognising the larger patterns of urban infrastructure. The park filter is composed of two thin linear structures of automated parking for 1,000 cars, a bus terminal, pedestrian and cycle paths, green roofs and hanging-tree gardens suspended in the steel cross bracing.

Brian McGrath and Victoria Marshall discern the newly resilient urban patterns that are emerging in the meta-city, shifting and adjusting to changing local and global conditions. Based on smart infrastructure, self-sufficiency and hybrid local models, highly adaptive design patterns take the form of responsive micropatches rather than overarching masterplans. As demonstrated by the featured projects, 'pattern recognition', sensory mapping techniques and sensitivity to a city's ecosystem are becoming essential tools to the urban designer.

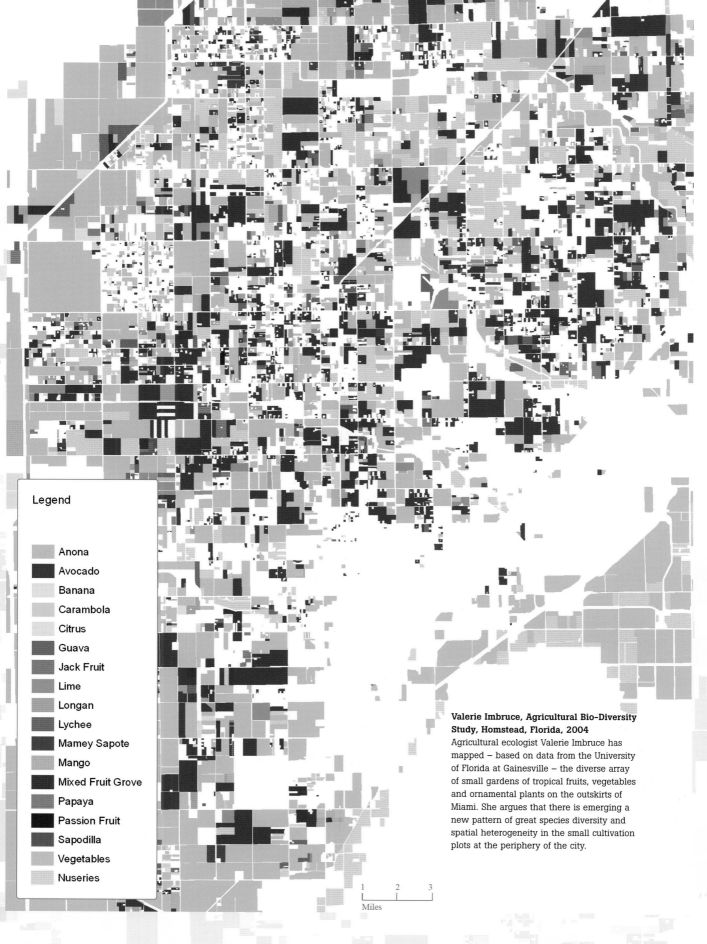

Legend

- Anona
- Avocado
- Banana
- Carambola
- Citrus
- Guava
- Jack Fruit
- Lime
- Longan
- Lychee
- Mamey Sapote
- Mango
- Mixed Fruit Grove
- Papaya
- Passion Fruit
- Sapodilla
- Vegetables
- Nuseries

Valerie Imbruce, Agricultural Bio-Diversity Study, Homstead, Florida, 2004
Agricultural ecologist Valerie Imbruce has mapped – based on data from the University of Florida at Gainesville – the diverse array of small gardens of tropical fruits, vegetables and ornamental plants on the outskirts of Miami. She argues that there is emerging a new pattern of great species diversity and spatial heterogeneity in the small cultivation plots at the periphery of the city.

1   2   3
Miles

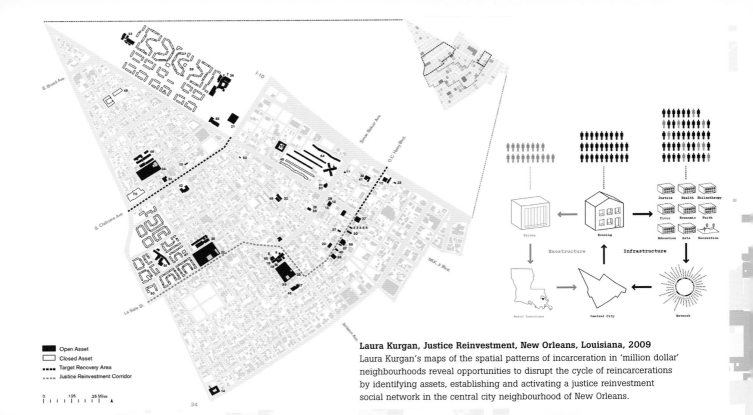

Laura Kurgan, Justice Reinvestment, New Orleans, Louisiana, 2009
Laura Kurgan's maps of the spatial patterns of incarceration in 'million dollar' neighbourhoods reveal opportunities to disrupt the cycle of reincarcerations by identifying assets, establishing and activating a justice reinvestment social network in the central city neighbourhood of New Orleans.

Self-propelled cyclists and biofuel commuters converge within the long vertical hall of Chicago Filter Park, a visionary infrastructural project by New York-based Leven Betts Studio. Architects David Leven and Stella Betts describe their design process as one of 'pattern recognition',[1] which in this project assimilates the layered logics of the expansive commercial street grid of the American city, the farms and forests of William Cronon's Nature's Metropolis,[2] Daniel Burnham's City Beautiful,[3] postindustrial inner-city fragments and exurban sprawl.

At the periphery of metropolitan Miami, beyond the monocultures of subdivisions and golf courses, agricultural ecologist Valerie Imbruce has studied the biologically and socially diverse patterns of micro-agricultural ecologies. Refugee farmers from Southeast Asia have cultivated a patchwork of small plots of tropical fruits, vegetables and ornamental plants. Proximity to Miami's port and interstate highways provides easy access to markets for exotic fruits and vegetables in East Coast Chinatowns.

In the central city neighbourhood of New Orleans, architect Laura Kurgan and the Justice Reinvestment project have devised a new pattern of social organisations to initiate one of the most strategic responses to the post-Katrina city. A new distribution system redirects the flow of public safety resources away from prisons and into reinvestment in the areas of New Orleans with disproportionate numbers of incarcerated residents. City justice patterns are being reimagined at the scale of the individual city block, organised through new physical and online social networking.

These three projects recognise, analyse and reassemble the flexible and dispersed postindustrial, agro-urban pattern of sprawling late 21st-century American cities.[4] While the bounded and centralised morphology of the 19th-century metropolis grew out of the metabolism of coal-burning and steam-powered industrial processes, the late 20th-century subsidised oil economy combined with the mobility of the private car produced a fractured and diffused urban pattern of the megalopolis. The post-Second World War breakdown of centralised metropolitan order also saw the easing of the enforced controls of rural migrations to the city and the emergence of megacities such as Rio de Janeiro, Johannesburg and Mumbai. What the megalopolis and the megacity have in common is a fractal-like growth pattern whose ordering systems are locally controlled, distributed and individuated, yet driven by the new-world economic order of the Bretton Woods System of global monetary relations. But the economies and metabolisms of megacity slums are highly efficient and resilient compared to the exurban landscape, which is currently under severe economic stress.

While the centrally planned and controlled colonial metropolis was splintered and fragmented by the late 20th-century megalopolis, this century's cities must confront the collapse of the former carbon-based urban model. New patterns of urban design are emerging based on smart infrastructure, self-sufficiency and hybrid local models that are able to scale up through new digitally enhanced social networks. The resulting 'meta-city' results in new resilient patterns of distributive managed micropatches rather than top-down masterplanned regional designs. The meta-city metabolism maintains flexibility and functional soundness by constantly readjusting and changing rather than returning to some fixed or equilibrium point after perturbation.[5] Resilient design patterns of the meta-city are based on the capacity of a system to adjust to changing conditions through maintaining tight electronic and bio-feedback loops.

Real-Time Actors in the Meta-City: Beijing, New York and Mumbai

During the 2008 Beijing Olympics, Sarah Williams clipped baton-like air-quality sensors on to reporters' and researchers' belts, backpacks and cars, in order to measure the impact of the closing of factories and traffic restrictions. The resulting environmental-monitoring relay race revealed continued high levels of particulate matter, but a temporary decrease in carbon monoxide during the games.

In New York City parks, Jordan and Efrem Press from Atlas Scientific, have planted solar-powered microcomputers, forming a network of sensors that monitor ground-water flow. They are able to quantify fluctuations and study new ways to manage the city's combined sewer outlet system. Their goal is to apply networked computer systems and expertise in biology and ecology to provide better understanding of urban ecosystem fluxes at a local level.

And in Mumbai, mobile phones serve as both input and output devices of information in Mobile Geographies, an urban-design game created by Colleen Macklin and Vyjayanthi Rao. Together with students at Parsons The New School for Design, the design and ethnography researchers aim to create a platform for the production and dissemination of geo-tagged urban information. Historical facts, individual experiences, neighbourhood statistics, planning and other information deemed important by a community of users provide a ghosted space where stories, histories and statistics reveal patterns of associations or visions of the future.[6]

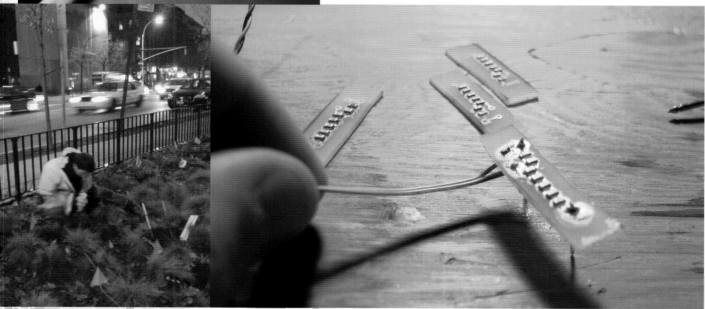

Sarah Williams, Air Quality Tracks: Beijing Olympics, Beijing, China, 2008
top: Sarah Williams dispersed portable air-quality sensors to volunteers in order to measure particulate matter and carbon monoxide matched with spatial location. She was thus able to map the change of air quality over time, tied to specific venue sites during the Beijing 2008 Olympics.

Jordan and Efrem Press (Atlas Scientific), Sensing New York's Ground water, New York, 2009
above: Jordan and Efrem Press from Atlas Scientific are developing ground-water flow sensors that can be planted like tulip bulbs in parks and green streets in New York City. The network of sensors provides spatial data in order to study new ways to manage the city's combined sewer outlet system.

The Taskforce on Sustainable Lifestyles (TSL) is a global network dedicated to redistributing resources and expertise between Europe and developing countries. TSL is part of a 10-year framework of programmes on sustainable consumption led by the UN Environmental Programme (UNEP) and Department of Economic and Social Affairs (UNDESA) to design the transition to a more sustainable global economy through changing everyday human behaviour and lifestyles. The Creative Communities for Sustainable Lifestyles (CCSL) project has been established to pinpoint emerging patterns of sustainable living. CCSL compares grass-roots innovations in everyday life in Europe with those in emerging countries like India, China and Brazil. Examples include production activities based on local resources and skills, healthy food, collaborative services for the care of children and the elderly, new forms of exchange, alternative mobility systems, and networks linking consumers directly with producers.[7]

abandoning the statistical sorting of the world into supposedly stable categories of race and class, and are now engaging more dynamic frameworks such as lifestyle choice and change over time. Collectively, these scientists and migratory citizens are translating their precise attention to ordinary patterns and processes that unlock existing orders of power, control and value. Together they are working with new non-equilibrium ecosystem models to imagine the design of the meta-city as comprising multiple stable transitions between states of material flux within fragments of the metropolis, in the formalisation of the informal settlements of the mega-city and a post-oil rehabilitation of the megalopolitan landscape of waste and sprawl.

New Patterns of Matter-Flux in the Meta-City

52 Famous Scenes of Newark is a patch-dynamic design model that reshuffles the New Jersey city's gateways into a low-cost sweat-equity participatory urban development project. Newark – sliced by the logic of aeroplanes, container ships, trucks, cars and trains – is here re-imagined as a geological ground of ridges, slopes, plains and rivers. The project asks residents, small businesses and artists to identify

The Emergence of the Meta-City

Meta-city patterns first appeared in the ruins of the fragmented metropolis during the first oil crisis of the mid-1970s. The logic of the meta-city combines both the techno-intelligence of the Dutch data-driven social democracy theorised by MVRDV in Meta City/Data Town[8] and the anarchitecture of creative social and environmental reorganisation within the ruins of what Naomi Klein has termed 'disaster capitalism'.[9] The social diversity of the meta-city lies at the intersection of suburban refugees who are increasingly ecologically literate, environmentally attentive and politically active, and rural migrants who bring with them self-sufficiency, hands-on skills and environmental intelligence. Together they are uniquely equipped to remake modern urban and suburban wastelands and bridge the urban/rural divide of the metropolitan urban pattern.

A feedback loop is emerging between specialised secluded research and distracted everyday urban life. Ecologists, geophysicists and climatologists – experts in the wild and the remote – have been venturing into cities since the 1970s. In addition, social scientists are

unique social and natural qualities at each gateway site. The city can license micro-economic activities tied to seasonal holidays – urban agriculture, vending, hawking, street performing. Digital feedback links these 'scenes' to a broad array of voices and audiences in the form of text messages, poetry, song, dance, rap, fashion and photography. The resulting cybernetic scenes are spectacular urban attractors, fantastic mixtures of vibrational matter-flux and new public spaces that are featured with mixed-use development marketing.

As all the projects illustrated here show, new urban design patterns are engaging cities, as living ecosystems, in the process of demolition and redevelopment through the monitoring of scientific research and attentive circuits of human bodies in movement. In a time of rapid urbanisation and climate change, more subtle and slower urban patterns of change demand our immediate attention. Many critical urban ecosystem processes, even when scientifically monitored, remain invisible in everyday life. The recent convergence of environmental attentiveness, ecological literacy and economic collapse, together with the rise in new digital and mobile communications technologies, new socionatural networks and smart infrastructure provides the context for the emerging pattern of the meta-city to thrive. ∆

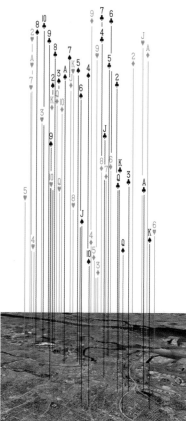

Colleen Macklin and Vyjayanthi Rao, Mobile Geographies, Mumbai, 2006
opposite: Text-messaging games serve as tools for participatory urban design activism in Mobile Geographies, a project involving students at Parsons The New School for Design and Mumbai's Urban Design Research Institute led by designer Colleen Macklin and anthropologist Vyjayanthi Rao.

Notes
1. David Leven and Stella Betts, *Pattern Recognition*, Princeton Architectural Press (New York), 2009.
2. William Cronon, *Nature's Metropolis: Chicago and the Great West*, WW Norton & Co (New York), 1991.
3. Carl Smith, *The Plan of Chicago: Daniel Burnham and the Making of the American City*, University of Chicago Press (Chicago, IL), 2006.
4. Robert Bruegmann, *Sprawl: A Compact History*, University of Chicago Press (Chicago, IL), 2005.
5. See Brian McGrath and David Grahame Shane, 'Metropolis, Megalopolis, Metacity', in Steven Cairns, Greg Crysler and Hilde Haynen (eds), *Handbook of Architectural Theory*, Sage Publications, forthcoming.
6. See http://a.parsons.edu/~mobile_geographies/.
7. See http://www.sustainable-everyday.net/ccsl/?page_id=4.
8. Winny Maas, *Meta City/Data Town*, MVRDV/010 Publishers (Rotterdam), 1999.
9. Naomi Klein, *The Shock Doctrine: The Rise of Disaster Capitalism*, Picador (New York), 2008.

Victoria Marshall and Brian McGrath, 52 Famous Scenes of Newark, Newark, New Jersey, 2009
above: The project establishes a network of places that link micro-economies and geographic distinctiveness to create a new image for the city. A detail of a gateway site where Interstate 280 meets an old industrial neighbourhood near Frederick Law Olmsted's Branch Brook Park, depicts flower vendors on Mother's Day.

Tracing Change Patterns in Landscape Architecture

For **Simon Swaffield**, landscape design can be regarded as the product of distinctive patterns formed through the intersection of site, technology and idealised nature. Across time and cultures, the interpretation of nature has shifted endlessly, and with it the manner in which the natural world is conceived, transformed and represented. Given its history, what might also be the future patterns of landscape design?

A Buddhist monk raking gravel into wave-like patterns in the Zen garden at the Zuiho-in Temple in Kyoto.

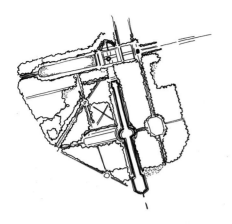
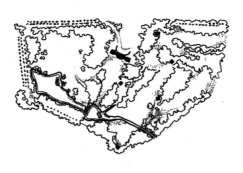
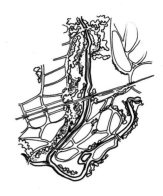

The distinctive patterns of the designed landscape are created at the intersection of site, technology and idealised nature. For landscape architecture is a hybrid art, and its patterns express the creative tensions between the very different imperatives embedded within the landscape medium. As both idea and artefact,[1] landscape is constructed from the interplay of imagined possibilities and the materiality of site, where 'beautiful' human order interrelates with the 'sublime complexity' of nature.[2] Such designed landscapes are always practically situated, both physically and culturally,[3] and their distinctive patterns express the way that ideals of nature are shaped conceptually and technically to the configurations and programmes of different sites.[4] They are, in effect, 'diagram[s] of process'[5] inscribed upon a particular terrain.

The primary imperatives that generate pattern in designed landscapes – technology, nature, and site form and function – are each complex and challenging realms of discourse. Site has always been a defining focus of landscape architecture. The patterns of designed landscapes express integrated systems of topography, ecology, water, structures and human uses, configured through design imperatives intended to 'amplify a site's latent character',[6] meet contemporary social needs and inscribe the signatures of prevailing cultural narratives.

One of the most ubiquitous of these cultural narratives is about the continually regenerating flux of energy and material we call nature, which is arguably the dominant metaphor of landscape architecture.[7] The patterns made by the discipline are thus expressions of nature conceived, transformed and re-presented. These ideals change over time, and so also does their design expression – from the visions of paradise of the premodern world to the God-given 'natural' order of the Enlightenment, and the self-organising and regenerating ecological systems of late modernity.

Technology provides the practical tools and potentials for design action. Each phase of culture has distinctive ways of communicating, processing material and obtaining energy, which both enable and limit the shaping of nature, real and imagined. The seminal moments of the discipline and the patterns through which they are expressed are typically those where innovative technologies are deployed to represent a new ideal of nature. Technology also shapes the patterns of landscape architecture reflexively, as each era of the discipline gives prominence to dimensions of nature that are revealed by the prevailing technologies of science.

What types of landscape pattern have these interrelated systems and imperatives created? Archetypical elements of landscape based upon long-established and regionally bounded cultural practices, uses and technologies provide the vocabulary for traditional patterns of landscape architecture. They include landform (promontory, terrace and theatre), vegetated space (clearing, bosque, alee and tree) and constructed space (cloister, yard, street and square), as well as water features – spring/fountain, pool and canal.[8] In premodern landscapes, these elements are typically combined to create landscapes of contemplation, enclaves shaped to express conceptually and experientially a sacred ideal of nature.

This inward focus contrasts with the grand visions of post-Enlightenment landscape architecture. In particular the Renaissance palace gardens of André Le Nôtre are notable for the way they explored the infinite potential of the Cartesian grid, extending conceptually and literally to the horizon and beyond. In these landscapes, the technologies of surveying and perspective are combined with advanced hydraulics to create a vast stage for the display of 'natural' and political order. Equally striking, but very different in pattern, are the improved rural estates of 18th-century England. These extensive 'pastoral' landscapes of open woodland, grass sward, water and isolated architectural features, were shaped through land engineering, stock husbandry and arboriculture to represent a naturalised arcadia of rural prosperity and wellbeing. These grand visions of order and wellbeing were subsequently reproduced and adapted to the precincts, parks and suburbs of the growing 19th-century industrial conurbations of the Western world, creating public and private settings for the celebration and restoration of body, mind and spirit.

Grand Visions: Patterns of Post-Enlightenment Landscape Architecture
opposite: The Cartesian geometry of Parc de Sceaux, Paris; the extensive rural arcadian landscape of Stowe, UK; and the suburban arcadia of Riverside, Chicago, by Frederick Law Olmsted.

Latz+Partner, Landschaftspark, Duisburg-Nord, Germany, 1991
left: Duisburg-Nord at night showing the combination of relict industrial geometry, light and organic regeneration.

The abstraction of 20th-century Modernism shifted creative thought away from landscape as a focus of cultural production, and suppressed the significance of site.[9] Landscape became relegated to the background, literally and figuratively, ordered as an 'outdoor room' through the extension of architectural functions and the placement of architectural objects. However, an important thread of landscape pattern development continued through the Modernist garden, in which abstract styles derived from painting and sculpture were adapted to the ecological, climatic and cultural particularities of a region and the new social functions of the consumer society.

By the mid-20th century, larger-scale landscape visions were again being more widely reasserted. In particular, Ian McHarg's agenda of a scientific stewardship of nature, based on multidisciplinary landscape analysis of the capability of 'natural' ecosystems to accommodate human uses, produced comprehensive, subregional landscape plans characterised by vivid patterns of discrete but interlocking zones of natural condition and human function.

Postmodernity has broken down the grand visions of modernity and replaced them with a pluralistic understanding of both culture and nature. This is notably expressed in the 'splintering'[10] and 'fragmentation'[11] of the unifying ideal of the grid, and its break up into a 'dislocated poly nucleated field'.[12] The shift to a new paradigm has offered a creative opportunity to recover landscape as a primary focus of cultural production, and the patterns of landscape architecture that have emerged over the past two decades express several new and contrasting imperatives. Digital technologies now play a major role, enabling dynamic multiple layering and shaping of data, empowered by remote sensing and techniques of virtual reality. The resulting designs are inspired by new conceptions of nature as chaos and cyborg, and draw particularly on artistic devices of collage[13] to valorise and reproduce the fractured mosaic of the late Modern city. Expressed in regional visions for extensive urban redevelopment, disciplinary boundaries have become blurred, enrolling architecture and infrastructure into an ambitious programme of landscape urbanism.

Alongside these ambitious expansionary programmes, there has also been a revitalisation of the central landscape architectural concern for the qualities of site, and in particular for its topography and its ecological regeneration. Degraded and abandoned brownfield sites, rivers and waste dumps are rehabilitated using ecological engineering techniques and new metaphors of nature, creating a 'sublime' post-industrial landscape.[14]

Renewable energy as a driver of future landscape patterns: An energy farm in Alameda County, California.

This refocus on process highlights the phenomenological and performative role of landscape, and a contemporary 'reclaiming' of site[15] creates palimpsest-like patterns in which earlier site histories are excavated, reinvented and reinscribed. Design action shifts from the transformation of extensive landscape mosaics to a more precise, tactical incision of particular design gestures.[16] The resulting patterns of designed landscape are marked as much by absence as by physical presence, creating openings that permit things to 'take place'.

What of the emerging, future patterns of landscape? The overriding imperative of the 21st-century designed landscape will surely be the need to respond to the global phenomenon of climate change and its human consequences. Designed landscape patterns will become increasingly shaped by the changing scientific understanding of climate and environmental systems, by the technologies deployed to influence their trajectories and to manage the local effects of change, and by the ability of society and culture to envision and implement redemptive action. There will be creative tensions between the imperative to engage with the sustainability agenda through regional and global transformations of

human ecosystems using new technologies and ever more complex datascapes, and the phenomenological need for 'a poetic mediation on existence'[17] at an individual and site level.

The complex systems created at the intersection of hydrology, topography and technological infrastructure will thus be interwoven by labyrinths of unfolding paths and performances that attempt to reconcile our 'senses with science'.[18] The patterns of landscape that result will, as before, express the coming together of contemporary technology, new ideals of nature and their combination in site programme, process and form. We might anticipate enhanced articulation of flows of recycled materials and water through divaricating networks, overlaid by grids of machines designed to capture renewable energy. Vegetation mosaics will regenerate the interstices of the infrastructure, revitalising ecosystem functions, converting solar energy into food and biofuels, and capturing carbon.

New aesthetic experiences and sources of delight will emerge both by design and serendipity from the newly emergent visual ecology of the 21st century.

The significance of time as 'the crucial dimension of landscape'[19] will be reasserted, and the fundamental design challenge will become how to shape landscape systems that sustain our material wellbeing at multiple spatial scales, from global to local, as well as our spiritual and experiential 'being' in place 'in a multiplicity of times'.[20] ᗄ

Notes

1. James Corner (ed), *Recovering Landscape*, Princeton Architectural Press (New York), 1999, p 1.
2. Patrick Condon, 'A built landscape typology: The language of the land we live in', in K Franck and L Schneekloth (eds), *Ordering Space: Types in Architecture and Design*, Van Nostrand Rheinhold (New York), 1994, pp 79–96.
3. David Leatherbarrow, *Uncommon Ground: Architecture, Technology and Topography*, MIT Press (Cambridge, MA), 2000, p 278.
4. Elizabeth Meyer, 'Site citations', in C Burns and A Hahn (eds), *Site Matters: Design Concepts, Histories, Strategies*, Routledge (New York), 2005, pp 93–129.
5. Simon Bell, *Landscape: Pattern, Perception and Process*, F&N Spon (London), 1999, p 33.
6. Meyer, op cit, p 97.
7. Laurie Olin, 'Form, meaning and expression in landscape architecture', *Landscape Journal*, No 2, 1988, pp 136–47.
8. Condon, op cit.
9. Meyer, op cit, p 114.
10. Steven Graham and Simon Marvin, *Splintering Urbanism – Networked Infrastructures, Technological Mobilities, and the Urban Condition*, Routledge (London), 2001.
11. Ross King, *Emancipating Space: Geography, Architecture and Urban Design*, The Guildford Press (New York),1996, p 114.
12. Albert Pope, 'The last horizon', in C Spellman (ed), *Re-Envisioning Landscape/Architecture*, Actar (Barcelona), 2003, p 179.
13. King, op cit, pp 47 and 130.
14. Michael Peter Lang, *The Post Industrial Landscape and the Sublime*, University of Virginia Press (Charlottesville, VA), 2000.
15. Sebastien Marot, 'The reclaiming of sites', in Corner, op cit, pp 45–58.
16. Georges Descombes, 'Shifting sites: The Swiss way, Geneva', in Corner, op cit, pp 79–86.
17. Mark Treib, 'Nature recalled', in Corner, op cit, p 37.
18. Christophe Girot, 'Four trace concepts in landscape architecture', in Corner, op cit, p 66.
19. Treib, op cit, p 37.
20. King, op cit, p 248.

EDAW AECOM, Gold Coast Intern Program, Intertidal Urbanity, 2007
This design vision for future urban structure in Queensland, Australia, by a team of student interns, expresses perfectly the hybrid geometries of the organic networked landscape of the 21st century.

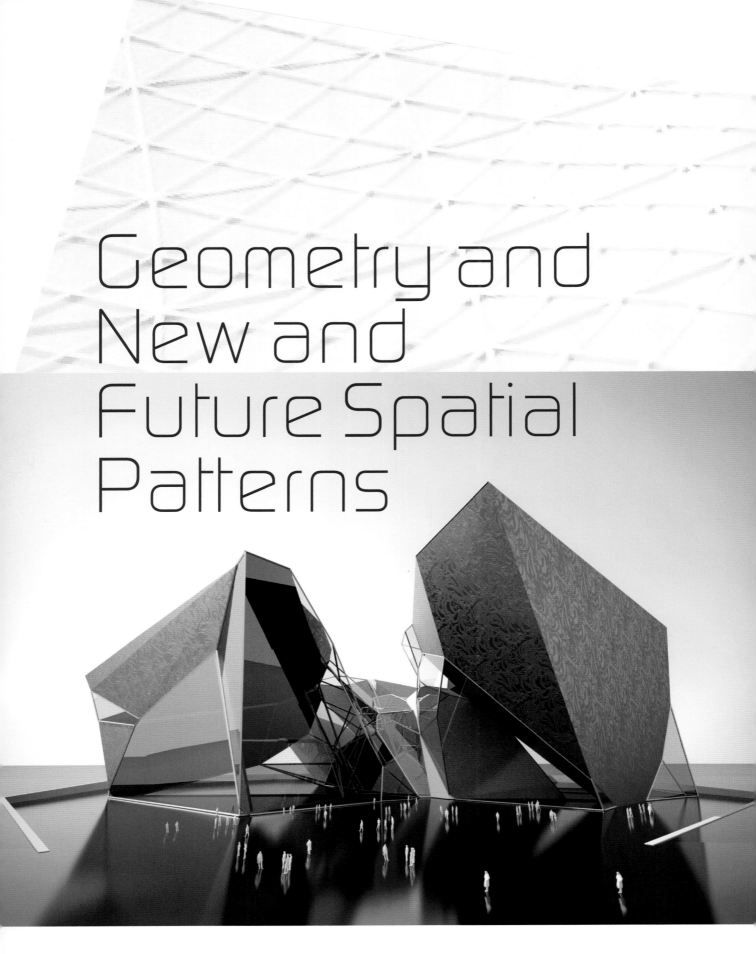

Geometry and New and Future Spatial Patterns

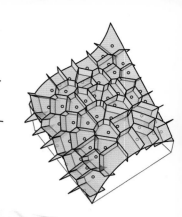

Despite architects' preoccupation with designing geometric surfaces, there has remained a gap between design and construction. The realisation of complex architectural freeform shapes and the generation of panel patterns continues to be especially challenging, limited by material and manufacturing constraints. Here, **Helmut Pottmann**, Head of Geometric Modelling and the Industrial Geometry Group within the Institute of Discrete Mathematics and Geometry at Vienna University of Technology (TU Vienna), explores the possibilities thrown up by new research employing fabrication-aware design software.

Geometric patterns have fascinated mankind since ancient times. Artists had an excellent understanding of the generation principles of patterns long before mathematicians devoted deep studies to this subject. A prominent example is furnished by Moorish architecture. In the 13th-century Alhambra Palace in Granada, Spain, we find all the essentially different types of pattern that can be formed by congruent tiles; the mathematical classification has only been achieved in the 20th century. Contemporary architecture generates a stunning variety of new designs and spatial patterns, but architects do not always have the right tools at their disposal to realise such structures. It is a challenging and exciting task for mathematicians to bridge the gap between design and construction and devise new fabrication-aware design tools for architectural application.

Patterns are a vast subject. Even in architecture they come in a variety of applications. The focus here is on recent research motivated by the realisation of complex architectural freeform shapes, where patterns arise naturally through the layout of panels and by supporting structures associated with freeform geometry. The generation of panel patterns is especially challenging on large seamless surfaces, since this is not only a matter of aesthetics, but also heavily influenced by material and manufacturing constraints.

Texture Mapping Versus Panelling

Computer graphics have intensively investigated the problem of mapping planar texture on to a double-curved surface while minimally distorting it. Texture mapping techniques may be useful in architecture for purposes of decoration and presentation, but for panelling they are hardly sufficient. Based on the choice of material and manufacturing technology, certain geometric shapes of panels are preferred; planar panels are always the simplest and cheapest. Curved panels should be cylindrical when working with glass; they can be more general, single-curve panels when metal is used; and should be ruled surfaces for certain technologies to manufacture curved glass-fibre reinforced concrete panels. However, available CAD software does not take such factors into account, hence patterns of panels and associated structures are an active topic for research and development.[1,2]

Companies that provide geometry consulting services in this field include Designtoproduction,[3] Evolute[4] and Gehry Technologies,[5] some of whom develop specialised software (based on optimisation algorithms) capable of solving basic panelling problems. The work featured here is the result of using software implemented at the Geometric Modeling and Industrial Geometry research group at TU Vienna and at Evolute.

Voronoi diagrams and their multiple generalisations are a rich source for the design of spatial structures. They associate nearest neighbour regions (Voronoi cells) to a set of input points. The concept works in the plane (top left), for input points on a curved surface (top right; only the part of the diagram close to the surface is shown) and in space (opposite).

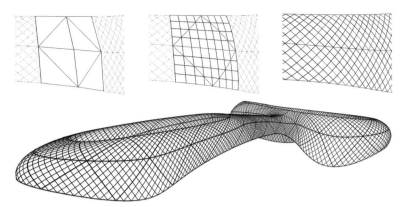

Asymptote Architecture, Yas Island Marina Hotel, Abu Dhabi, 2009
The quad pattern of supporting beams computed for the grid shell of
the Yas Island Marina Hotel receives structural stability through the
formation of especially strong beams arranged in a triangular macrostructure. The geometric computation and optimisation of the beam
layout by Evolute, Gehry Technologies and Waagner Biro Stahlbau,
Vienna proceeds as follows: (top row) An initial quad mesh is refined
via subdivision; part of the resulting mesh together with its diagonal
mesh contains the desired triangular macrostructure and is finally
optimised towards high aesthetics while staying close to the
design surface and meeting a number of
constraints (bottom).

Subdivision Techniques

Subdivision is a popular approach to shape modelling and
is based on the successive refinement of a coarse input
mesh. Subdivision algorithms, a first simple variant of
which led Buckminster Fuller to his geodesic domes, tend
to produce aesthetically pleasing meshes and are
therefore particularly interesting for architecture. They may
be used to generate meshes formed by triangles, quads or
hexagons, or even more complicated patterns, some of
which are addressed below in connection with circle
patterns. Subdivision may also be part of the geometric
optimisation strategy for an architectural structure.

Patterns from Planar Quads

For Asymptote's Yas Island Marina Hotel in Abu Dhabi
(2009), the panels are mounted with gaps to the
structure and thus planarity of the quadrilateral mesh
faces has not been an issue. However, for watertight quad
structures, planarity of faces may be essential. Recently,
important progress has been achieved in the design and
computation of freeform quad meshes with planar faces
(known as PQ meshes).[6] Recent geometric research has
revealed a close relation between PQ meshes and the
curvature behaviour of the underlying surface. If the quad
panels need to be close to rectangles, the layout is guided
by the principal curvature lines of the surface, and these
curves follow the directions of locally extreme normal
curvature. The resulting patterns may be intriguing, but
also limiting when specific requirements on the panel
layout for an already designed surface need to be met.
The design of PQ meshes with the help of subdivision,
interleaved with optimisation, is much easier and ready
for practical use.

Supporting Structures

Special types of PQ meshes such as the so-called conical
meshes can be embedded into a sequence of meshes of the
same type that lie at a constant distance from each other. The
distance may be measured in different ways, leading to different
mesh types. For example, conical meshes possess offset meshes
where corresponding faces lie at constant distances. Related to
this are layouts of supporting beams with torsion-free nodes;
that is, at each vertex the central planes of the beams are
coaxial. On the other hand, hybrid meshes can be associated
with offsets at variable distances; however a torsion-free beam
layout can generally only be achieved in an approximate way via
an optimisation algorithm.

Hexagonal Structures

Buckminster Fuller, Frei Otto,[7] Lars Spuybroek[8] and others have
been fascinated by the shapes and structural efficiency of the
siliceous microskeletons of radiolaria whose shapes are often
based on hexagonal meshes. Hexagonal meshes representing
freeform shapes are a geometrically very interesting subject.
Focusing on the planarity of faces yields surprising patterns,
since panels in negatively curved (locally saddle-shaped) areas
will not be convex. To generate a 'hex mesh' with planar faces,
one may start with a triangle mesh and intersect tangent planes
at mesh vertices; the result will be a mesh formed by mostly
hexagonal panels. This is a numerically very sensitive process,
accompanied by difficulties in controlling the behaviour in areas
where Gaussian curvature changes its sign.[9] Thus, achieving
high aesthetic quality in a hex mesh with planar faces is a
challenging and largely unexplored topic. It should be
mentioned that patterns of planar panels with more than four
edges per panel always exhibit non-convex panels in the areas of
negative Gaussian curvature.

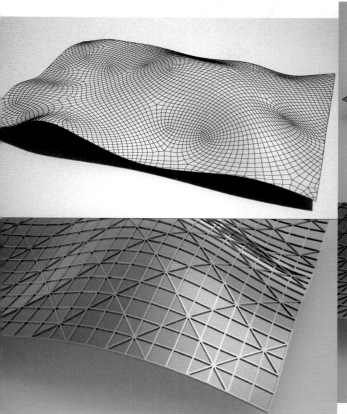

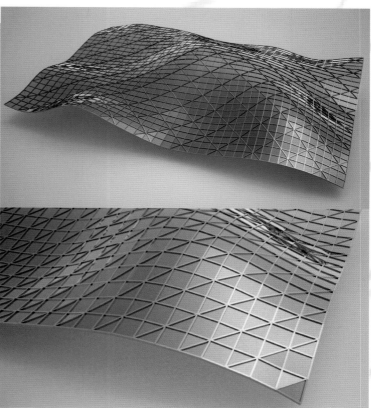

Patterns of planar quads strongly reflect the curvature behaviour of a surface. These may exhibit extraordinary points at undesired locations, a strong variation in panel sizes and incompatibility with boundary conditions. A practical solution to meet imposed constraints can be achieved by hybrid meshes of triangles and planar quads since they offer more degrees of freedom. The dataset for this example comes from the design of an Islamic Art department in the Louvre, Paris, by Mario Bellini and Rudy Ricciotti. The mesh on the lower right (by Evolute and Waagner Biro Stahlbau, Vienna) has been chosen as the solution to be realised.

Multilayer structures are spatial patterns around a surface-like pattern. This image shows a structure based on a conical mesh and formed by planar quads only.

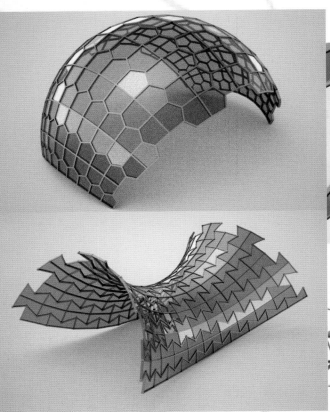

Circle Patterns and Derived Structures

Motivated by the work of Future Systems (Selfridges department store, Birmingham, 1999), researchers at TU Vienna and TU Graz are currently investigating patterns associated with special arrangements of circles and spheres on surfaces which are derived from so-called 'circle-packing' (CP) meshes. These are triangle meshes where the in-circles of neighbouring triangles have the same contact point at their common edge. CP meshes enjoy a high aesthetical value and lead to various remarkable surface patterns as well as to a number of unsolved mathematical problems. Neighbouring in-circles of CP meshes are tangent to each other and thus they form an arrangement of circles that in mathematics may be called a 'packing'. However, this packing is not complete, since each circle has only three neighbouring circles tangent to it, while in a complete packing six tangent neighbours (for most of the circles) would be preferable. One could say that there is a circle missing at each vertex. Complete circle packings exist only in the plane and on the sphere. On surfaces, it is necessary to move to an approximate solution, for which CP meshes provide various possibilities. Meshes formed by hexagons and triangles can also be computed from CP meshes. In these tri-hex meshes, the presence of triangles allows the use of nearly planar and almost regular hexagons in a structure where there is no longer the structural disadvantage of non-convex panels.

Pentagonal and hexagonal meshes with planar faces feature non-convex panels in negatively curved areas, so structural feasibility may require additional elements. The shown meshes are so-called 'edge offset' meshes that allow for a particularly clean layout of supporting beams. At each vertex, beams of constant height meet, perfectly aligned, on both sides and without torsion; that is, their central planes are coaxial.

Conclusion and Future Research

The design and fabrication of geometrically complex architectural structures will no doubt benefit from the interaction of architects with mathematicians and engineers. This has been illustrated by a number of recent solutions to, for example, panelling problems (with planar quads, planar hexagons and hybrid meshes) and supporting structures (in particular those which exhibit torsion-free nodes) for freeform hulls. Mathematics also offers promising tools for the design of fully 3-D spatial patterns such as Voronoi diagrams and shape evolution algorithms. In recent years, though shape evolution has received a lot of interest within mathematics and geometric computing, this has really only been in terms of computer vision and image processing applications rather than in architecture.

A related and highly challenging topic for future research is the computation of 4-D patterns in the form of animated facades and other flexible space structures. Ideas for such dynamic architectural designs have been contributed by, for example, Kas Oosterhuis and his co-workers within the Hyperbody research group at Delft University of Technology. These could provide the basis for further investigations from a mathematical/computational/engineering perspective to promote flexible architectural structures on a larger scale. **Δ**

Notes

1. Helmut Pottmann, Andreas Asperl, Michael Hofer and Axel Kilian, *Architectural Geometry*, Bentley Institute Press (Exton, PA), 2007.
2. Helmut Pottmann, Axel Kilian and Michael Hofer (eds), *Proceedings of Advances in Architectural Geometry*, Vienna, 2008.
3. See http://www.designtoproduction.com.
4. See http://www.evolute.at.
5. See http://www.gehrytechnologies.com.
6. Sigrid Brell-Cokcan and Helmut Pottmann, Supporting structure for freeform surfaces in buildings, Patent AT503.021 31.
7. Klaus Bach (ed), *Radiolaria*, Vol 33 of *Publications of the Public Institute of Lightweight Structures*, University of Stuttgart, 1990 (series editor: Frei Otto).
8. Lars Spuybroek, *NOX: Machining Architecture*, Thames & Hudson (London), 2004.
9. Christian Troche, 'Planar hexagonal meshes by tangent plane intersection', in Pottman, Kilian and Hofer, op cit, pp 57–60.

Left: Circle–packing (CP) meshes are triangle meshes where the inscribed circles of neighbouring triangles are tangent to one another and give rise to sphere packings on surfaces, to hexagonal patterns and to torsion-free beam layouts.

Centre: A tri-hex structure derived from a CP mesh, where the hexagons are nearly planar and regular.

Right: A supporting framework of a tri-hex mesh that makes use of the triangles in the mesh. The framework was inspired by that of Nicholas Grimshaw's Eden Project (2001) in Cornwall. However, the Eden Project represents spherical shapes, and a different layer in the framework takes on the role of the roof.

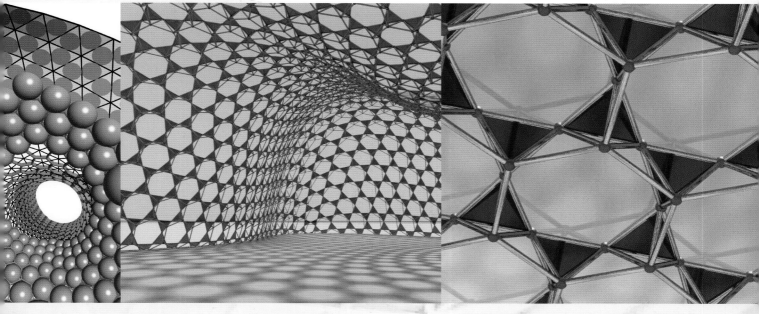

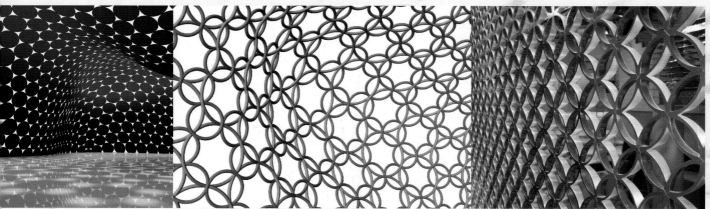

Left: Approximate circle packing of a freeform shape derived from a CP mesh.

Centre: CP meshes also serve as the basis for the computation of freeform circle patterns.

Right: A planar circle pattern in the Louis Vuitton store, Paris (architects: Eric Carlson and Peter Marino, Barthélémy & Griño, LVMH architecture, 2005–06).

For the structural engineer, patterns provide vast potential, ranging from the meta- to the microscale. Here, guest-editor Mark Garcia captures the ebullient enthusiasm Hanif Kara of Adams Kara Taylor has for this infinite topic, which is open-ended in its application, providing endless representational possibilities while also embracing both natural models and artificial forms and forces.

Reductive Engineering
An Interview with

Microscopic section of mahogany wood (*Pinus sylvestris*). Another part of the ongoing research by Hanif Kara and AKT is with regard to the patterns found in living organisms and nature, from plants and animals down to the micro-scale patterns of cells and systems of biological components.

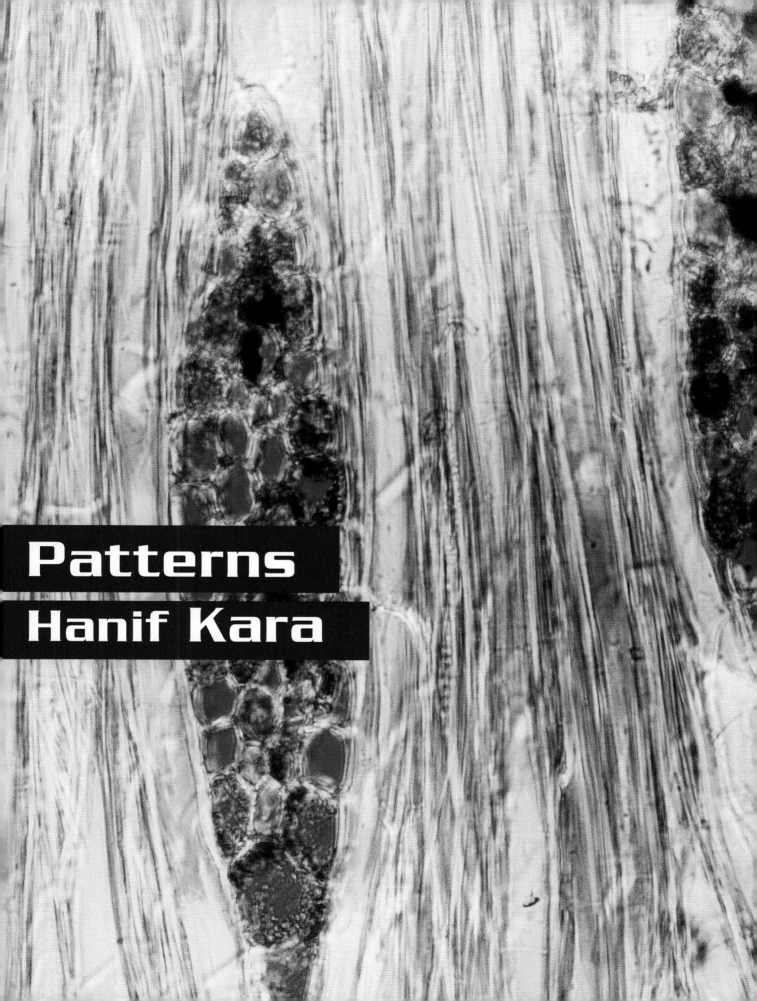

Patterns
Hanif Kara

A photomicrograph of the patterns of a sample of pure tungsten magnified 2.7 million times. This image was produced using a new superpowered Müller field ion microscope. Investigations of the pattern properties of crystals, metals, chemicals and synthetic, man-made materials are part of the ongoing engineering research of Hanif Kara and AKT.

Hanif Kara of Adams Kara Taylor (AKT) is one of the world's most sought-after engineers. Working with architects such as Zaha Hadid, Will Alsop, Foreign Office Architects, Foster + Partners, Thomas Heatherwick, David Chipperfield Architects, Hopkins, AHMM and Future Systems, the AKT portfolio is an index of the most significant, original and rigorous research, spanning avant-garde architecture, infrastructure, urbanism, engineering and design. Hanif Kara is Pierce Anderson Critic of Creative Engineering at GSD Harvard University, a visiting professor at the Arkitekturskolan, Stockholm, and a CABE commissioner. It is perhaps this unique mix of fundamental academic teaching and research, combined with a diversity of international experience in real, built projects, that makes him such an essential collaborator for architects seeking extraordinary solutions to difficult new types of design problem.

The world's top engineers are the *éminences grises* behind the world's best architects, and this is one of the reasons why architects and urban designers are only now able to deploy the most sophisticated kinds of pattern in their designs. As well as their specific disciplinary knowledge bases, engineers are expanding their capabilities and disciplinary links with current and emerging technologies. As a consequence of their multidisciplinary excursions, proactive engineers like Kara are also making significant innovations in the fields of computation, formal analysis, and structural, functional and other building and design performance developments. Being able to operate with and deliver the new kinds of high-performance and creative patterns that

are the hallmarks of some of the most original and successful spaces being designed today requires a complex set of organisational and behavioural holding patterns. Because Kara and AKT have been the structural engineers for so many of the innovative pattern-dependent architectures of the last five years, Kara is crucial to the future development of the field.

In this first published reflection on AKT's designed and built research into patterns in design engineering, Kara identifies the catalytic role of cutting-edge computational and production technologies (software programming, CAD/CAM, computational performance simulations and analyses) in the materialisation of patterned aesthetics and in the increased effectiveness of transfers of patterns from nature and biology into engineering. He also outlines the ways in which these processes require new patterns in the organisation and systems of AKT itself, as well as in the management and processes of specific projects and research activities. Together these have instigated an explosion of original and complex pattern typologies that are moving from the imagination into a built, high-performance, practical reality.

Nature, Scale, Material and Aesthetics in Pattern Engineering

How these factors have combined together to produce this new pattern paradigm is, as Kara explains, partly due to the work of engineer Cecil Balmond at Arup:

'In order to give coherence to the limited scope of an interview such as this, it is important to acknowledge the work of Cecil Balmond who has for some time been concerned with, and brought to the fore, the use of patterns in structural engineering. This has encouraged us to take the initiative to understand "patterns" that allow us to collaborate with architects and schools that are experimenting with the subject, not only to affect the conceptualisation of form, but also in the use and

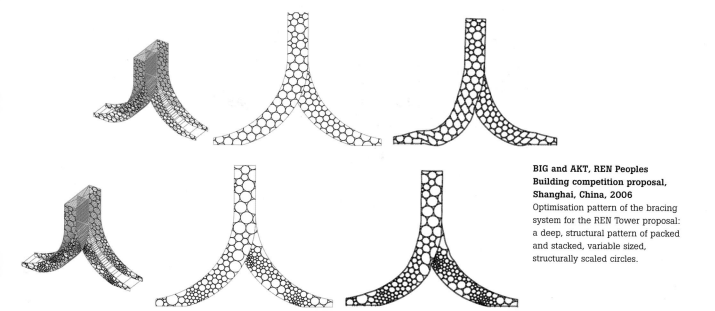

BIG and AKT, REN Peoples Building competition proposal, Shanghai, China, 2006
Optimisation pattern of the bracing system for the REN Tower proposal: a deep, structural pattern of packed and stacked, variable sized, structurally scaled circles.

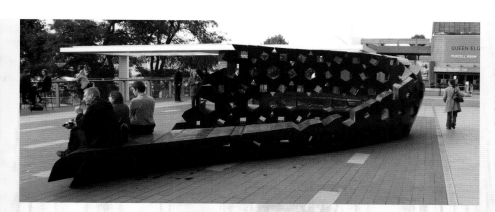

Zaha Hadid Architects and AKT, Urban Nebula, South Bank, London, 2007
For this sculptural installation, the parameters of the masonry units are varied to generate a unified but dynamic form.

nature of materials at the micro/macroscales. Straightforward correlation between patterns and any engineering can be a very reductive path, but for structural engineers the triumph of recent technologies is proving to be the simple, most powerful force in shaping new understandings and control of patterns. Clearly nature remains the best model we can follow at all scales when we are trying to get to grips with the vast subject of patterns at the meta- macro- object and microscales.

'As an office that has a propensity to engineer the practice of design itself, it is inevitable that the fascination with "patterns" as an instrument of the way in which the organisation behaves, the processes we go through, for studies in form generation and material organisation is of interest.

'Collaborations with architects and schools include research into the potential of patterns for "resemblance and representation" in aesthetics, but, more scientifically, AKT's interest goes beyond that to help reveal any other intelligence that can be brought to the fore in part of a

construction, or the whole building and site as it appears to the sight. We are mostly concerned with the artificial patterns that we can simulate and create from the daily rigorous production of load paths, force fields, connections, understanding topological geometry, and the "make-up" of materials.'

New Technologies and Computational Analyses in Pattern Engineering

Kara's identification of the five critical loci of patterns research in design engineering is crucial to his understanding of, and work in, this field. He is clear about the genealogy of his thinking in respect to these five key areas and the specific origins of each in the historical and theoretical design precedents and context of engineering in general. The case studies from AKT that he references in support of his position on patterns provide a clear diagram of his particular achievements and the legacy of patterns engineering as a whole. As he notes:

'This started with the tools of the late 1950s that allowed, for instance, the visualisation of stress fields on stress trajectories that eventually led to the advent of finite element modelling (FEM), a common computation technique for stress analysis today. Sophisticated FEM techniques now allow us to reveal stress contour

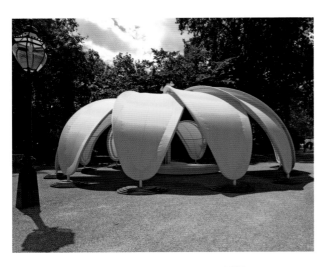

Tonkin Liu Architects and AKT, Flower Pavilion, 2008
View of the pavilion showing the fabric patterning by
engineering analysis and design consultants Tensys.

Tensys pattern diagrams of wind stresses.

FILL STRESS
(kN/m)

1.6
1.4
1.2
1.1
0.9
0.8
0.6
0.5
0.3
0.2
0.0

0.0

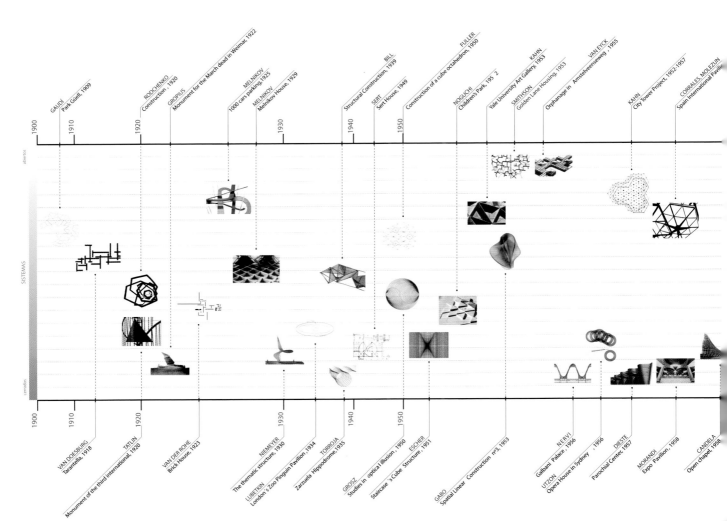

GAUDI
Park Güell, 1909

RODCHENKO
Construction, 1920

GROPIUS
Monument for the March dead in Weimar, 1922

MELNIKOV
1000 cars parking, 1925

MELNIKOV
Melnikov House, 1929

BILL
Structural Construction, 1939

SERT
Sert House, 1949

FULLER
Construction of a cube octahedron, 1950

NOGUCHI
Children's Park, 195_2

KAHN
Yale University Art Gallery 1953

SMITHSON
Golden Lane Housing, 1953

VAN EYCK
Orphanage in Amstelveenseweg, 1955

KAHN
City Tower Project 1952-1957

CORRALES, MOLEZUN
Spain International Pavilli

VAN DOESBURG
Tarantella, 1918

TATLIN
Monument of the third international, 1920

VAN DER ROHE
Brick House, 1923

NIEMEYER
The thematic structure, 1930

LUBETKIN
London's Zoo Pinguin Pavilion 1934

TORROJA
Zarzuela Hippodrome 1935

GROSZ
Studies in optical illusion, 1950

ESCHER
Staircase's Cube Structure, 1951

GABO
Spatial Linear Construction nr3, 1953

NERVI
Galbani Palace, 1956

UTZON
Opera House in Sydney, 1956

DIESTE
Parochial Center, 1957

MORANDI
Expo Pavilion, 1958

CANDELA
Open chapel, 1958

GEOMETRIAS DEL SIGLO XX ▌ GEOMETRIES D

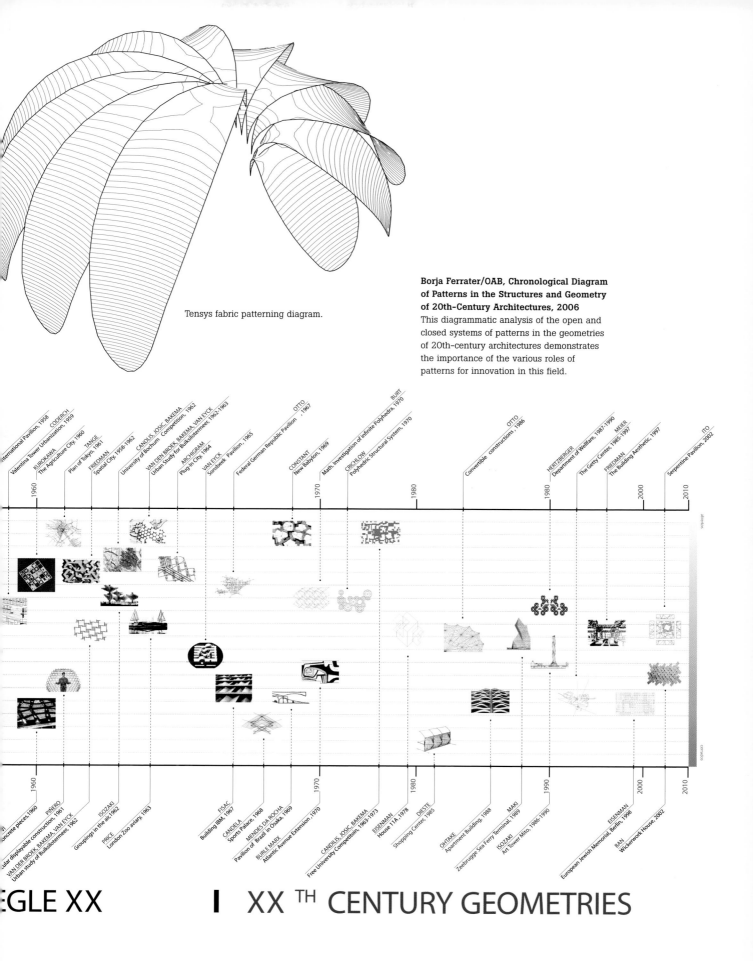

Tensys fabric patterning diagram.

Borja Ferrater/OAB, Chronological Diagram of Patterns in the Structures and Geometry of 20th-Century Architectures, 2006
This diagrammatic analysis of the open and closed systems of patterns in the geometries of 20th-century architectures demonstrates the importance of the various roles of patterns for innovation in this field.

International Pavilion, 1958
CODERCH
Valentina Tower Urbanization, 1959
KUROKAWA
The Agriculture City, 1960
TANGE
Plan of Tokyo, 1961
FRIEDMAN
Spatial City, 1958-1962
CANDILIS, JOSIC, BAKEMA
University of Bochum Competition, 1962
VAN DEN BROEK, BAKEMA, VAN EYCK
Urban Study for Buikslotermeer, 1962-1963
ARCHIGRAM
Plug in City, 1964
VAN EYCK
Sonsbeek Pavilion, 1965
Federal German Republic Pavilion
CONSTANT
New Babylon, 1969
OTTO , 1967
CRICHLOW
Polyhedric Structural System, 1970
BURT
Math. Investigation of Infinite Polyhedra, 1970
OTTO
Convertible constructions , 1986
HERTZBERGER
Department of Wellfare, 1987-1990
MEIER
The Getty Center, 1985-1997
FRIEDMAN
The Building Aesthetic, 1997
ITO
Serpentine Pavilion, 2002

1960   1970   1980   1980   2000   2010

1960   1970   1980   1990   2000   2010

cular displayable construction 1961
ncrete pieces,1960
PIÑERO
VAN DEN BROEK, BAKEMA, VAN EYCK
Urban study of Buikslotermeer, 1962
ISOZAKI
Groupings in the air,1962
PRICE
London Zoo aviary, 1963
FISAC
Building IBM, 1967
CANDELA
Sports Palace, 1968
MENDES DA ROCHA
Pavilion of Brazil in Osaka, 1969
BURLE MARX
Atlantic Avenue Extension 1970
CANDILIS, JOSIC, BAKEMA
Free University Competition, 1963-1973
EISENMAN
House 11A ,1978
DIESTE
Shopping Center, 1985
OHTAKE
Apartment Building, 1988
MAKI
Zeebrugge Sea Ferry Terminal, 1989
ISOZAKI
Art Tower Mito, 1986-1990
EISENMAN
European Jewish Memorial, Berlin, 1998
BAN
Wickerwork House, 2002

I XX ᵀᴴ CENTURY GEOMETRIES

patterns which give an incomplete picture but can inspire new ways of thinking about the next steps in the process of design iteration. Finite element techniques owe much to the understanding (of the previous half a century) of internal stresses that photoelastic models had provided. Photoelastic stress analysis relied on the property of certain transparent materials to transform polarised light into patterns as it passes through in proportion to the stresses inside the material.

'Currently the "images" produced by FEM analysis, when shown and understood by architects, can be manipulated to not only change the way materials will behave but to zoom out and develop forms that become more optimal and simultaneously allow new architectural concepts that relegate "style and rhetoric" if need be. This control gives us the confidence to look at reorganising the materials of structures – and let's face it, there are five principal structural materials: masonry, fabric, concrete, steel and timber.

Interior of the Dome of the Hall of Comares (Hall of the Ambassadors), Nasrid Palace, Alhambra, Granada, Spain, *c* 1338–90
The pattern here is a representation of the seven heavens of the Islamic paradise. This shallow dome is made from hundreds of thousands of pieces of interlaced cedarwood which form a complex interlacing of a number of geometrical patterns within patterns.

'Starting with patterns of steel bracing systems as an example, past models of "x", "k", "w" systems can be integrated and combined to be appropriated where they are needed the most, as the tools now allow new integrations and optimisations. Take, for instance, the REN Peoples Building by Bjarke Ingels Group (BIG) which AKT worked on. REN is a hybrid of two types: the tower and the bridge. Here, the architects' desire to use circles was seen as an opportunity for an exercise in "packing and stacking" different sizes of circle. Digital tools automate the optimisation of the circles through gathering and scaling in response to stresses. This can only be achieved by bespoke scripting that allows conversations between FEM packages and other architectural digital tools. A further demonstration of the power of such technologies is that biology-like processes are scripted to pack the circles.

'Taking "masonry" as an example material system, the Urban Nebula project on London's South Bank, in which we supported Zaha Hadid, explores the use of compression, but also of another hybrid form that is read as furniture, shelter and sculpture at the same time. "Variety of brick" sizes are used to produce a pattern of apertures of different sizes maintaining "block to block" contact of the masonry to ensure the predominant compression forces are transferred.

'Similarly, the early work of Frei Otto in developing the "analysis/patterning" software necessary for fabric structures revolutionised the understanding of "tension" and the patterns that develop when shape is used to transfer load. While fabric has less use today, it still fascinates some, and companies like Tensys have continued to develop highly sophisticated software for fabric structures, which can be adapted for analysing "patterning" and designing extremely complex surfaces.'

Kara's analysis of the importance of patterns in the history of design engineering is borne out in the diagram of 20th-century structural systems by ETAB Professor and Barcelona-based architect Borja Ferrater and his practice OAB (Office of Architecture in Barcelona). This chronological taxonomy of open and closed configurations of pattern systems in the geometry of architectural engineering of the period shows the importance and predominance of patterns as the level on which fundamental solutions and research innovations were grounded. It also shows how just a simple, small diagram or pattern can revolutionise architecture and engineering. Kara's analysis is both contained in, and goes beyond, the diagram.

Polydisciplinary Patterns in Engineering
Kara's own designed and built work in this field is successful partly because of the open, collaborative 'polydisciplinary' way in which AKT operates. As he explains, with reference to the Ferrater diagram:

'Now that we have new computational visualisation and analyses tools, one can pick out ideas from this work on patterns (that goes back to Nervi, Gaudí, Dieste and others) and advance them in new ways that could not have been achieved at the time. In our particular case this happens through our internal "polydisciplinary" group (P art) that helps the engineers (re)search such models. What is learnt from this is then reapplied and exploited by the "hardcore"

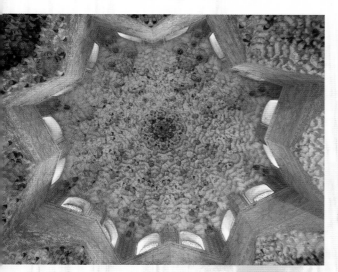

Interior of the 16-sided Dome of the Hall of Abencerrajes, Nasrid Palace, Alhambra, Granada, Spain, c1338–90
The image shows the 'honeycomb', 'mocarabe' or 'stalactitic' vaulting. The Alhambra is an architectural archive of hundreds of thousands of complex, mathematically and geometrically designed patterns that influenced many later spatial pattern designers such as MC Escher.

engineers. Stephen Wolfram in his simple principle of conceptual equivalence sums up the approach that we enjoy the most: "that whenever one sees behaviour that is not obviously simple – in essentially any system – it can be thought of as corresponding to a computation of equivalent sophistication".[1] Wolfram's discoveries in physics, mathematics, computer science, biology and other fields have been inspirational and an important reference point. At the macroscale, the modelling of flow patterns is another instance that has helped engineers understand cities and people and infrastructure projects. We have just been working on a project in Farringdon in London to investigate the possibilities of using these new simulations in a scheme to bridge over the station.

'Finally, I am fascinated by many kinds of patterns, some more controlled than others, like those of Escher and Pollock. I think the work done by Keith Critchlow on Islamic patterns has a lot of potential.[2] I don't fully understand the Islamic patterns, but there is no question that there is a certain way to go to learn from the scientific and aesthetic theory of vision and beauty in them.[3] The symmetry groups in Islamic geometric patterns and the frequency with which they appear in Islamic art and the built environment needs closer examination. I think, however, that the recent explosion (due to the market in the East) in the use of such patterns among designers can be dangerous. The patterns are often stretched, misused and ubiquitously proliferated to take away their original meanings and intentions.'

The Futures of Pattern Engineering/Engineering Patterns

For Kara, the futures of patterns in engineering lie in a number of larger-scale, interconnected, collaborative research programmes. His conclusions about the futures of patterns in engineering centre on extending both his academic and engineering work to a joint discourse with leading schools and architects:

'Prototypes and practical transfers with larger projects are a way forward. For example, spacesuits and other space technologies have some secret, high-performance features. If these micro-advances were shared and transferred to the building scale, for example to building skins, we could make some real progress. We are fascinated by things like emergent patterns and metallurgical, chemical and ligneous patterns, not just for their performance and efficiencies, but also for their beauty. New man-made materials are developed by understanding and creating new patterns at nano and molecular levels. Even failure patterns (where there is a crack) are fascinating and useful in understanding new, better and more efficient spaces. What I also find fascinating are those people who are scripting new patterns. In the right hands, these new patterns, with the right intelligence and expertise behind them (whether it is that of biologists, computer scientists, programmers, materials experts or technologists) can bring the highest levels of patterns to bespoke projects and techniques. What will unify all researchers and research projects in pattern design is the integration of the variety of digital tools.'

The scale of the projects and capabilities being built at AKT and through Kara's global academic and industrial networks, then, is set to be a defining factor in the future generation of innovations in pattern engineering. Kara's explanation of how AKT is designed to maintain the firm's current position as one of the leaders in this sector of engineering is (like both Kara and AKT itself), reassuringly honest, ambiguously pragmatic, poetic and mercurial:

'Internally, the way we organise ourselves and the way we organise teams around specific projects, people and firms also has a specific pattern in the sense of process and methodology. We adapt our own non-linear patterns to certain starting points to fit with the starting point of the project or architect and the methods used in their own patterns of working, thinking, making and their visions. These are all current and future projects we are working on, but there is still a long way to go. I would conclude with something Francis Bacon said: "I am greedy for … what chance can give us … far behind anything I can calculate logically."'[4] ⌂

Notes
1. Stephen Wolfram, *A New Kind of Science*, Wolfram Media (Canada), 2002.
2. Keith Critchlow, *Islamic Patterns: An Analytical and Cosmological Approach*, Thames & Hudson (London), 2008.
3. Valerie Gonzalez, Beauty and Islam: Aesthetics and Islamic Art and Architecture, IB Tauris Publishers (New York), 2001.
4. Louise Cohen, *The Times*, London, 9 September 2008. See http://entertainment.timesonline.co.uk/tol/arts_and_entertainment/visual_arts/article4706909.ece.

Biomimetic Patterns in Architectural Design

Julian Vincent, Professor of Biomimetics and Director of the Centre for Biomimetics and Natural Technologies within the Department of Mechanical Engineering at the University of Bath, identifies three distinct levels at which patterns can be translated from biology to architecture. Emphasising the importance of pattern recognition in the transfer of the most abstract derivations, he demonstrates that the greatest potential for biomimetics lies in its application for problem solving rather than straightforward mimicry of biological shapes and forms.

Swirling mass of bigeye trevally (*Caranx sexfasciatus*) in the sea off Papua New Guinea. The shoal is a hierarchical or emergent structure whose behaviour and expression are made up of separate units (the fish) closely choreographed.

Biomimetics, also referred to as bionics, biomimicry, bioinspiration or bioinspired design, can be defined as the implementation of design principles derived from biology. These principles can be applied, literally, with a biomorphic[1] approach, or can be applied to an approach that is more orientated towards systems. The more abstract the derivation, the more one relies on the recognition of pattern in the data rather than the shapes of physical objects. Abstraction thus simplifies technology transfer by emphasising the main principles to be used, and so makes the technology more powerful and pervasive: powerful because it introduces techniques from biological systems in a more adaptive manner; pervasive because this adaptive manner makes it easier to blend the biological approach with conventional engineering. Ideally it should also be subversive, since there is little point in introducing new concepts unless they are going to change the fundamental nature of engineering and design. The goal is to produce engineering that has basic attributes of biological systems such as low energy usage, easy recycling, extreme durability and versatility from few readily available starting materials.

Three distinct levels can be recognised at which patterns can be translated from biology to architecture.

The lowest level, and the most obvious, is direct copying of biological objects. There is not much pattern here; however, there are many patterned examples such as leaves, shells, trees and bones. Primary patterns are not much use because biological structures and

mechanisms can be torn from their context with little realisation of their reliance on adjunct features. For instance, the strength of shells depends on the distribution of different types of structure through the thickness of the shell, which changes with the size of the animal and is different for species that have to resist different types of attack. Even so, the shape of a shell can be a useful starting point, and some bivalve shells are stiffened economically with radial ridges.

Unfortunately, simple copying can also become urban myth, such as the idea that the Eiffel Tower has design progenitors in the medullary structure of the head of the human thigh bone, or that the design of the roof of the Crystal Palace was inspired by the leaf of the *Victoria amazonica* lily. There is no evidence, written or observational, for either of these popular interpretations. Indeed, the ridged roof structure of the Crystal Palace was based on a design that allowed more sunlight into the greenhouse at Chatsworth Park and is echoed in the topmost external layer of the Albert Hall which has a ridged ruff around the central axis of its roof.

But this approach is not sufficiently general and can be applied only in specific cases – pinpricks in the engineering corpus. There is a need to look more deeply into biological materials and structures to see where their success lies, and this requires deeper levels of analysis.

The second level of translation is the recognition of patterns in the way problems are solved in biology and engineering. A major part of design is the recognition, solution and elimination of problems. Any design could therefore be described or classified in terms of the problems that it solves, or which were solved in its genesis. It is possible to identify the main factors involved in the solution of a problem in answer to the question: 'What did I have to change in order to achieve a resolution?'

left: Comparison of materials processing and properties in biology and technology. We are gradually moving from the technology stream to the biology stream, but at present we have neither a roadmap nor a compelling reason to follow one.

opposite: Pathogen patterns. The outer pattern of the HIV virus (light blue) is made from the membrane of the host cell in which the particle developed. The membrane encloses an icosahedral patterned layer which surrounds the inner genetic core (purple/yellow). The patterned surface knobs (yellow) allow the virus to attach to cells.

BIOLOGY	ENGINEERING
Light, common, elements	Many heavy elements, some rare
Na P Cl K Ca H C N O Si Fe Ni Al Zn Cr	
Growth by adaptive accretion	Fabrication from powders, melts, solutions
Environmentally influenced self-assembly	Externally imposed form
Hierarchical structure	Mostly monolithic; little or no hierarchy
Interfaces allow separate control of stiffness and fracture	Few interfaces, therefore poor fracture control
Environmentally responsive	Very little environmental response
EXTERNAL Adaptive in function and morphology INTERNAL Growth repair	Obsolescent

Using the headings 'substance', 'structure', 'energy', 'space', 'time' and 'information', the Centre for Biomimetic and Natural Technologies (CBNT) at Bath University has thus classified the main design problems. Even with such a crude and general resolution of the control parameters available to implement change, strong patterns can be identified and useful differences between biology and technology quantified. The CBNT has classified some 5,000 examples from technology and 2,500 from biology, covering a size range from nanometres to kilometres. At the nanometres to millimetres level, the observations are equated with the synthesis and processing of materials; from millimetres to metres we are mostly concerned with structures and mechanisms; and from metres to kilometres and beyond the concern is more with populations and ecosystems.

The CBNT research found that materials processing technology commonly depends on the control of energy (for 70 per cent of all problems) and the choice or synthesis of starting materials.[2] Remarkably, the production of almost exactly the same range of specific properties of materials is achieved in biology using only two polymers (proteins and polysaccharides) plus a few additives, by generating a wide range of structures whose definition and design are derived from the information encoded in DNA, which drives and directs the intimate chemistry of the two polymers. The idea that in biology material is expensive but shape is cheap (the opposite is

true in the case of technology) has been around for some time,[3] and this confirms the concept. Energy is the controlling parameter in only 5 per cent of all problems in biology.

Unfortunately we do not have sufficient control over the intimate chemistry of the polymers to generate such structures by self-assembly. But whereas biological materials and structures are 'inside' the system – they 'become' – engineering is outside the system, so that materials and structures are 'made'. This opens up a range of assembly techniques and mechanisms, relying less on the self-assembly observed in biological systems. Even so, total energy input could be reduced by taking bond energy into account. Stronger intermolecular bonds tend to need higher energy input for their formation during processing, since they are at a higher energy level, so higher-energy bonds should be used only where greater loads are to be taken. In engineering, structures are graded such that the material and structure are related to the loads to be borne, thus the top of a skyscraper is lighter than the base. Bamboo, one of the most efficient woody materials, has a morphological gradient that has been mapped radially but not vertically.[4] This gradient has structural (volume fraction of solid material) and material (degree of cross-linking) components. Bamboo would therefore yield an interesting pattern for structural gradients in tall buildings. In this context, Foreign Office Architecture's Bundle Tower (the office's proposal for the World Trade Center site) is a good but not quite perfect example.

Taking the hint from biology that structure at all size levels is paramount, and that by using a wide range of structures we can reduce the number of substances and increase the versatility of the materials, we should see which structures dominate. There has been much

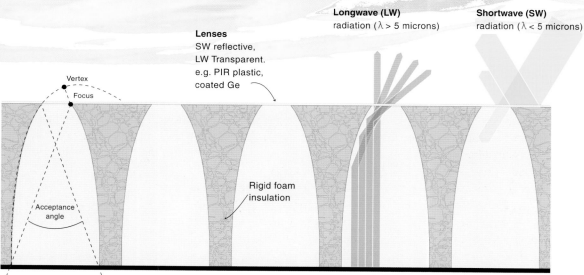

Lenses
SW reflective,
LW Transparent.
e.g. PIR plastic,
coated Ge

Longwave (LW)
radiation (λ > 5 microns)

Shortwave (SW)
radiation (λ < 5 microns)

Vertex

Focus

Acceptance
angle

Rigid foam
insulation

Compound Parabolic Concentrator (CPC) guides
Longwave radiation up & out. 3:1 ratio shown.
Highly reflective internal conical surface

Radiator cools below ambient temperature
via radiant exchange with the sky. Structured
insulation minimises convective and solar gains

Salmaan Craig, Buro Happold, Heat Selective Insulation, 2009
above: A cool roof system for hot arid climates, where the thin
atmosphere permits large amounts of radiant heat to escape into
space. A combination of structure and shape allows passive
cooling below ambient temperature. The concept was developed
using a TRIZ-based framework for biomimetics.

opposite: Transverse section of a bamboo stem
showing gradient from low density on the inside of the
stem (left) to high density on the outside (right). The
'butterfly' patterns are sections of tubes that transport
water and nutrients up and down the stem.

Pharaoh cuttlefish (*Sepia pharaonis*) mating. The male at the centre of the picture is protecting the egg-laying female (below) from a rival male (above). The dark stripes and raised arms are threat displays. Like all cuttlefish, this variety can change the colour, texture and patterns of its skin for camouflage and communication.

success with fairly simple and obvious patterns such as tensile structures and the computation of shapes to remove stress concentrations.[5] The Eiffel Tower, for example, has demonstrated the advantages of structural hierarchy largely ignored by engineers,[6] yielding a life six times longer than its designed 20 years. The hierarchical structure of its struts results in significantly greater resistance to catastrophic failure; the hierarchical arrangement of holes in wood gives control over fracture.[7] This could easily be imitated in structural concrete by controlling the sizes and distribution of voids in the structure, except that we have no idea of the optimum ratio of void-to-material or of the ratio of size of small-to-large voids. In hardwoods this ratio is probably 1:10. The interfaces between different size levels within a hierarchy allow the levels to be decoupled; for instance, stiffness (arising from interatomic bonds: nanometre interactions) can be separated from fracture (arising from starter cracks: micrometre to millimetre interactions).[8]

The third level of translation is more closely integrated with current practice in engineering and design. It is founded on the TRIZ system (a name derived from the Russian acronym of 'Theory of Inventive Problem Solving'), which was developed specifically for solving engineering problems. The patterns are more abstract, but are there, in that problems are defined and solved within a closely defined framework based on a large number (probably more than 3 million) of published patents. The method of interrogation is to ask not just 'What did I have to change?', as at the second level, but 'What did I want to improve and what was stopping me making that improvement?' This is a very well-established construct that can be traced to Heraclitus in ancient Greece, but is easily recognised in the dialectic motion between thesis and antithesis based on Hegelian philosophy (taught routinely in Russian schools) that leads to synthesis – the solution to the problem.

This is probably the most powerful pattern, and TRIZ formulates it so that it is almost impossible not to achieve a novel solution. The novelty is based in the ability of TRIZ to ignore the walls that most people erect between their areas of expertise or knowledge, enabling access to 'unknown knowns' – things you didn't know you knew – which are not recognised because they seem irrelevant to the problem. The three main rules to follow are: 1) to imagine the ideal result irrespective of the technology required to deliver it; 2) to state that result in terms of the function required rather than the means of delivery; 3) to list and be aware of all of the available resources (including time, gravity, space and so on).

TRIZ has other tricks, too, some of which show that technology evolves in a way similar to evolution. For instance, objects become more complex and compartmentalised in ways that not only parallel organic evolution, but can be used to predict technical developments. These evolutionary trends of technology have been used to write patents for machines and structures that have yet to be invented.

Biomorphic design might take on a new significance if, instead of ignorantly copying the shapes of animals and plants, we were to acknowledge that biomimetics teaches that shape is the most important parameter of all.

Even so, the ways in which biology and technology solve problems can be very different. Using analysis at levels two and three we have developed some simple design tools. These have been used by Salmaan Craig at Buro Happold to design a form of insulation that will allow the re-radiation of heat to the night sky and control the temperature of a building without recourse to an air conditioner or any other machine.[9] The secret is to introduce orientated tubes into the insulation so that the long-wave radiation of heat can pass straight through them. Biomorphic design might take on a new significance if, instead of ignorantly copying the shapes of animals and plants, we were to acknowledge that biomimetics teaches that shape is the most important parameter of all. ⚙

Notes
1. Hugh Aldersey-Williams, *Zoomorphic: New Animal Architecture*, Laurence King (London), 2003.
2. Julian FV Vincent, Olga A Bogatyreva, Nikolay R Bogatyrev, Adrian Bowyer and Anja-Karina Pahl, 'Biomimetics – its practice and theory', *Journal of the Royal Society Interface* 3, 2006, pp 471–82.
3. Julian FV Vincent and Paul Owers, 'Mechanical design of hedgehog spines and porcupine quills', *Journal of Zoology* 210, 1986, pp 55–75.
4. Ulrike GK Wegst, 'The mechanical performance of natural materials', PhD thesis, University of Cambridge, 1996, pp 1–128.
5. Claus Mattheck, *Design in Nature – Learning from Trees*, Springer (Heidelberg), 1998.
6. Rodney S Lakes, 'Materials with structural hierarchy', *Nature* 361, 1993, pp 511–15.
7. David G Hepworth, Julian FV Vincent, Graham Stringer and George Jeronimidis, 'Variations in the morphology of wood structure can explain why hardwood species of similar density have very different resistances to impact and compressive loading', *Philosophical Transactions of the Royal Society* A 360, 2002, pp 255–72.
8. Julian FV Vincent, 'Biomimetic materials', *Journal of Materials Research* 23, 2008, pp 3140–7.
9. Salmaan Craig, David Harrison, Anne Cripps and David Knott, 'Biotriz suggests radiative cooling of buildings can be done passively by changing the structure of roof insulation to let longwave infrared pass', *Journal of Bionic Engineering* 5, 2008, pp 55–66.

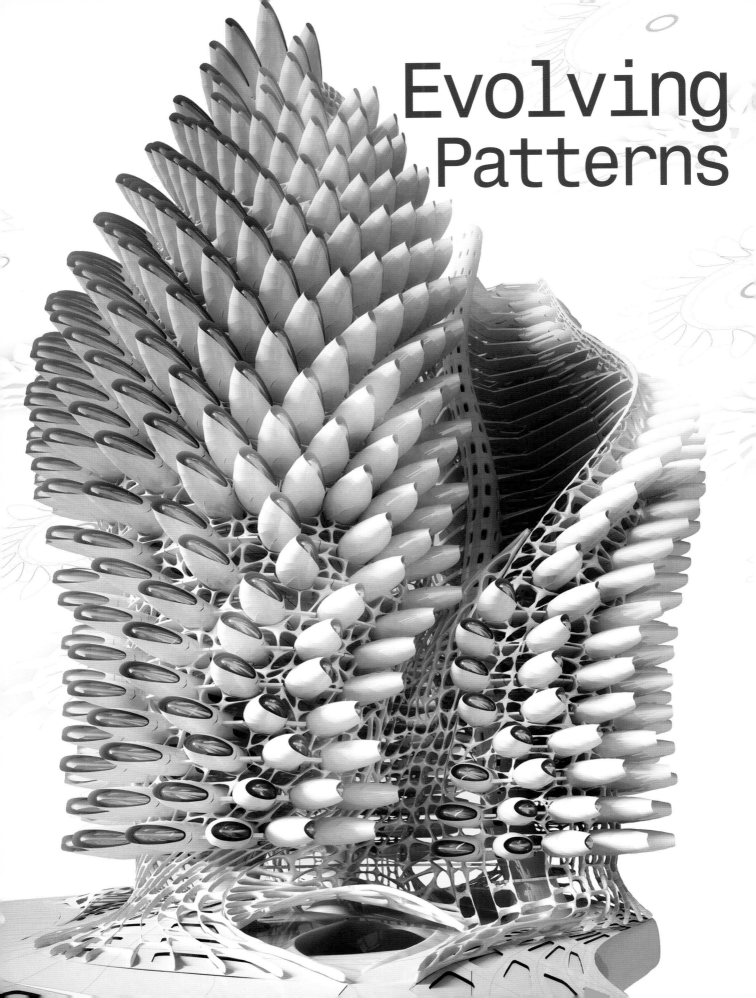

Evolving
Patterns

Correlated Systems of Interaction

Over the last four decades, the onset of computation has enabled architects and designers to employ generative patterns in their exploration of emergent social, material and spatial systems. Theodore Spyropoulos provides an overview of the field and discusses how it has been developed by the Design Research Lab (DRL) at the Architectural Association into an 'Adaptive Ecologies' agenda. In the context of parametric urbanism, the DRL has explored models of living through behavioural patterns found in nature, examining the role of the singular and the collective.

What was mere noise and disorder or distraction before, becomes pattern and sense; information has been metabolized out of noise.

WM Brodey and N Lindgren, 'Soft architecture: The design of intelligent environments', 1967[1]

Living systems are units of interaction; they exist in ambience.

Humberto Maturana, *Biology of Cognition*, 1970[2]

Patterns have served historically as instruments of description and construction. Varied pursuits of designers have wrestled to construct systems that perform and communicate through patterns.

Influential science writer Philip Ball reminds us that 'many of the most striking (pattern) examples that we encounter around us are evidently the products of human hands and minds – they are patterns shaped with intelligence and purpose, constructed by design'.[3]

Through the development of new forms of systemic practice, architecture has pursued computation as a tool for the construction of alternative models of space and time. These explorations have employed generative patterns to examine architecture and design as an emergent social, material and spatial system. Examples of this could be identified in 1967 when two famed research departments were founded at MIT: the Architecture Machine Group founded by Nicholas Negroponte to develop digital tools for architecture through computation, and the Center for Advanced Visual Studies founded by György Kepes as a platform for research in art and technology.

Negroponte's and Kepes' groups explored novel concepts of cross-mediated constructions that engaged art/architecture, computation, science and technology as part of an emerging new class of design. Parallel to this, Experiments in Art and Technology (EAT), founded by engineers Billy Klüver and Fred Waldhauer and artists Robert Rauschenberg and Robert Whitman, was established as an association to couple art and engineering practices. The following year the pioneering exhibition curated by Jasia Reichardt brought together scientists, mathematicians, artists and designers under the name 'Cybernetic Serendipity' at the Institute of Contemporary Arts (ICA) in London. The same year the British Computer Arts Society was founded.

This period saw the issues of pattern recognition – participation, interaction, intelligence and evolution – emerge through pioneering collaborations and applications. Ten years later, in 1977, Christopher Alexander in his seminal book *A Pattern Language* pursued patterns as an associative networked system to enable designers to become what he called 'pattern authors'.[4] His work examined generative scenarios that he described in the 253 unitary patterns based on traditional architecture. Alexander's approach was far-reaching as his work influenced computer science and engineering, and it became required reading in MIT's AI Lab. Architectural thinking in the work of Negroponte's Architecture Machine Group (AMG), like Alexander, radically influenced systemic design as it evolved into what is known today as the MIT Media Lab. Architecture, though instrumental in opening up new terrains of design research, abandoned the built environment in favour of systems of mediated communication.

Team Chimera (Pierandrea Angius, Alkis Dikaios, Thomas Jacobsen, Carlos Parraga), Mangal City, Design Research Lab (tutor: Theodore Spyropoulos), Architectural Association, London, 2009
Chimera's project explores an urban model of an ecology based on the social associative principles of the mangrove plant and its collective, the mangal forest.

Nicholas Negroponte, Seek, The Jewish Museum, New York, 1970

Seek is potentially the most radical of all proposals developed by the AMG, as it constructs an environment that embeds live agents (gerbils), scanning arm systems and building blocks in an evolving fitness landscape. The experiment is set in motion when the gerbils are placed in the container and begin the process of appropriating their new environment. The gerbils' activities continually reorganise the initial block deployment, pushing and pulling blocks into new configurations. After a period of inhabitation, the container becomes a display of the negotiated space of interaction through its newly formed configuration. The gerbils, blocks and scanning arm have reached a balanced negotiation through the allowance of a co-evolutionary process of becoming.

In 1980, John Frazer, working at the Architectural Association, published his seminal book *An Evolutionary Architecture*. In his foreword, the cybernetician Gordon Pask described what he perceived as a fundamental cybernetic thesis:

> The fundamental thesis is that of architecture as a living, evolving thing. In a way this is evident. Our culture's striving towards civilization is manifested in the places, houses and cities that it creates. As well as providing a protective carapace, these structures also carry symbolic value, and can be seen as being continuous with and emerging from the life of those who inhabit the built environment. It is appropriate to stress an important cybernetic feature of the work; namely that unity is not uniformity, but is coherence and diversity admixed in collusion.[5]

Frazer's work explored, above all, computation as a conceptual modelling process. He states: 'Perhaps … computing without computers is the most important lesson to be learned by designing these tools. The real benefits are found in having to rethink explicitly and clearly the way in which we habitually do things.'[6] Through the evolution of correlated systems of interaction, computation serves as a tool to control material and behavioural patterns for the production of new forms of structured spatial organisation.

It is with this spirit over the last three years that the Architectural Association Design Research Lab (DRL) has pursued its 'Adaptive Ecologies' agenda as part of its focus on parametric urbanism. The research has been exploring models of living through the collective

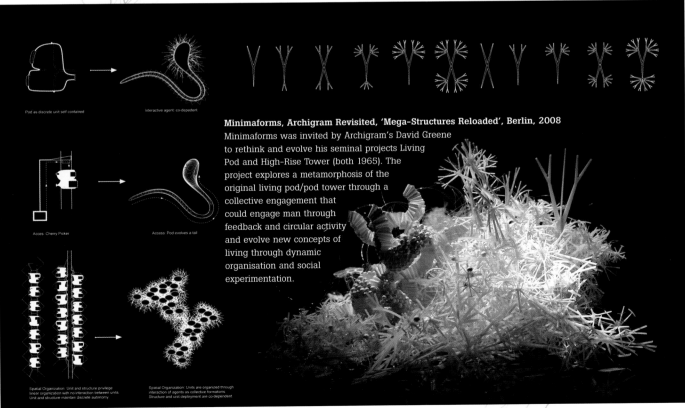

Pod as discrete unit self contained   Interactive agent: co-depedent

Acces: Cherry Picker   Access: Pod evolves a tail

Spatial Organization: Unit and structure privilege linear organization with no interaction between units. Unit and structure maintain discrete autonomy.

Spatial Organization: Units are organized through interaction of agents as collective formations. Structure and unit deployment are co-dependent.

Minimaforms, Archigram Revisited, 'Mega-Structures Reloaded', Berlin, 2008
Minimaforms was invited by Archigram's David Greene to rethink and evolve his seminal projects Living Pod and High-Rise Tower (both 1965). The project explores a metamorphosis of the original living pod/pod tower through a collective engagement that could engage man through feedback and circular activity and evolve new concepts of living through dynamic organisation and social experimentation.

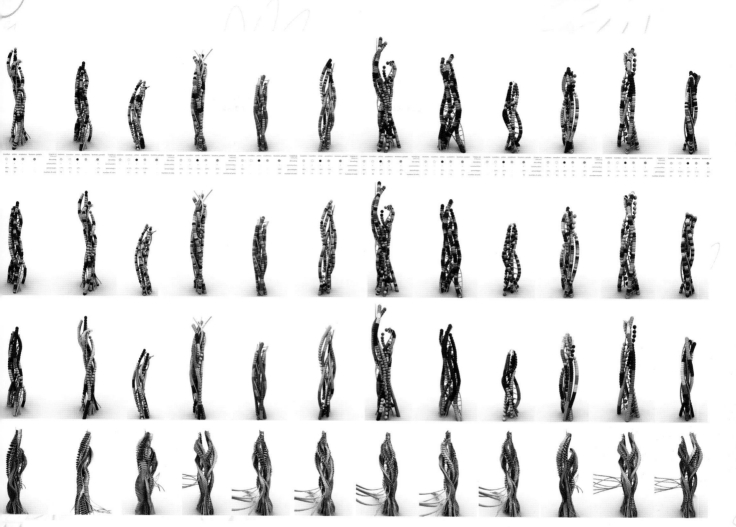

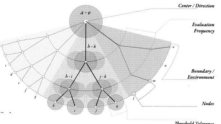

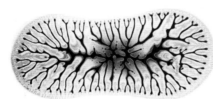

Team RED.pdf (Dominiki Dadatsi, Rena Fountoulaki, Eleni Pavlidou), Plantis, Design Research Lab (tutor: Theodore Spyropoulos), Architectural Association, London, 2007
above: RED.pdf's research explores adaptive growth models based on phyllotaxis as a parametric system constructing algorithmic iterations for an urban housing development located in the Thames Gateway in Greater London.

Team Egloo (Pankaj Chaudhary, Jwalant Mahadevwala, Mateo Riestra, Drago Vodanovic), Connective Neighbourhoods, Design Research Lab (tutor: Theodore Spyropoulos), Architectural Association, London, 2008
left: Egloo proposes a decentralised connective neighbourhood model developed through the interplay and transcoding of material and digital computation.

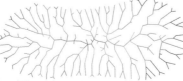

behavioural patterns found in nature, examining the role of the singular in the collective. The projects evolve design systems that interface between urban, building and material scales of operation. The city is understood as a model of ecology that actively participates and engages the proposals through feedback and negotiation.

Projects are developed through the construction of analogue and digital-driven architectural machines, data-mining behaviours that can inform the formation and organisational principles of generative and parametrically controlled design systems. Agent-based models are developed through pattern logics of growth and adaptation, allowing systems to develop high-order goals. Examples of these systems have developed computational machines exploring rule-based polyp growth, stigmergic and phyllotactical patterns that are dynamically correlating as systems of interaction. Models such as coral reefs, termite mounds, Portuguese Man o' War (*Physalia physalis*) and mangal forests all suggest intimate collective orders that are constructed through the interplay of local agency and environmental stimulus.

Stimergy, for example, allows termites to construct their nest through locally controlled deposits signalled through pheromone trails. Environmental stimulus gives rise to structures of elaborate complexity as the termites are continuously adaptive to local and global signalling. The architectures of these structures are not embedded in a blueprint as with most man-made structures, but rather are correlated series of operations that are governed through pheromone trails that emerge through collective interaction.

Embodied patterns emerge through goal-oriented systems that exhibit life-like tendencies. These social orders allow a synthetic interplay to construct a new breed of proto-animalistic architectures that evolve through negotiated interactions. Such interactions create a hybrid fusion of digital and analogue computation that draws on the landmark work of renowned neurophysiologist Dr W Grey Walter. Through his interests in cognitive operations and biological systems, Walter developed his Machina Speculatrix (a machine that watches) robotic agents that could demonstrate how simple organisms could exhibit non-linear complex interactions. He created Elsie and Elmer, the first autonomous robots that took the form of phototropic tortoises inspired by a character in Lewis Carroll's *Alice in Wonderland*.

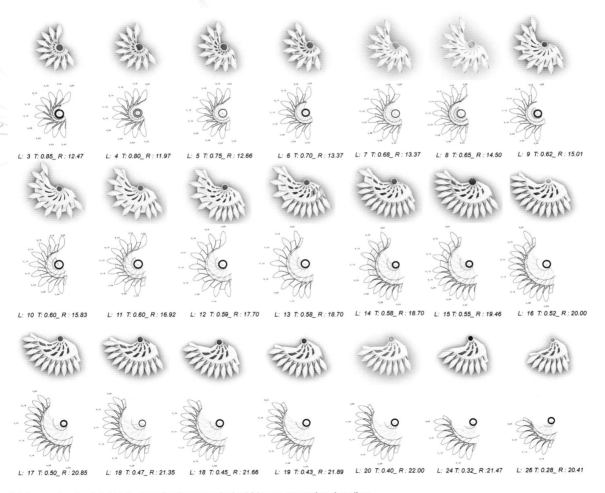

L: 3 T: 0.85_ R: 12.47   L: 4 T: 0.80_ R: 11.97   L: 5 T: 0.75_ R: 12.66   L: 6 T: 0.70_ R: 13.37   L: 7 T: 0.68_ R: 13.37   L: 8 T: 0.65_ R: 14.50   L: 9 T: 0.62_ R: 15.01

L: 10 T: 0.60_ R: 15.83   L: 11 T: 0.60_ R: 16.92   L: 12 T: 0.59_ R: 17.70   L: 13 T: 0.58_ R: 18.70   L: 14 T: 0.58_ R: 18.70   L: 15 T: 0.55_ R: 19.46   L: 16 T: 0.52_ R: 20.00

L: 17 T: 0.50_ R: 20.85   L: 18 T: 0.47_ R: 21.35   L: 18 T: 0.45_ R: 21.66   L: 19 T: 0.43_ R: 21.89   L: 20 T: 0.40_ R: 22.00   L: 24 T: 0.32_ R: 21.47   L: 26 T: 0.28_ R: 20.41

Catalogue of proto-slab distribution of units networked within one tower that describes the parametrically controlled phyllotaxis radii through core slab and subsystems.

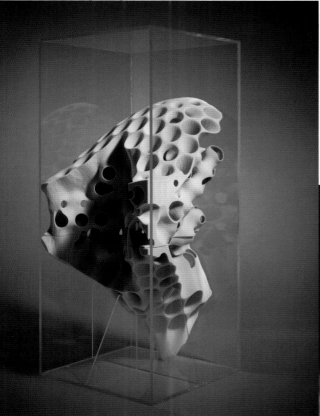

Team Farm (Marga Busquets, Sebastien Delagrange, Iain Maxwell), Stigmergic, Design Research Lab (tutor: Theodore Spyropoulos), Architectural Association, London, 2009
left: Farm's research explores stigmergy as the pheromone-based interaction ecology of agents created to generate highly differentiated and interconnected architectural typologies. The image shows a prototypical section developed for the Hudson Yards West Development in New York.

Team Shampoo (Pavlos Fereos, Konstantinos Grigoriadis, Alexander Robles Palacio, Irene Shamma), Urban Reef, Design Research Lab (tutor: Theodore Spyropoulos), Architectural Association, London, 2009
below: Prototype exploring a detailed development of fibre-based structure system and unit deployment. A coral growth principle (increase growth rate at areas of high curvature) informs the distribution and positioning of the housing units within the proposed network.

Designed with a primitive nervous system, the tortoises' constructed complex social behaviour and self-organisational patterns were characteristic of animal behaviour and ritual.

Walter's genius was in his ability to recognise complex adaptive behaviours in simple interconnected systems that focused on goal orientation and adaptation through learning. This allowed the robots to be free-ranging autodidacts that built up intelligence through interaction. Through a fusion of synthetic and natural systems, architecture can construct machines that are generative, evolving relationships that engage new forms of spatial organisation and fabrication. The ability to shift preoccupations from object to system would allow our built environment to play an active and participatory role in the construction of adaptive forms through feedback.

In concluding, Philip Ball explains that:

Scientific descriptions of phenomena do not fully capture reality, nor do they claim to. They are models. This is not a short coming of science but strength, since it allows scientists to make useful predictions without getting bogged down with intractable details. Much of the scientist's art lies in the working out what to include and what to exclude in a model.[7]

In many ways architecture shares this strength in constructing alternative models, evolving patterns of spatial practice that question both social and material practice. In the continued experimentation through the works of Alexander, Negroponte and Frazer in the age of computation, we may shortly see an architecture that displays a new nature combining the biological and computational as an adaptive and evolving organism, reinforcing Karl Friedrich Schinkel's belief that 'architecture is the continuation of nature in her constructive activity'.[8] ᗄ

Notes
1. Warren Brodey and Nilo Lindgren, 'Soft architecture: The design of intelligent environment', *Landscape*, Vol 17, No 1, 1967, pp 8–12.
2. Humberto R Maturana, *Biology of Cognition*, Biological Computer Laboratory Research Report BCL 9.0, University of Illinois (Urbana, IL), 1970, p 9.
3. Philip Ball, *Shapes*, Oxford University Press (Oxford, New York and Tokyo), 2009, p 7.
4. Christopher Alexander, *A Pattern Language: Towns, Buildings, Construction*, Oxford University Press (New York), 1977.
5. Gordon Pask, 'Foreword', in John Frazer, *An Evolutionary Architecture*, Themes VII, Architectural Association Publications (London), 1995, p 6.
6. Ibid, p 24.
7. Ball, op cit, p 31.
8. Goerd Peschken, *Das Architektonishce Lehrbuch*, Deutscher Kunstverlag (Munich), 1979, p 36.

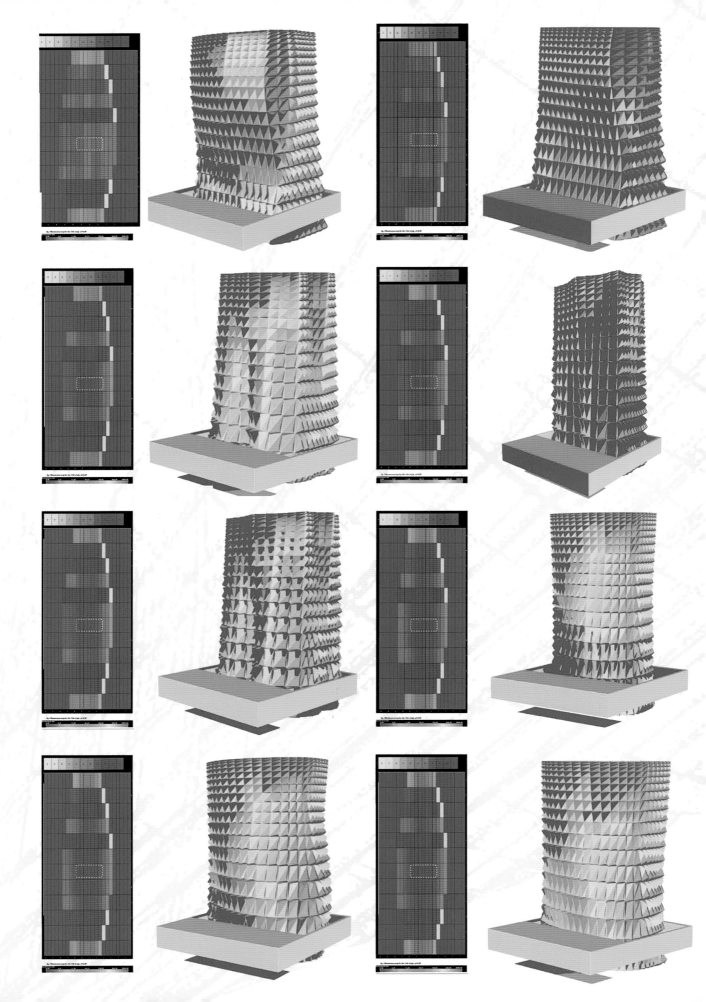

Patterns in Performance-Oriented Design

An Approach towards Pattern Recognition, Generation and Instrumentalisation

The question of pattern in architecture generally divides architects into two distinct groups: those with an aesthetic interest in man-made ornament; and those who take a deeper interest in the processes that underlie the formation of pattern in the natural world. An investigation of the performative, though, enables an exploration of pattern that arises out of the interaction of man-made interventions with the natural environment. **Michael Hensel**, Professor for research by Design at AHO, the Oslo School of Architecture and Design, and **Achim Menges** of the Emtech (Emergent Technologies and Design programme) at the Architectural Association in London, explore this arena based on their research and educational work at the AA and other international institutions, which focuses on aspects of performance in the built environment.

Patterns occur in nature, as well as in man-made designs and artefacts, and are commonly described as specific recurring events and repetitive material formations. This broad description is interesting in that it implies that patterns can range from energy to matter – a realisation of key importance to the argument pursued below, and even more so if one considers that in natural systems most patterns are generated by the interaction and mutual modulation of both energy and matter.

Simple man-made patterns may be based on repetition and periodicity; however, this is not the case with all patterns and certainly not with most natural ones. In his seminal book *The Self-Made Tapestry: Pattern Formation in Nature*, Philip Ball describes patterns as 'arrays of units that are similar but not necessarily identical, and which repeat but not necessarily regularly or with a well-

defined symmetry.'[1] In contrast to pattern, Ball posits form 'loosely as the characteristic shape of a class of objects. Like the elements of a pattern – objects with the same form do not have to be identical, or even similar in size; they simply have to share certain features that can be recognised as typical.'[2]

In natural systems patterns arise from self-organisation; that is, irreversible processes that lead to the emergence, development and differentiation of complexity in non-linear dynamic systems, based on interaction and feedback between the system elements, and when open systems exchange energy, matter and information with the environment in a far-from-equilibrium state.[3] The science of 'pattern formation' examines the outcomes of the process of self-organisation and the common characteristics and principles that underlie similar patterns. The detection of underlying patterns is called 'pattern recognition'.

Ioannis Douridas, Adaptive Surfacescape, Emergent Technologies and Design programme (tutors: Michael Hensel, Achim Menges and Michael Weinstock), Architectural Association, London, 2004–05
The envelope surface of the Piraeus Tower in Athens is here derived through an iterative algorithmic procedure based on peak time and average daily solar exposure analysis. Multiple surface generations are computationally evolved and analysed in relation to a number of environmental fitness criteria in order to explore the self-shading capacity of both the global envelope shape and the local articulation of the skin components.

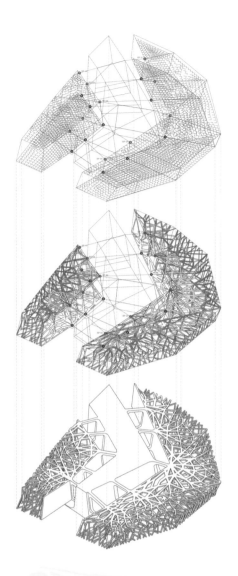

Christina Doumpioti, Adaptive Growth of Composite Structures, Emergent Technologies and Design programme (tutors: Michael Hensel, Achim Menges and Michael Weinstock), Architectural Association, London, 2006–08
The project explores the computational process of stress-driven growth for fibre-composite structures. The overall shape is derived through an iterative generation and tessellation process (Figure 1) in which surface nodes work as receptors for detecting local stress peaks triggering a homeostatic growth process based on the recurring structural analysis of displacement, stress intensity and principal force flow (Figure 2). The resultant fibre layout can be produced by computer numerically controlled (CNC) steered-fibre lay-up manufacturing (Figure 3).

Figure 1

OCEAN and Scheffler + Partners, New Czech National Library, Prague, competition entry, 2006
Through an analytic computational procedure the stress distribution within the envelope of the Czech National Library's cantilevering volumes is evaluated and mapped as a vector field of principal forces (top). According to this structural information, combined with other parameters such as the angle of incident of sunlight, view axes and spatial characteristics, a network of merging branches is derived (centre), which is developed into a structural envelope of the volumes cantilevering from the central national archive (bottom).

If, as is the case for natural systems, both form and pattern arise out of processes of self-organisation, it is debatable to what extent a strict generalised distinction between these two notions remains useful. Ball suggests that 'patterns are typically extended in space, while forms are bound and finite', but warns that this should be taken as a guideline and not as a general rule,[4] and that it is not always possible to maintain a clear distinction between the two.[5] In this regard, the reduction of pattern to an exclusively material condition seems counterproductive, as does the reduction to appearance only, which ignores the processes that underlie the formation and transformation of patterns. For example, the recurring patterns of the structure and organisation of fibrous proteins in connective organic tissues can only be understood in relation to their stress-driven growth process, in which fibroblast cells lay down the fibres in direct response to the flow of forces within the tissue.

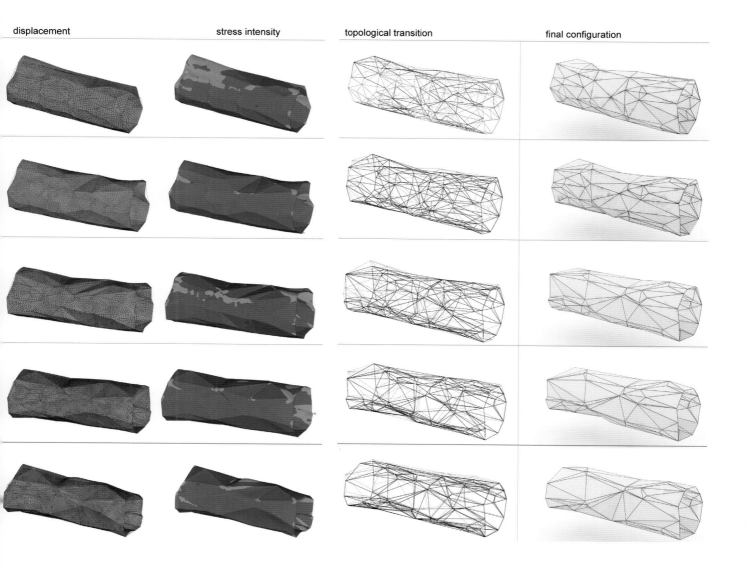

displacement	stress intensity	topological transition	final configuration

Yet, the question may remain of what relevance this understanding can be for architectural design. If pattern-generating, self-organisational processes are the locus of interest, one may question how, and in response to which conditions, patterns arise and what their related behavioural capacities and performative potentials are; or in other words, why and how such processes and their outcomes might be instrumentalised.

A significant part of the authors' research conducted at the Architectural Association and other academic institutions in the last couple of years has so far focused on developing differentiated and performative material systems that are based on and derived through the relationship between material characteristics and behaviour, and related self-organisational processes, manufacturing constraints and assembly logics, as well as performative potential.[6] In so doing, the research aims at establishing an alternative design approach, one in which material formations arise from the feedback between internal constraints and capacities of a material system and a specific environment. Material elements and components are evolved into varied arrays of parametrically defined and interrelated units and systems. Differentiation and variation is driven by processes of self-organisation within the limits of manufacturing and assembly, behavioural capacities in exchange with environmental influences, and, in due course, by performative capacities. The three projects illustrated here, for example, provide an insight into how highly specific morphology can be evolved through continuous feedback loops of analysing the behaviour and capacity of material systems in relation to external influences, from the flow of forces to the distribution of solar energy and related thermodynamic phenomena.

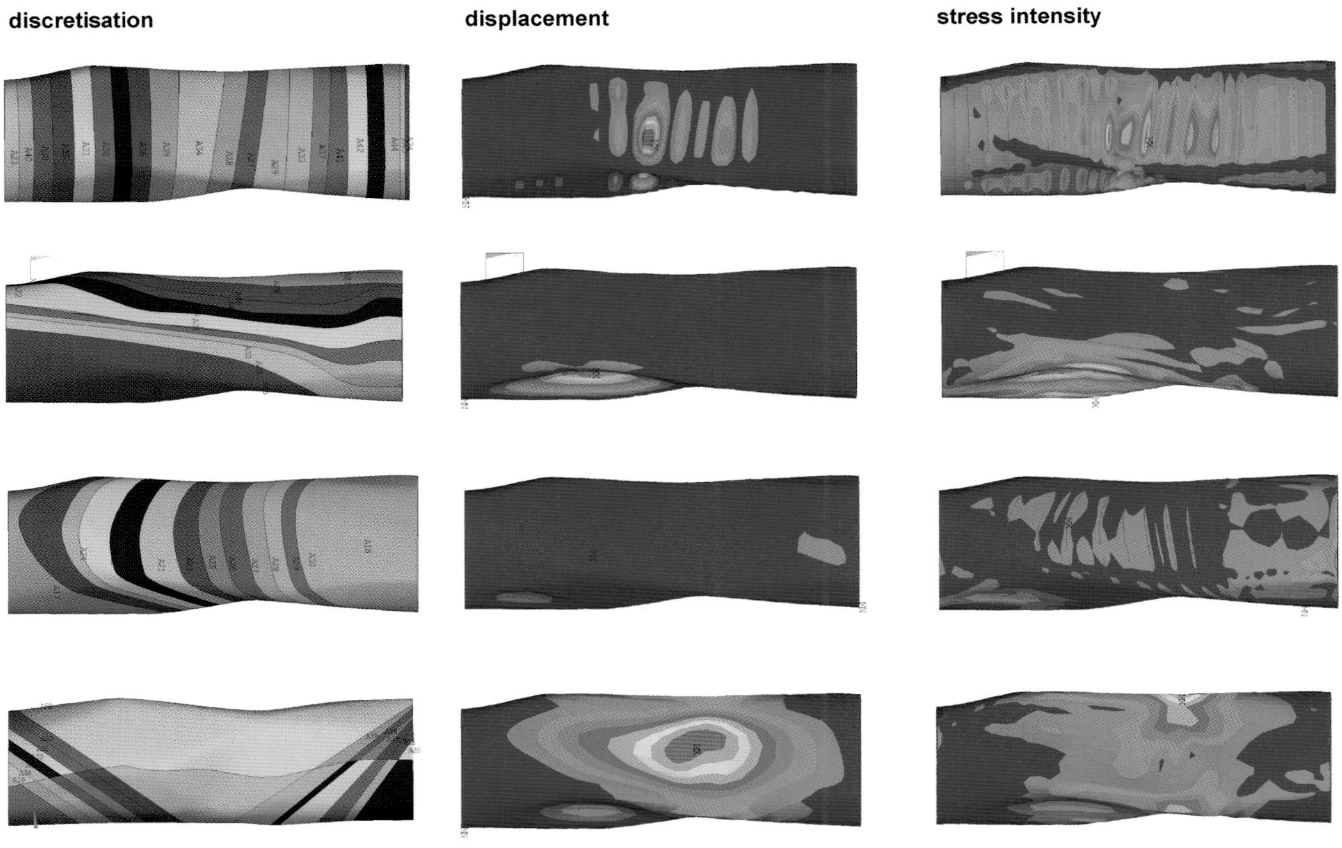

discretisation **displacement** **stress intensity**

Figure 2

As a consequence it is important that the predominance of form definition so often emblematic of architectural design is profoundly questioned. Instead, the finely calibrated synthesis of formation and materialisation processes characteristic of self-organisational natural systems should also underlie the logic of the definition and differentiation of the material systems under development. From the (potentially varied) material make-up and behaviour to the definition and differentiation of the varied elements and subassemblies to the overall system, multiple hierarchical features and logics arise that share these characteristics of natural systems. From their integral articulation come behavioural capacities and patterns in which every interaction between object and environment has consequences, whether prohibitive or accelerating, and registers in the pattern formation and surface articulation of the material systems.

Harnessing generative processes based on self-organisation involves relinquishing the logic of linear, one-way causal effects that architectural design is so commonly based on, and instead deploying logics of interaction. From the interaction of material system and environment unfolds a multitude of behavioural patterns of the modulation of both the system and the environment. The latter includes thermodynamic, luminous, sonic or similar modulations; the former usually less recognisable aspects such as the changing distribution of internal forces, frequencies, sound waves or aspects of building physics such as changes in moisture content and temperature gradients. Understanding that the development of a material system must always be derived through its interaction with external environmental stimuli opens up the design space beyond the common articulation of material artefacts and structures towards the modulation of related behavioural patterns of light, thermodynamics, sound and so on, in turn expanding design opportunities for architects and offering the possibility for performance-oriented design.

force flow

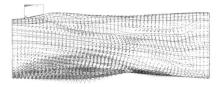

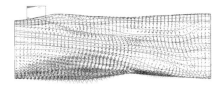

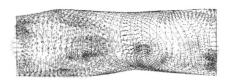

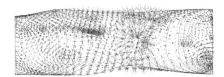

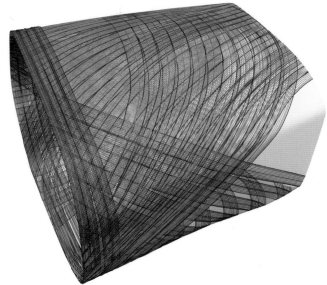

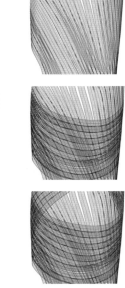

Figure 3

When behavioural tendencies and patterns are instrumentalised they can be put to task or, in other words, they can become performance oriented. Design is then grounded in recognising these patterns and unfolding from them the performative capacity of the material systems that articulate the built environment and human habitat. The notion of performance in this context is based on two-way relationships and interaction, and thus exceeds the tendency in architecture for simple one-way causal functionality. When such higher-level functionality is based on the presence of multiple interrelated capacities embedded in an overall assembly that does not specify single-function subsystems but, instead, locates multiple capacities already on the level of pattern-based subsystems that are extensive, it becomes necessary to employ behavioural pattern recognition to develop an understanding and sensibility towards this new level of functional integration and related, inevitable complexity.

The relationship between development patterns (*Entstehungsmuster*) and behavioural patterns (*Verhaltensmuster*) can be synthesised towards performance-oriented design. Here, design unfolds in a perpetual and synergetic process of pattern generation in feedback with pattern recognition for both material articulation and environmental modulation. ⌂

Notes
1. Philip Ball, *The Self-Made Tapestry: Pattern Formation in Nature*, Oxford University Press (Oxford, New York and Tokyo), 1999, p 9.
2. Ibid.
3. W Ebeling, 'Grundzüge evolutionärer Selbstorganisation', *Prozeß und Form 'Natürlicher Konstruktionen'*, SFB 230, Ernst & Sohn (Berlin), 1996, p 24 (authors' translation).
4. Ball, op cit, p 10.
5. Ibid, p 9.
6. See Michael Hensel and Achim Menges (eds), *AD Versatility and Vicissitude*, 2008, and Michael Hensel and Achim Menges (eds), *Morpho-Ecologies*, AA Publications (London), 2006.

Pattern Deposition From Scripts to Applications

Is the widespread adoption of existing design software appropriated from other disciplines limiting architects' potential for pattern-making? Could the development of complex code applied to equally complex pattern problems open up alternative avenues of expression? **Mike Silver** illustrates work by himself and other architects and artists that suggest that new kinds of software-driven pattern recognition and simulation computer models are opening up the field.

We need to take the computer back from the large developers that control the software most artists use.
— Golan Levin, 'High-Bandwidth Magic Show' (Interview), *RES* Magazine, 2006, p 80[1]

The building that houses Pixar Animation studios in Emeryville, California, is divided down the middle with artists occupying one half of its interior spaces while the other half is filled with computer programmers. The plan of the complex institutionalises the connection between art and engineering, producing a collaborative model typical of the many disciplines dependent on the production of new and constantly evolving software. This culture of exchange, customisation and craft has been adopted in recent years by sculptors who build computer-controlled art, and by artists who make drawings with home-made algorithms rendered on software platforms of their own creation. (Daniel Rozin, Casey Reas and Ben Fry immediately come to mind.)

In architecture, however, the rote operation of existing software appropriated from other fields has delayed the radical integration of computation and design. In a very real sense computers have not really entered the discipline as a transformative medium because designers and engineers do not write programs together. Limited to the constraints of borrowed code, most architects today are forced to squeeze their imaginations through the prefabricated structures of existing protocols. To a certain extent this situation has begun to change with the introduction of custom scripting where designers are able to tweak the constraints of their tools. But even these developments are at best a contingency aimed at the deeper, more comprehensive practice of full-blown application development. Through this approach, the production of complex code, designed from the ground up, offers architects an opportunity to engineer tools that facilitate creativity while engaging the myriad challenges of building design and construction.

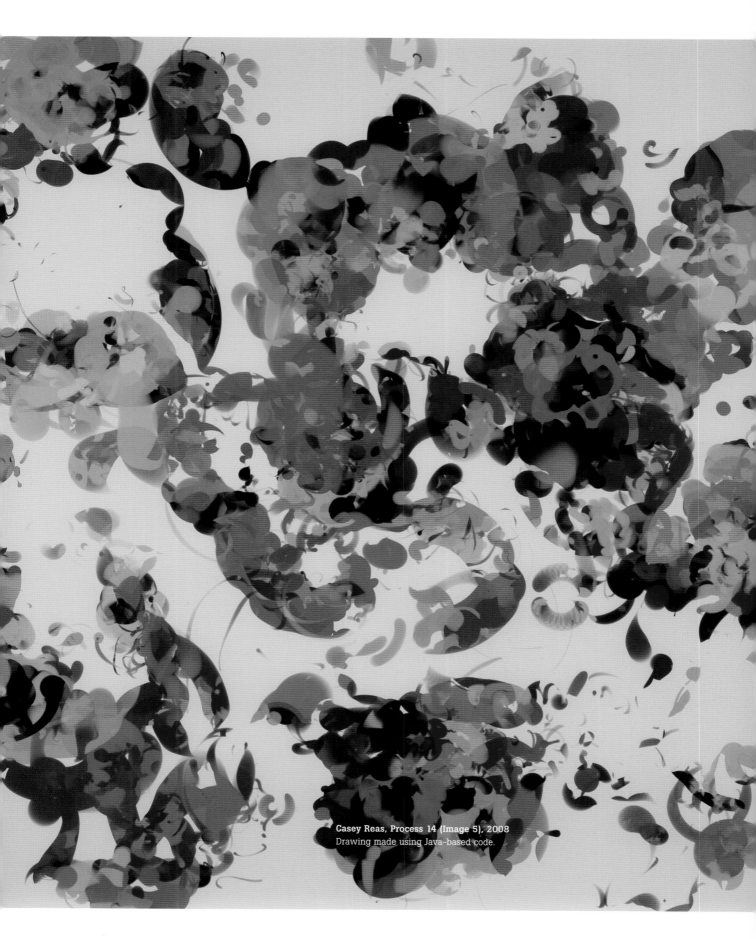

Casey Reas, Process 14 (Image 5), 2008
Drawing made using Java-based code.

Undermining the move towards a broader, more empowered culture of architectural programming is the avant-garde's fascination with rule-based patterns and their decorative functions. One of the guiding principles motivating a new generation of computationally inspired architects is the idea that simple programs can produce complex forms. From flocking patterns to fractal geometry, the reduction of complexity to a single set of abstract rules has shifted attention away from the messy, embodied realities of existence towards the very real need to create working methodologies that are inclusive, process based and physical. Emblematic of this emphasis on mathematical abstraction is Stephen Wolfram's extensive study of simple programs or cellular automata (CA). In a recent review of his book *A New Kind of Science*,[2] Ray Kurzweil writes:

> There is a missing link ... in how one gets from the interesting, but ultimately routine patterns of a cellular automaton to the complexity of persisting structures that demonstrate higher levels of intelligence ... Wolfram would counter that rule 110 automaton could be used as a 'universal computer.' However, by itself a universal computer is not capable of solving intelligent problems without ... 'software.' It is the complexity of the software run on a universal computer that is precisely the issue.[3]

Mike Silver, Architects, AutomasonMP3 software, 2009
An iPhone digital music player displaying a class 4 cellular automaton. AutomasonMP3 is a free, stand-alone application that was designed for constructing complex brick buildings in Dhaka, Bangladesh. The tool was developed for the International Masory Institute by Mike Silver, Architects in collaboration with programmers Yee Peng Chia, Eric Maslowski and Chipp Jansen.

The projects below explore the development of complex code applied to equally complex problems. The aim here is to open up alternative avenues of expression and new ways of working with the computer as a design tool. Perhaps it is only a question of time, as the careers of Reas and Fry suggest, before the programmer and the architect become the same individual and when the ability to write code replaces 'drawing' as 'the true mark of one fully socialised into the profession'.[4]

CAD/CAM in an Expanded Field

Mike Silver, Architects' first attempts to build a full-scale brick wall with simple programs (CAs) employed a set of 17 templates repeatedly used to determine the position and state of individual masonry units. Expert masons devised a technique that limited the influence of errors to single masonry units and horizontal courses. (These mistakes could be detected late in the construction process and corrected even after the mortar of the wall was dry.) The system allows workmen to build complex masonry patterns without literally executing a cellular automaton program on site. A 'Run Length encoding' (RLE) module was written into the latest version of AutomasonMP3 so that encoded information could be stored as audible files played on a mason's smart phone or digital music player. With a bluetooth headset, workmen can access block-stacking commands leaving their hands free to do physical work. The production of a-periodic masonry patterns is therefore based on an efficient technical synergy employing home-made code, traditional materials, local craftsmen and existing computer technologies. In other words, simple programs require elaborate software that makes complex architecture easy to build.

Daniel Rozin, Wooden Mirror, Israel Museum of Art, Jerusalem, 1999
Rozin's mirror uses computer software, servo controllers and wood blocks to create a pixellated reflection of its viewers.

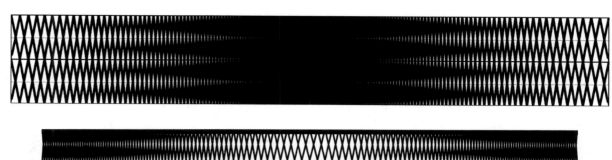

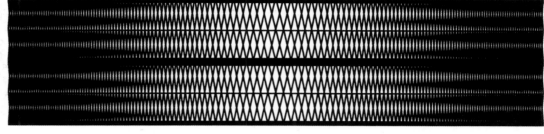

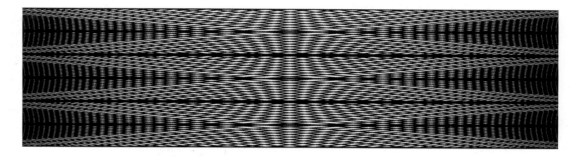

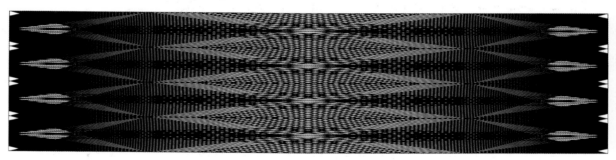

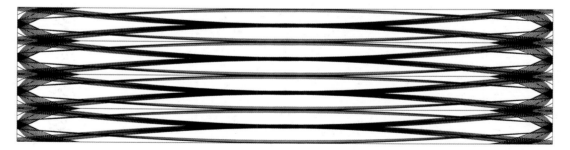

Mike Silver, Architects, Java-based taping patterns for an s-glass fibre-placed truss, 2008
With a reusable mould, a variety of patterns can be produced by simply varying the data that
drives the fibre-placement process. Increased fibre plies in section help mitigate surface
buckling while allowing for a less densely packed fibre layout in elevation. Here, the window
and the wall, the frame and the panel no longer exist as distinct systems. The resulting
penumbra (top image) also provides a flexible way to control natural light.

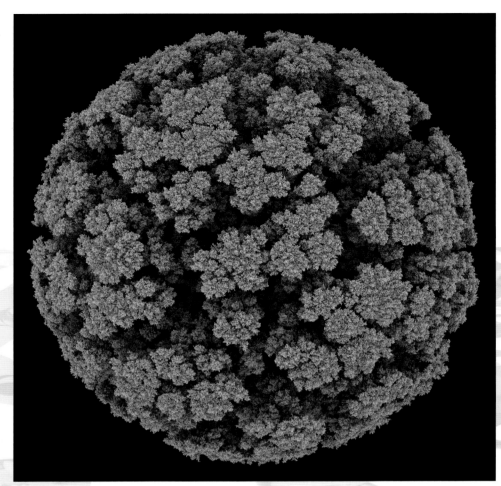

Andy Lomas, Aggregation 27, 2005
left: 3-D diffusion limited aggregation (DLA) model produced by artist and visual effects supervisor Andy Lomas. This simulation is based on the same algorithm as lighting.

Mike Silver Architects, Fibre-placed truss, 2007
right: Robot laying down strands of s-glass tape on an aluminium mould. This small-scale prototype was produced by New York-based composite manufacturer Automated Dynamics. The final production part, spanning 30 metres (100 feet), would be 10 times lighter than a conventional concrete beam and 1.5 times as strong.

AECOM Consult, Inc, TRANSIMS project, Atlanta, Georgia, 2009
opposite top: Traffic volumes on roadways in Atlanta generated using the TRANSIMS output visualiser. While both images display a common morphology, their embodied reality is quite different.

Roadrunner supercomputer, Los Alamos National Laboratory, New Mexico, 2008
opposite bottom: The Roadrunner supercomputer is used to create high-throughput, interactive simulations.

Complexity Without Excess

Fibershop Version 1.0 (beta) was developed in collaboration with artist and programmer Chipp Jansen and was used to robotically produce high-strength, composite skins for spanning the courtyard of the Cleveland Museum of Art in Ohio. Because fibre-placement machines are traditionally used to construct aeroplanes, new code was needed to make components for use in buildings. The limits of the existing composites software necessitated the creation of complex visualisation and fabrication tools designed from the ground up. Through a collaborative process of testing, coding and recoding it was possible to build an ultra-light, 'frameless' truss incorporating windows, walls and structure into a single design.[5] This was achieved by controlling the variable deposition of individual fibre-reinforced plastic strands laid down on a reusable mould.

Rather than producing components that were homogeneous and structurally overdetermined (I-beams, T-sections, bearing walls and so on), this design achieved its efficiency by increasing material density where stresses were high and decreasing them where they were low. The complexity of the final component was produced for free by simply changing the data in the taping software. In this way the internal stresses of the truss became visible as an expressive field of both straight and non-geodetic lines (the corners of the truss are curved). Instead of pursuing patterns that tend towards excess – solutions that create more problems than they solve – robotically fabricated composites facilitated an organic complexity through integrated geometries that achieved more with less but without standardisation. In other words, diversity was produced through the conservation of mass and energy.

Supercomputation

Applied to problems that require complex calculations, supercomputers have been used by scientists and engineers to study a wide variety of environmental and spatial phenomena ranging from climate change and weather forecasting to nuclear explosions and urban traffic patterns. Supercomputers have become the technical benchmark by which we judge advances in processing speed and power. With the constant introduction of new machines and new technologies, the development of ever more complex and computationally sophisticated simulations will continue well into the future. This steady increase in power is revolutionising the way we understand different patterns of behaviour and their real-world consequences. Projects like

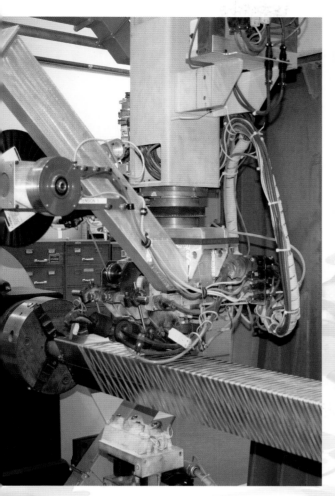

TRANSIMS, a high-throughput simulation of the vehicular infrastructure of Atlanta, Georgia, have allowed programmers to visualise and experiment with complex patterned systems that exceed the operational scope of traditional media. Each vehicle in TRANSIMS, for example, 'is coded for operating characteristics … such as engine type, exhaust system, tire pressure and speed';[6] as virtual cars (modelled according to real-world census data) circulate through the traffic network they generate emissions that are processed by a program responsible for calculating air quality. An increasingly sophisticated understanding of how large urban settlements impact the environment, changes in their patterns of use, as well as new insights into future design strategies are especially important features of these new kinds of models.

At first they appeared on his fingernails as small white blotches. Eventually, minute patterns began to form in legible rows of finely hollowed points. These grew from underneath his cuticles and inched their way slowly across the soft corona of pale tissue that beamed like an eclipse most prominently on his thumbs. From the trimmings of each nail, coherent forms could be assembled, piece by piece, into a translucent mass. Over time, one could discern the contours of a miniature landscape, crystalline shapes and even the city with its street-light glitter, floating in storm clouds like a distant nebula. ⊿⊅

Notes
1. Golan Levin, 'High-Bandwidth Magic Show' (Interview), *RES* Magazine, Vol 9, No 4, 2006, p 80.
2. Stephen Wolfram, *A New Kind of Science*, Wolfram Media (Champaign, IL), 2002.
3. Ray Kurzweil, 'Reflections on Stephen Wolfram's *A New Kind of Science*'; see http://www.kurzweilai.net/articles/art0464.html?printable=1. Accessed June 1 2009.
4. Reyner Banham, 'A black box', in *A Critic Writes*, University of California Press (Berkeley, CA), 1996, p 10. A stress on applications does not necessarily render the use of conventional software tools obsolete. For instance, if an architect needs to draw simple plans and sections then AutoCAD is quite sufficient. However, the development of new tools will help the discipline break free of the operational limits of existing code.
5. The surface strength of a fibre-placed membrane is produced by laminating fibre-reinforced plastic strips. The strength and stiffness of composite shells are acquired through the precise control of their fibre's orientation and density. With these materials and manufacturing techniques a complete enclosure is created without structurally distinguishing frame from infill.
6. John Casti, *Would-be Worlds: How Simulation is Changing the Frontiers of Science*, John Wiley and Sons, Inc (New York), 1997, p 133.

Psychology and Perception of Patterns in Architecture

Pattern perception is often regarded as highly subjective, dependent on individual taste and preference. Neurologically, however, it has been proven that distinct areas of the brain are stimulated differently by different pattern design and colour combinations. Here **Patricia A Rodemann** probes into the very real physical and psychological consequences of product design finishes and surface patterning.

Acoustic dot pattern walls in the Weigel Hall Music Rehearsal Room, Ohio State University, Columbus, Ohio, 1990.

Does architecture express personality? Does architectural pattern design have the ability to affect behaviour or physiological outcomes? Home owners express themselves through colour and pattern, but the close connection between design as an expression of identity extends to commercial spaces as well. Sixty-one per cent of the respondents in the syndicated *Rooms of America III* survey[1] had high to complete agreement with the statement 'I think of my home as an extension of me', and 25 per cent agreed somewhat. One aspect of the masters degree research study conducted at the Ohio State University and published in the book *Patterns in Interior Environments: Perception, Psychology and Practice*[2] uncovered which patterns respondents thought belong in which spaces, proving

the powerful psychological and cultural associations we make with pattern design. Often, architects see these unwritten, unspoken cultural 'design rules' as constrictive and superfluous to 'good design'.

There are significant demographic considerations behind pattern preference, as has been revealed in large-scale quantitative design surveys of over 25,000 US home owners, probing colour, style, pattern, finishes, products and plans for the interiors and exteriors of homes for commercial clients. Though the initial commercial focus of the *Rooms of America* and *Homes of America*[3] survey series was wall-covering design, later research moved into patterns for flooring, upholstery and drapery textiles, bedding and other elements of a space for manufacturing/retail clients. This research could be replicated with adaptation in other countries and global contexts.

Beyond expressed preference, however, every moment of the day we see colour, light, pattern and texture. We are processing rapidly at a

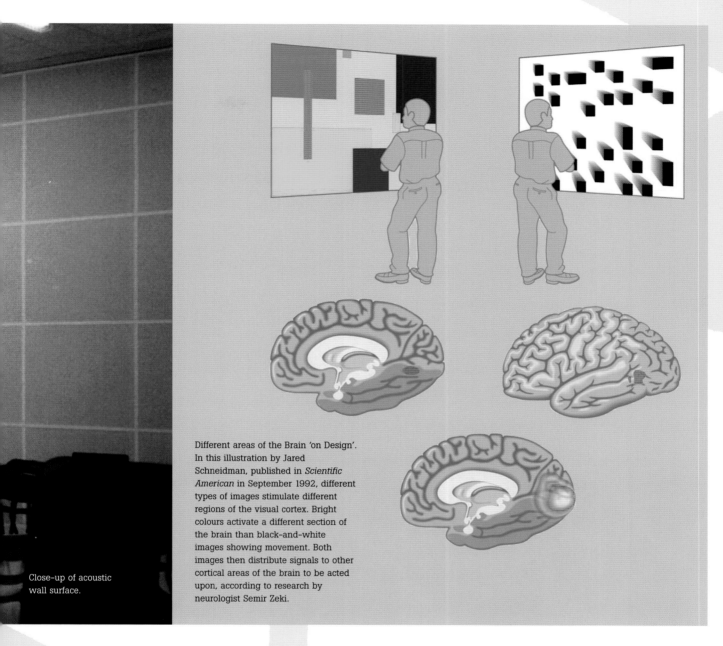

Different areas of the Brain 'on Design'. In this illustration by Jared Schneidman, published in *Scientific American* in September 1992, different types of images stimulate different regions of the visual cortex. Bright colours activate a different section of the brain than black-and-white images showing movement. Both images then distribute signals to other cortical areas of the brain to be acted upon, according to research by neurologist Semir Zeki.

Close-up of acoustic wall surface.

subconscious, automatic level and at a highly aware, focused level. There are unintentional physiological consequences from product design finishes and patterns such as dots in ceiling tiles (going dotty), headaches or epileptic seizures triggered by exceptionally narrow mini-blinds and specific light phenomena, moving escalator stair gratings, high-contrast closely spaced floor tiles, geometric carpets in hospitality and healthcare installations, and even visual distress for seamstresses sewing Oxford cloth garments that were jokingly termed 'astigmatism shirts'.

Secondary research across medical literature indicated that neurologists have found that 82 per cent of migraine sufferers will experience a migraine after looking at certain types of pattern stimulus – most notably stripe

gratings. After several preliminary studies with individual designs in six pattern categories using design boards, slides and scale models, and interview, survey and semantic differential, full-size rooms with what are known as acuity patterns were installed. Psychological and neurological research reveals what is actually happening in this type of architectural pattern perception.

Neurologically, different areas of the brain are stimulated differently by different pattern designs and colour combinations, as illustrated here. The response to pattern is more pronounced for some types of people than others; in addition to migraine patients, schizophrenics and Parkinson's patients have a greater sensitivity to verticality, wavy patterns or flickering lights. This may also true of those suffering post-traumatic stress syndrome.

In a post-occupancy evaluation of a site with an acoustic dot wall-surface pattern, a high degree of perceived 'wave motion' and reports of visual fatigue, distraction and even feelings of nausea were reported. Though it was a small sample, 64 per cent of the musicians interviewed perceived some degree of movement to the surface and 36 per cent perceived a significant degree of movement.

This post-occupancy evaluation revealed that most perceived the dot pattern as 'distracting', 'busy', 'vibrating', 'overbearing', 'wearying' and 'disruptive' using a semantic differential versus 'soothing', 'calming', 'stationary', 'graphic', 'simple', 'refreshing' and/or 'comfortable'. Subjects with glasses, bifocals and trifocals were significantly more sensitive to the objectionable patterns as were those with physical conditions such as migraines or motion sickness.

Three things stood out regarding the use of pattern design across several surveys in the masters degree research and subsequent 13 years of national preference studies. Whether a design was perceived as 'dated' was not only important to the bottom line but also triggered a host of related perceptions and assumptions. The second and third considerations were 'a perception of movement' or 'seeing after-images' caused by viewing certain designs. These designs, known as 'acuity' patterns, include certain types of high-contrast stripes, a high-contrast chequerboard and

highly regimented geometric, graphic and dot patterns – also higher contrast. There are potential issues with each pattern category so making the best selection is important.

The thesis research focused on acuity patterns because whether a design such as grey marble is perceived as 'cold', 'morgue-like' or 'boring' does not affect us from a physiological point of view, though

Looking at the design, smaller scale, on a presentation board or as a 30.5-centimetre (12-inch) custom sample directly on, the carpet is attractive and striking. Walking across the extensive sweep of floor, however, produces a feeling of being on an undulating surface not unlike sea billows.

there are psychological, marketing and economic implications. For example, as we look around a dental office with a dated textured vinyl wall-covering vaguely reminiscent of burlap textile, we are apt to wonder about the age of the dentist's equipment. This could contribute to our anxiety when facing a root canal procedure, for example. In an anecdotal example, a national hospitality/restaurant brand design

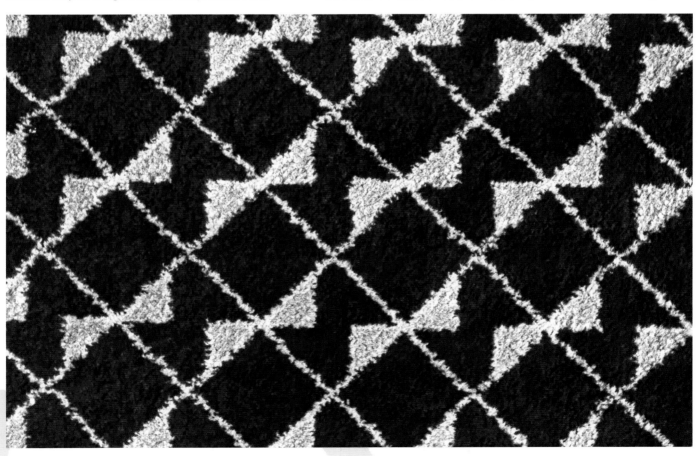

concept utilised patterns similar to those the research showed as 'busy', 'dated' and 'annoying', and colours in the blue family that were known to have negative associations with food. Traffic dropped once the new designs were installed, and people left sooner. Presumably sales also declined and it was noted that locations closed.

A custom geometric chevron design carpet was photographed in the lobby area of a performing arts centre located in a bank building. Looking at the design, smaller scale, on a presentation board or as a 30.5-centimetre (12-inch) custom sample directly on, the carpet is attractive and striking. Walking across the extensive sweep of floor, however, produces a feeling of being on an undulating surface not unlike sea billows. This is not uncommon. A facility manager told of a graphic ladybug custom design carpet installed in a smaller diagnostic/treatment lobby of a children's hospital. Nurses had selected the design because it was 'cute'. Apparently, children standing, sitting or crawling across the floor vomited at a higher rate with the optic pattern in place. When the carpet had to be removed and replaced, the incidence plummeted with the unpatterned lower contrast carpet. Thus principles of vision plus common illusion effects coupled with illness and/or medication may not lead to optimal outcomes.

top: Example of chequerboard acuity pattern used in the research study from a common wall-covering collection in black-and-white.

above: Example of a ticking stripe acuity pattern used in the research study from a common wall-covering collection in black-and-white.

left: Movement illusion occurring with carpeting installed in a performing arts centre on the second floor of a bank tower building.

opposite: Example of a geometric carpet pattern leading to a perception of movement – a fairly common illusion.

Also as part of the masters research project, a graphic black-and-white ticking stripe was installed in a graphics/marketing services department, and a black-and-white chequerboard in another similar office for a specified period of time with behaviour mapping before, during and after, including the kind of supplemental video-camera observation a security camera might record. Follow-up interviews with subjects and staff revealed that 51 per cent of those dropping off/picking up work in the chequerboard space noticed the wall-covering immediately, as one might expect. (This is a good design to attract attention as one fast-food restaurant chain does on its marquee and brand/graphics.) Context is everything. However, in this particular usage, avoidance behaviours shot up to 38 per cent from less than 2 per cent, and subjects were 17 per cent less likely to engage others in conversation. Subjects were 21 per cent more likely to move quickly through the space to another area and, because the customers were 10 per cent less likely to wait for work being done with the pattern up, it appeared the staff had to work 13 per cent harder to engage them in conversation.

The black-and-white stripe got the attention of 71 per cent of subjects; 24 per cent exhibited avoidance behaviours. Avoidance behaviours on the checklist included downcast eyes, looking away, body stance orientation, 'tightness' of motion, head movement and so on. Other behaviours observed, such as glancing around, rapid gestures, nail biting and fidgeting, had not been noted in the period prior to the installation of the acuity patterns and there did not appear to be other contributing causes. Observed behaviour goes beyond expressed preference, which is why multiple research techniques and measures were used for greater validity.

Subjects were 21 per cent less likely to engage others in conversation in the presence of the optical stripe pattern. Staff also began to avoid the area, leading to a 43 per cent decline in conversations initiated. Subjects were 32 per cent more likely to move through the space away from the striped surface, with head and eye motion increased in the presence of both patterns. Subjects were also 35 per cent more likely to leave work to be picked up later rather than sit in the striped area waiting room. Twenty-five per cent of the staff interviewed noticed the design less over time (a common response), and while 25 per cent said they avoided the design or spent less time in the area, 75 per cent said there was no change in their behaviour (though this was not confirmed).

When one considers that in a lifelong career people spend between 86,000 and 129,000 hours in the workspace, this is significant 'exposure' to designs. It is only in the last 200 years that we have 'come indoors'

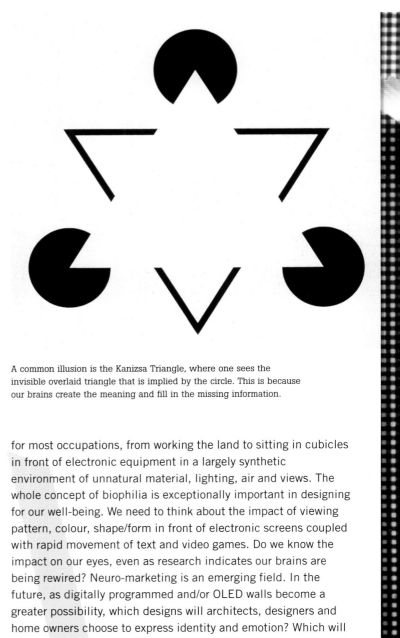

A common illusion is the Kanizsa Triangle, where one sees the invisible overlaid triangle that is implied by the circle. This is because our brains create the meaning and fill in the missing information.

for most occupations, from working the land to sitting in cubicles in front of electronic equipment in a largely synthetic environment of unnatural material, lighting, air and views. The whole concept of biophilia is exceptionally important in designing for our well-being. We need to think about the impact of viewing pattern, colour, shape/form in front of electronic screens coupled with rapid movement of text and video games. Do we know the impact on our eyes, even as research indicates our brains are being rewired? Neuro-marketing is an emerging field. In the future, as digitally programmed and/or OLED walls become a greater possibility, which designs will architects, designers and home owners choose to express identity and emotion? Which will contribute to healing/well-being? The possibilities are immense. △

Notes
1. Patricia Rodemann, *Rooms of America III* survey, 1998, Table 33, N=2,056. Data projectable nationally with an error rate of 0.07. (Unpublished.)
2. Patricia Rodeman, *Patterns in Interior Environments: Perception, Psychology and Practice*, John Wiley & Sons (New York), 1999. The book explores the behavioural aspects of patterns in interior architecture, such as sociological, cultural and environmental implications behind selections, and examines considerations of pattern design: the historic origin of designs, rendition and aesthetics, type and categorisation of patterns, demographics, and the physiological affect and psychological-cognitive, emotional and economic impact of our design choices.
3. An outgrowth of the *Rooms of America* survey. *Homes of America I* survey, 2003, N=3,011. (Unpublished.)

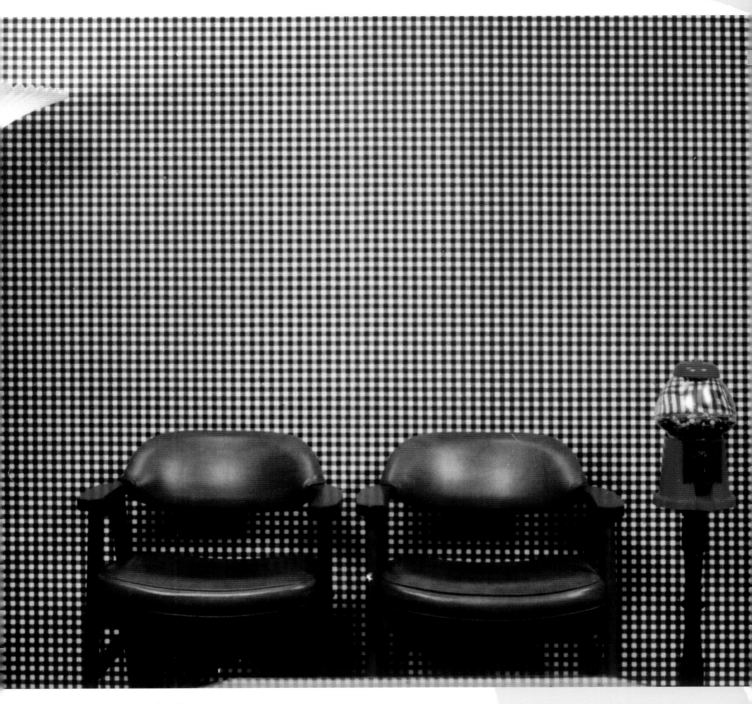

Geometric chequerboard pattern installed
in the marketing/graphics office of a
printers' service in Columbus, Ohio.

Contributors

Mark Garcia is the Research Co-ordinator and an MPhil/PhD Supervisor in the Department of Architecture at the Royal College of Art (RCA). He has worked for Branson Coates Architecture and has held academic research posts at St Antony's College (Oxford University) and the Department of Industrial Design Engineering (Royal College of Art) as well as lecturing in universities across Japan, Switzerland and the UK. He was guest-editor of *AD Architextiles* (Vol 76, No 6, Nov/Dec 2006) and is editor of *The Diagrams of Architecture* (John Wiley & Sons, January 2010).

Michael Hensel is an architect, researcher and writer. He is Professor for Research by Design at AHO, the Oslo School of Architecture and Design, a board member of BIONIS (the Biomimetics Network for Sustainability), editorial board member of *AD* and the *Journal for Bionic Engineering*, and founding member of OCEAN Research and Design Network. He has taught, lectured, published and exhibited worldwide.

Hanif Kara is a London-based structural engineer. Since co-founding his practice, Adams Kara Taylor, his particular 'design-led' approach and interest in innovative form, material uses, prefabrication, sustainable construction, and complex analysis methods have allowed him to work on award-winning and unique projects with leading architects. His approach extends beyond the structural engineering disciplines and led to his appointment as a commissioner for CABE, the first structural engineer to hold this post. He was selected for the master jury for the 2004 cycle of the Aga Khan awards for Architecture and was made an Honorary Fellow of RIBA the same year. He co-tutored a Diploma Unit at the Architectural Association in London from 2000 to 2004, has accepted a position as the Pierce Anderson Lecturer in Creative Engineering at Harvard School of Design, and is a visiting professor of architectural technology at Kungliga Tekniska Högskolan (KTH) in Stockholm, Sweden.

Brian McGrath is Associate Professor of Urban Design at Parsons The New School for Design and the founder of urban-interface (www.urban-interface.com), a studio that works at the intersection of media, urban design and ecology. He is the author of two books published by John Wiley & Sons: *Digital Modelling for Urban Design* (2008) and, with Jean Gardner, *Cinemetrics: Architectural Drawing Today* (2007). He was co-editor, with David Grahame Shane, of *AD Sensing the 21st Century City: Close up and Remote* (Vol 75, No 6, Nov/Dec 2005). He served as a Fulbright senior scholar in Thailand in 1998/99, recently completed a two-year fellowship at the New School's India China Institute, and is a co-principal investigator for the Baltimore Ecosystem Study, an interdisciplinary long-term ecological research project (www.beslter.org).

Victoria Marshall is a practising landscape architect and urban designer living and working in Newark, New Jersey. She is the founder of TILL as well as Assistant Professor of Urban Design at Parsons The New School for Design. She completed her graduate studies at the University of Pennsylvania and has taught at that school as well as Columbia University, Pratt Institute, the University of Toronto and Harvard University. Her current research engages urban design at the small scale, in particular the practice, performance and potential of drawing as a tool for situated action.

Achim Menges is Professor and Director of the Institute for Computational Design at Stuttgart University. He has been teaching at the Architectural Association in London as Studio Master of the Emergent Technologies and Design masters programme since 2002, and as Unit Master of Diploma Unit 4 from 2003 to 2006. His research projects have been published and exhibited worldwide and have won numerous international awards.

Helmut Pottmann received a PhD in mathematics from Vienna University of Technology (TU Vienna) in 1983. From 1992 he was professor at TU Vienna and head of the Geometric Modelling and Industrial Geometry research group. He is currently Director of the KAUST Geometric Modeling and Scientific Visualization Research Center, Saudi Arabia. His recent research focuses on geometric computing for architecture and manufacturing.

Patricia A Rodemann has over 25 years' experience in product, graphic and interior design, research, corporate/brand image, marketing, communications, business development, licensing and strategic planning. She is currently the owner of Designed for Success strategic visual consulting, and was previously a vice-president with the Borden Worldwide Decorative Products group. Her masters degree from the Ohio State University is in industrial/interior/visual communications design research. She is a chair-holder of the Colour Marketing Group, and a member of the Market Research Association. She is author of the book *Patterns in Interior Environments: Perception, Psychology and Practice* (John Wiley & Sons, 1999).

Patrik Schumacher is a partner at Zaha Hadid Architects and founding director of the Architectural Association Design Research Lab (DRL). He joined Zaha Hadid in 1988. He studied philosophy and architecture in Bonn, London and Stuttgart, where he received his diploma in architecture in 1990. In 1999 he completed his PhD at the Institute for Cultural Science, Klagenfurt University. He founded the AA DRL with Brett Steele in 1996, and continues to serve as one of its co-directors. Since 2004 he has also been tenured professor at the Institute for Experimental Architecture, Innsbruck University. He is currently a guest professor at the University of Applied Arts in Vienna.

Mike Silver holds a masters of Building Design from Columbia University, and is a LeFevre '29 research fellow for the Knowlton School of Architecture in Columbus, Ohio, and a Sanders Fellow at the University of Michigan. He is the former Director of Digital Media at the Yale School of Architecture and has taught at Harvard's Graduate School of Design and Cornell. He is the author of numerous books and articles on the relationship between technology and design, including *Pamphlet Architecture #19: Reading/Drawing/Building, Mapping in the Age of Digital Media* (John Wiley & Sons, 2003), and *AD Programming Cultures* (Vol 76, No 4, July/Aug 2006). He currently directs a multidisciplinary design laboratory based in New York.

Theodore Spyropoulos co-directs the Architectural Association Design Research Lab (DRL) in London. With Stephen Spyropoulos, he also co-directs the London- and New York-based experimental architecture and design studio Minimaforms (www.minimaforms.com). He has been a visiting research fellow at MIT since 2006, and curates the AA New Media Research initiative. He has taught in the graduate schools of the University of Pennsylvania and the Royal College of Art, studied at the AA, Bartlett School of Architecture and the New Jersey Institute of Technology, and worked for the offices of Peter Eisenman and Zaha Hadid Architects.

Simon Swaffield is Professor of Landscape Architecture at Lincoln University in New Zealand, where he has been a teacher and researcher since 1982. His research focuses on three linked areas: landscape values and perceptions; landscape change and public policy; and theory in landscape architecture. He is the editor of a widely used reader on *Theory in Landscape Architecture* (Penn Press, 2002), and is also co-authoring a text on research strategies for Wiley.

Mark Taylor is an associate professor and Head of Interior Design at Queensland University of Technology, Australia. He has held visiting positions at several universities and taught, lectured, exhibited and published in Europe and Australasia, including as guest-editor of *AD Surface Consciousness* (Vol 73, No 2, March/April 2003), and co-editor of *Intimus: Interior Design Theory Reader* (John Wiley & Sons, 2006). He recently had work exhibited at the Melbourne Museum as part of the 'Homo Faber: Modelling Ideas' exhibition (2007), and at the 2008 Venice Architecture Biennale (Australian Pavilion – Abundant). He is currently completing a PhD at the University of Queensland.

Julian Vincent was educated at Cambridge and Sheffield universities. He spent most of his career in the Department of Zoology at the University of Reading. In 2000 he was invited to take a chair in the Department of Mechanical Engineering at the University of Bath. Here he has developed applications of biology to engineering, producing some novel machines and objective methods for developing biomimetics.

Alejandro Zaera-Polo is an architect and theorist and co-founder of London-based Foreign Office Architects (FOA). He trained at the Escuela Técnica Superior de Arquitectura de Madrid, and went on to do a masters in architecture at Harvard's Graduate School of Design. He collaborated with OMA in Rotterdam between 1991 and 1993, prior to establishing FOA in 1993. He is currently visiting professor at Princeton School of Architecture, and occupies the Berlage Chair at the Technical University in Delft, the Netherlands, where he is also a member of the institute's research board. He was Dean of the Berlage Institute in Rotterdam from 2000 to 2005. He has been visiting critic at Columbia GSAPP, Princeton and UCLA, and led a Diploma Unit at the Architectural Association in London for eight years.

AD+ CONTENTS

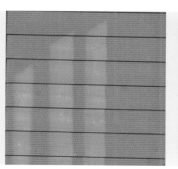
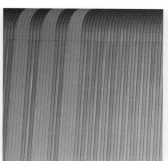

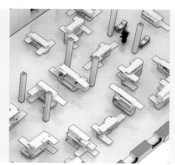

SAI Consultants

The work of Bangkok-based Bundit Chulasai runs the full gamut of building types from palace restorations to private houses, resorts and even discount supermarkets. **Brian McGrath** describes how Chulasai's successful adaptive practice with SAI Consultants creates a critical mirror to reflect the last 30 years of Thai society.

SAI Consultants with Bundit Chulasai (centre).

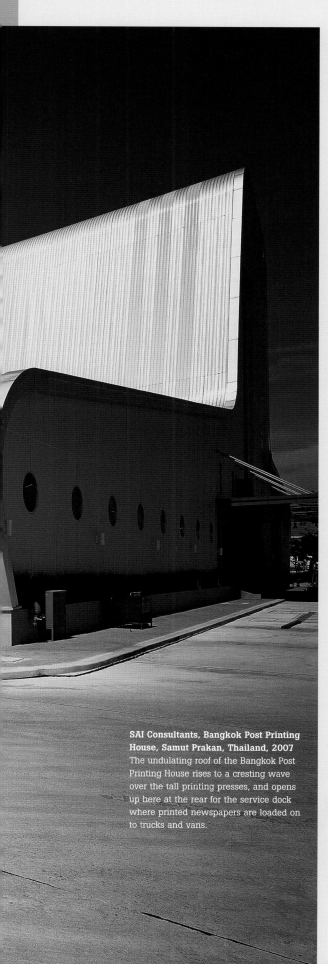

In the age of globalisation, architects must develop creative agility in order to keep pace with fluctuating economic, environmental and cultural contexts. Over the past three decades, architectural practice in Thailand has been exceptionally tumultuous as the country emerged after the Second World War as a Cold War bastion of capitalism to become the world's fastest growing economy between 1985 and 1995. While the kingdom of Thailand quickly catapulted itself into a newly industrialised country, Thais maintained strong ties to cultural traditions through Buddhism, allegiance to the Chakri royal family, and a devotion to simple forms of sustained sociability. Additionally, Thai society has a long legacy of cultural adaptation, first as a key entrepôt between Persia and Japan, secondly through the royal assimilation of European colonial lifestyles, and later an enthusiastic adoption of American consumer culture. The great cultural and economic wealth slowly acquired, carefully preserved and recently accumulated has been unevenly distributed in this still emerging democracy, and new competition from the historical regional hegemonies of India and China has exposed economic and social vulnerabilities.

Since setting up a design studio in Bangkok in 1978 with his brother Kunchorn, Bundit Chulasai has established an extremely diverse architectural practice – SAI Consultants – in this context of dynamic change in Thailand over the last 30 years. During the same period of time, he has also been teaching at the Faculty of Architecture, Chulalongkorn, where he was named dean in 2008. He completed a trilateral education in Thailand, the US and France, and his career is exemplary of the agile navigation of maintaining Thai cultural values and knowledge while at the same time embracing this period of cultural assimilation and modernisation. Remarkably, he has created a distinctive body of contemporary designs while working on some of the kingdom's most important conservation projects, royal commissions, tourist resorts, and some of Thailand's most blatantly commercial projects. From palace restorations to discount supermarkets, Chulasai's successful 'adaptive practice' creates a critical mirror to reflect the last 30 years of Thai society.

Wandering down the narrow alley, Soi Kasemsan 2, in the heart of Bangkok, one leaves the world of high-rise commercial developments, malls, spas and resorts and enters a canalside enclave of small bungalows. Along a canal at the end of the alley, Chulasai has designed two buildings which form a gateway to the house the American Jim Thompson built for himself during the 1950s and 1960s while helping to create an international market for the Thai silk industry when not busy serving as a US military intelligence officer. Thompson inverted and reassembled six traditional Thai teak houses into a spacious villa along the San Saeb Canal, and Chulasai's additions create a threshold between the hard concrete city and the cool, verdant retreat of the Jim Thompson Museum. The architect first designed a café/restaurant and banquet room, and later a museum shop and temporary exhibition hall. With a growing number of tourists flocking to the site, the additions enhance and support the existing original house compound by freeing all support functions from the historical structure, and lengthen and deepen the experience of the visitors by providing ancillary facilities and gardens.

SAI Consultants, Additions to the Jim Thompson House and Museum Compound, Bangkok, Thailand, 1997 and 2001
The Jim Thompson House is well known not only for its legendary owner and exquisite Thai silk products, but also for its adaptation and conservation of traditional teak construction. The original consists of a complex of six old Thai-style houses purchased from several owners and reassembled at the present location in 1959. Bundit Chulasai designed two new pavilions to house a café, restaurant and banquet room as well as a museum shop and temporary exhibition hall. The additions accommodate visitors' basic needs and expand and lengthen their experience. The new constructions were designed as contemporary reinforced-concrete structures, yet they harmonise with the pre-existing teak structures and the lush tropical environment through complementary scale, detailing, open verandas and the use of traditional Thai terracotta roof tiles.

Bundit Chulasai's design for support facilities for the Jim Thompson House and Museum in Bangkok provides visitors with a comfortable waiting area at the gate to the museum.

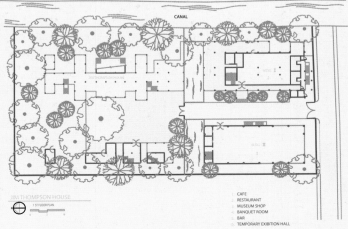

The floor plans of the house and museum compound show Chulasai's two additions to the right, which form a gateway to the historical house and gardens to the left. An extension of the canal (top of plan) provides a buffer between the additions and the museum, crossed by a small bridge.

The museum has become a contemporary cultural venue as well as a historical attraction with the ground-floor modern shop and upper-level gallery Chulasai completed in 2002.

A reflecting pool separates the concrete-frame café and banquet hall, right, from the old teak museum to the left.

The café and banquet rooms open up on a covered porch and veranda overlooking a pool which reflects the entryway into the museum, making the site a cool midday retreat even for those with no intention of joining the house tour. The temporary exhibition hall floats above the new museum shop, supported by a colonnade which provides another shady garden veranda. Chulasai clearly distinguishes between the new buildings and the historical structures through the use of new materials, but the new buildings conform to the portion, scale and spatial disposition of the older house. His adaptive modern style provides a solution for the new extension of the museum which respects the context of the existing museum, as well as representing contemporary Thai style in the new design. While wood, especially teak, is the material of choice for the construction of traditional Thai houses, it is impractical for present-day construction because of cost and availability. Instead Chulasai employs a reinforced-concrete structure and masonry lightweight brick wall for the museum extension, for cost-effectiveness, climate control and practical local construction.

Southeast of Bangkok, across from the tourist-friendly crocodile farm in Samut Prakan province, hundreds of young girls and boys assemble in front of the striped, army-green lattice-covered facades of Chulasai's Rim Khob Fa Youth Center. An urban camp site, the facility provides simple shelter, food facilities and a convention hall for cub scouts at Muang Boran, or Ancient Siam – an 80-hectare (200-acre) cultural theme park roughly in the shape of Thailand. Ancient Siam houses an enormous assembled and reconstructed collection of abandoned artefacts of Thai architecture as well as replicas of famous existing monuments and fantastical mythical structures of the ancient kingdom. The original structures and the outstanding replicas were built with the assistance of experts from the National Museum, and they make Muang Boran one of the world's largest outdoor cultural museums and experiential learning classrooms. Hundreds of thousands of Thai schoolchildren join international tourists in exploring the site, and in 2007 the youth center was constructed to provide a three-storey dormitory and a large multipurpose hall to accommodate cub scouts on overnight camping trips and jamborees.

Scouting was first introduced in Thailand in 1911 by King Vajiravudh, who was influenced by his educational experience at the Royal Military College at Sandhurst and Oxford University in England – the first Thai monarch to study abroad. He established the Wild Tiger Corps modelled on the British Volunteer Force, and created a junior branch – the Tiger Cubs – based on Robert Baden-Powell's boy scouts movement. Chulasai's design arranges the two main buildings along a north–south axis adjacent to Ancient Siam. On the north is a three-storey building for overnight accommodation and to the south is an 8-metre (3.2-foot) high multipurpose hall and supporting facilities for indoor functions and activities. There is a service court between the two buildings, an assembly yard to the north of the dormitory, and a more ceremonial garden with a statue honouring King Vajiravudh south of the multipurpose hall. The king is fondly remembered as the father of Thai scouting and every year on 1 July, for Scout Day, scouts take part in parades and pay homage to his image.

The dormitories for the Thai cub scouts at Ancient Siam cultural heritage park are located in twin buildings with an open entry and circulation breezeway between, all wrapped in horizontal-striped lattice sunscreen.

SAI Consultants, Rim Khob Fa Youth Center, Samut Prakan, Thailand, 2007

The Rim Khob Fa Youth Center is made up of two buildings: a three-storey cub-scout dormitory comprised of two single-loaded-corridor lodging blocks facing one another to form an open court with conjoining bridges and a staircase in the middle, and a 6,000-square-metre (64,583-square-foot) assembly hall and supporting facilities raised above a below-ground parking level. The facilities are used by the Tiger Cub scouts of Thailand as an urban camp and jamboree facility adjacent to Ancient Siam, an outdoor museum of rebuilt, copied and fantastical Thai architecture. The youth centre buildings are modern, simple and humble, yet utilise indigenous knowledge of building in a flood-prone tropical delta. The dormitory's court opens under a translucent roof providing natural lighting and ventilation. Both buildings have a second outer sunscreening wall, the horizontal pattern of the lattice covering most of the facade like Venetian blinds.

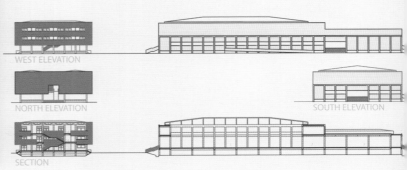

WEST ELEVATION

NORTH ELEVATION

SECTION

SOUTH ELEVATION

Scouts assemble at the dormitory entry. Administration offices are on the ground floor, and a double open stair leads to open corridors and two levels of dormitories above. The breezeway is covered with a translucent roof that provides daylighting but shelters the scouts from monsoon rains.

Elevations show the relationship between the dormitory, to the left, and the large multipurpose hall to the right. Three exterior spaces are defined: a parade ground in front of the dormitory, a service court between the buildings, and a ceremonial garden behind the multipurpose hall to the far right.

This view from within the open vestibule of the dormitory shows how effectively the lattice screens the strong tropical sun, and frames the parade grounds where the scouts assemble.

The lattice continues to wrap the interior of the dormitory atrium and becomes handrails for stairways and connecting corridors to the rooms.

The two buildings are framed with reinforced-concrete light steel supporting a sheet-metal roof. The dormitory structure comprises two single-loaded-corridor lodging blocks facing one another across an open court with conjoining bridges and a staircase in the middle providing natural ventilation throughout. A translucent roof shelters the open court from monsoon rains, and provides natural daylighting throughout the building. The architect says the buildings' proximity to the historically and culturally significant Muang Boran museum dictated a simple, respectful and humble design. Both buildings open to the east and the west, facing strong heat from the direct sunlight all day. The architect arrived at a climate-control solution by creating a 'double surface system' of autoclaved aerated concrete, a lightweight material, for the inner wall to reduce building structural load as well as heat transfer, and a fibre-reinforced cement lattice for the outer surface screen. The striped lattice screen reduces direct heat to the buildings and softens the intensity of strong sunlight for the interior. The pattern of the lattice screen covering most of the facade also emphasises the buildings' horizontality and creates marvellous patterns of diagonal shadows over the course of the day.

Visitors departing from Bangkok can take the elevated Bangna-Chonburi expressway – a marvel of French-engineered post-stressed cantilevered concrete – to the new international aerotropolis, named Suvarnabhumi by the king. The royal name honours the rich cultural diversity of the ancient Golden Land of Southeast Asia before the surveyed boundaries and national identities of European colonisation. Beyond the airport, the eastern seaboard industrial area stretches for miles towards the deep-water port of Laem Chabang and the beach resorts of Rayong. Along the expressway, a large wave of standing seam metal seems to cascade into a concrete surf. A tall cathedral-like window at the crest of the wave briefly allows a view straight through the building, and for a moment a glance at a giant four-storey printing press. The Bangkok Post was founded by Alexander MacDonald, from the Office of Strategic Services, the US intelligence agency that was the predecessor of the CIA. While the American State Department helped finance this Cold War information outlet, its new multinational owners asked Chulasai to relocate its venerable printing house from a central location to a new printing and distribution centre at the periphery of the city. This new facility provides a striking modern image at the gateway to Thailand and ensures just-in-time delivery of the English-language daily newspaper to tourist resorts and ex-pat enclaves around the country, as well as to its Bangkok-based, English-literate Thai middle-class constituency.

The north side of the printing press hall has eight tall concrete piers supporting a crane on rails, awaiting installation of more presses to fill an empty bay. In the cool morning air, huge barn doors open this great hall, which acts like a giant breezeway to the highway. Above, a projecting second floor supports a balcony mezzanine catwalk. A third-level mezzanine houses the printing control room, with a glass wall overlooking the four-storey presses. The wavy ceiling is perforated by seven deeply recessed skylights. Morning daylight lights and natural ventilation cools the printing machines before the presses are started at noon. The lower portion of the facade is

The building presents itself as a figuration of paper running through the presses with the Bangkok Post staff head directed towards the traffic leaving Bangkok on the elevated Bangna-Chonburi Expressway.

SAI Consultants, Bangkok Post Printing House, Samut Prakan, Thailand, 2007

The Bangkok Post Printing House is a large steel and reinforced-concrete structure that supports a giant wave-like metal standing seam sheet-roof surface, strikingly visible from the Bangna-Chonburi elevated expressway. Not just a facility for traditional newspaper printing, it also houses a high-tech digital control centre and a distribution warehouse. The distinctive profile of the building not only reflects the image of rolls of paper coming off a printing press, but also provides the necessary headroom clearance as the rolls climb through the towering presses and out to the flat space of the warehouse and distribution room. The red sign on the roof facing the highway seems redundant as the building itself, while primarily utilitarian, is a symbol of the vibrancy of newspaper journalism in a 21st-century democracy.

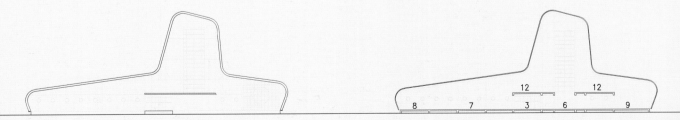

While the elevation view shows the profile the building presents to those travelling on the elevated expressway, the section shows that the interior is in fact one large space under a continuously waving roof, through which the newsprint has the privileged promenade under, up over, through and out the back.

The interior of the great hall holding the presses is lit by large windows, one facing the expressway, the other the sea. The space is opened up to the cool night air and is only closed and air-conditioned while the presses run during the afternoon.

A detail view of the rear window shows the printing press hall and, in the foreground, a warehouse for rolls of newsprint ready to be wheeled over to the presses.

punctured by porthole windows like a ship caught under the giant roof wave. A warehouse in the back stores rolls of newsprint paper which are wheeled over to the presses, then pivoted on a turntable and rolled into place. After travelling through the presses and cutters, the rolls of paper are printed into newspapers and sample pages are conveyed to the control tower for final inspection. Ribbons of skylights emit sunlight reflecting on the printed newspapers which fly in on rails above. The finished newspapers are diverted into four different tracks over a sparkling blue speckled floor for sorting, shrink-wrapping and piling on distributing bales ready to be shipped to sale destinations around the country. Open to the east, the wave wall is flipped open like a hatchback for the shipping dock, a raised platform overlooking a sports field for the staff.

Chulasai's work covers a wide variety of building types and cultural histories that is unique to Thailand, yet exemplary in its mindfulness, simplicity and adaptability to different budgets, social contexts and programmatic demands. In addition to the unusual buildings detailed above, his other notable projects include the renovation and extensions of the Sofitel Centara Grand Resort & Villas in Hua Hin from 1989. In collaboration with Professor Pussadee Tiptus and others, Bundit has designed several buildings on the Chulalongkorn University campus, of which the Institution 2 Building (1982) and Chulachakrabongse Building (1986) received awards from the Association of Siamese Architects under royal patronage. His most prominent project is the Sala Rajakarunya Memorial Museum (1992) in Trat border province, a monument to commemorate Queen Sirikit's act of kindness in giving aid to Cambodian refugees in 1979. The monument is mentioned as one of the distinctive examples of 20th-century architecture in Thailand in Sir Banister Fletcher's *A History of Architecture* (20th edn, 1996).

The force of Chulasai's work lies in his capacity to maintain a profound balance between respectful attention to Thai building and social traditions while contributing to the further evolution of modern Thai architecture. His work attests to the originality of Thai contributions in the further elaboration of contemporary architecture in an era of globalisation where restraint and adaptability are necessary skills. ∆+

Brian McGrath is an architect and founding partner of urban-interface, a collaborative practice that explores the relationship between urbanism, ecology and media. He is also an associate professor of Urban Design at Parsons The New School of Design, a Fulbright senior scholar in Thailand and a Fellow of the India China Institute. He has published many essays for *AD*, and was guest-editor, with David Grahame Shane, of *AD Sensing the 21st Century City: Close-up and Remote* (Vol 75, No 6, Nov/Dec 2005). He is the author of two books published by John Wiley & Sons: *Digital Modelling for Urban Design* (2008) and, with Jean Gardner, *Cinemetrics: Architectural Drawing Today* (2007).

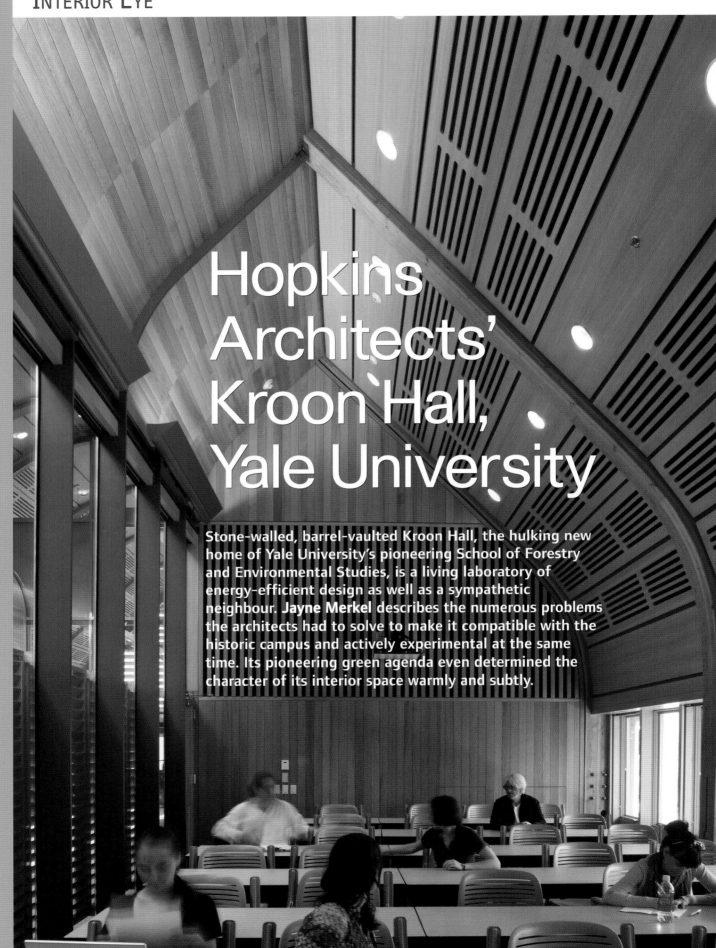

Hopkins Architects' Kroon Hall, Yale University

Stone-walled, barrel-vaulted Kroon Hall, the hulking new home of Yale University's pioneering School of Forestry and Environmental Studies, is a living laboratory of energy-efficient design as well as a sympathetic neighbour. **Jayne Merkel** describes the numerous problems the architects had to solve to make it compatible with the historic campus and actively experimental at the same time. Its pioneering green agenda even determined the character of its interior space warmly and subtly.

Kroon Hall has a soaring, rather enigmatic presence. It looks like a cross between a cathedral and a sports arena because of the high pitch of its curved roof, rough stone walls and elongated proportions. It nods both to Eero Saarinen's whale-shaped hockey rink across the road and to the old brownstone Collegiate Gothic laboratories on each side, while vastly improving the neighbourhood by burying a service delivery area and creating a welcoming courtyard with a pool full of wetland plants that filter rainwater from the roof so that it can be used in toilets and for irrigation.

'We tried to make a building that feels like it belongs to Yale, rather than one that says, "Oh look, I've got lots of bits of sustainable technology from circa 2006" that in 20 years' time will look completely out of date,' Michael Taylor of London-based Hopkins Architects explained. Certainly a building that goes out of style and is soon replaced is the least sustainable of all. But the architects' goals here were not in conflict. As it turned out, the building's mostly traditional materials, long thin shape and solar orientation did more to help it save

energy than all the high-tech devices combined, though they all work in carefully conceived unison.

The shape of the elongated curved roof and the red oak panelling that lines the vaulted skylighted meeting rooms beneath it have also created some of the most unusual and welcoming public spaces on the Yale campus. Their character was almost solely influenced by the mandate to make the building as energy efficient as possible. Hopkins worked with Centerbrook Architects of Connecticut on the building; Atelier Ten consulted on sustainable design; Arup was responsible for structural and mechanical engineering.

The building is four storeys high, though the ground floor is buried in the hillside on the north side for thermal insulation, so it is 20 metres (65 feet) tall on the south but rises only 16.5 metres (54 feet) on the north side. It is only 17 metres (57 feet) wide but 66 metres (218 feet) long because its roof was designed to hold 1,008 photovoltaic panels that convert sunlight to electricity. The south facade also contains four evacuated tube solar collectors that heat the building's potable water. But the shape of the building itself conserves energy the way the shapes of Gothic cathedrals (which are warm in winter and cool in summer) do.

Hopkins Architects with Centerbrook Architects, Kroon Hall, Yale University, New Haven, Connecticut, 2009
opposite: Red oak panelling covers the walls and vaulted ceilings in small chapel-shaped reading rooms at the top of the building. The wood gives interiors texture and symbolises the activities that Kroon Hall was built to house.

below: Kroon Hall is nestled into a hilly site on Yale's Science Hill where its blonde rough stone walls offer insulation and relate to those of the historic brownstone laboratories nearby. Wide gutters under the roof shade the bands of windows just beneath them and collect rainwater that is filtered in the plant-filled 'cleansing pond' on the new south courtyard accessed from a colonnade off the ground-floor library. Runoff water is then buried and stored for use in toilets and for landscape irrigation.

above: The soaring vaulted space at the top of the building houses informal meeting areas, conference facilities, an auditorium and a café with views out on to Science Hill and Sachem's Wood.

right: Douglas fir louvres on the glazed ends of Kroon Hall filter natural light while providing vistas of the landscaped campus beyond. The west facade looks down on the 1913 brownstone Osborne Laboratories to the southwest, which form a gateway to Science Hill from the south.

opposite: The photovoltaic panels at the top of the roof are encased in glass to provide dramatic skylighted spaces in the barrel-vaulted rooms on the top storey where conferences and informal meetings take place. Warm red-oak walls and skylights make them welcoming and dramatic in an unusual way that particularly befits a School of Forestry and Environmental Studies – serious of purpose but informal at the same time.

The 48 photovoltaic panels at the top of the roof are embedded in glass to create skylights in the dramatic vaulted 175-seat auditorium, café and conference rooms beneath them, where red oak-panelled walls, constantly changing light, asymmetrical form and spaciousness makes them a fitting climax to the procession up the staircase in a series of gentle flights. Although photovoltaic panels can be used as roofing, the ones covering Kroon Hall are attached to a metal surface so that they can be replaced as more efficient photovoltaic technology is developed. They already provide 100 kilowatts of renewable energy – a quarter of that used in the building.

Kroon Hall's stone side walls are rough hewn like those of the old dark-brown laboratories on either side, but they are made of yellow Briar Hill sandstone from the same quarries that supplied the stone for many of the Gothic Revival 'colleges' (dormitories) in the older part of the Yale campus to the south. Luckily, though the quarry was three states away in Ohio, it was (barely)

within 500 miles (805 kilometres) – the distance permitted by the dictate to use only 'local' materials. Much of the red oak panelling inside, however, which gives the building a rather Scandinavian feel, came from the university's own nearby sustainable Yale-Myers forest.

The roof is supported by a series of 21 glue-laminated Douglas fir arches. Since they were made from thin layers of wood glued together, small pieces of wood could be used instead of large tree trunks from old-growth forests. All the wood in the building was sustainably harvested as befits the home of the first professional forestry programme in the US, founded in 1901.

The warm wood panelling inside Kroon Hall not only symbolises the programme that the building houses, but also softens the effect of the exposed-concrete interior walls and ceilings on the bottom three floors. Here, 0.3-metre (1-foot) thick concrete was used because its high thermal mass can store and slowly release warmth in winter and cooling in summer. Most of the structural system is also reinforced concrete. The concrete used contains 25 per cent ground granulated blast furnace slag, a fire-resistant recycled postindustrial material. A by-product of steel smelting, it decreases carbon-dioxide emissions normally associated with concrete production.

A soaring 175-seat auditorium occupies the western end of the barrel-vaulted space on the top storey of Kroon Hall. It, too, has wood-panelled walls and ceilings and dramatic views of the landscape, as well as comfortable upholstered seats. Mechanical features are almost invisible.

Wooden window frames, louvres and furnishings carry the decorative and symbolic generous use of wood into faculty and staff offices that occupy most of the building. Natural light is provided as well as highly efficiently fluorescent lighting that shuts off when it is not needed or when rooms are vacated.

The library and informal meeting areas on the ground floor flow into a covered walkway on the south side of the building and out to one of the courtyards that the building's orientation created on Science Hill where outdoor space was badly needed.

The difficult thing about creating a sustainable building is that you do not just have to design one that will conserve energy when it is being used, you also have to conserve energy. And conserving energy in New England is a lot harder than it is in the UK, as Taylor, whose firm was chosen for its expertise in sustainable design, pointed out.

Summers in New England are warm and humid, winters are cold and icy, so it only makes sense to open windows in spring and autumn. Those in Kroon Hall have lights that glow green when it is wise to do so, red when it is not. The building's operable windows are highly insulated so they perform well closed. The thick stone walls on the sides of the building allow more light to enter during winter when the sun is low. In summer, when the sun is high, deep window frames and aluminium shades block its rays. Douglas fir louvres covering the glass facades on the east and west ends keep out unwanted heat and glare. Light and occupancy sensors dim the efficient fluorescent artificial lighting when it is not needed.

Kroon Hall houses a library, meeting rooms, faculty and staff offices, and conference facilities, but no laboratories, so the high-tech equipment inside is there mainly to monitor the building's performance and is not particularly visible. Heating and cooling is achieved by heat pumps rather than conventional boilers and chillers. Four 457-metre (1,500-foot) deep wells and ground-source heat pumps extract water to help heat and cool the interior from the earth below Sachem's Wood, an area that was deeded to the university years ago with the understanding that it remain green space. But it was not much used before Kroon Hall was built, as it is a good 10 minutes' walk from the more urban historic areas where Yale grew up. Although there have been laboratories on Science Hill, as the area is called, since 1912, and Eero Saarinen prepared a master plan for it in 1951, there were not many usable outdoor gathering spaces. The new building, which replaces an oil-fired power plant, creates a backdrop to the hilly underused land, buries service drives, greenhouses and dumpsters, and adds new footpaths as well as two new courtyards landscaped by the Olin Studio with 25 varieties of native plantings.

It took decades for the faculty of the School of Forestry and Environmental Studies to convince university officials to make a pioneering commitment to energy-efficient design, but it has done so beautifully in this $33,500,000 building, which they describe as 'a Modernist blend of cathedral nave and Connecticut barn'.

Hallways and skylighted staircases in Kroon Hall are sheathed in red oak panelling, much of the wood harvested from Yale's own sustainable forest, to make transition spaces that invite casual interchange. They also warm the well-insulated deep concrete walls and ceilings behind them, both physically and psychologically.

Kroon Hall manages to be high-tech without looking it. It has the warmth of a traditional academic building and, with its variegated wood panelling juxtaposed with smooth concrete, the subtle polish of some of Yale's best modern ones, such as Louis Kahn's Center for British Art. And yet there is a pleasant quirkiness derived from its proportions and a certain mystery evoked by rows of closed office doors. Since the school's laboratories are housed elsewhere there is none of the grit of a wet lab building. It is a restful, inspiring place in which to figure out how to save the earth. **∆+**

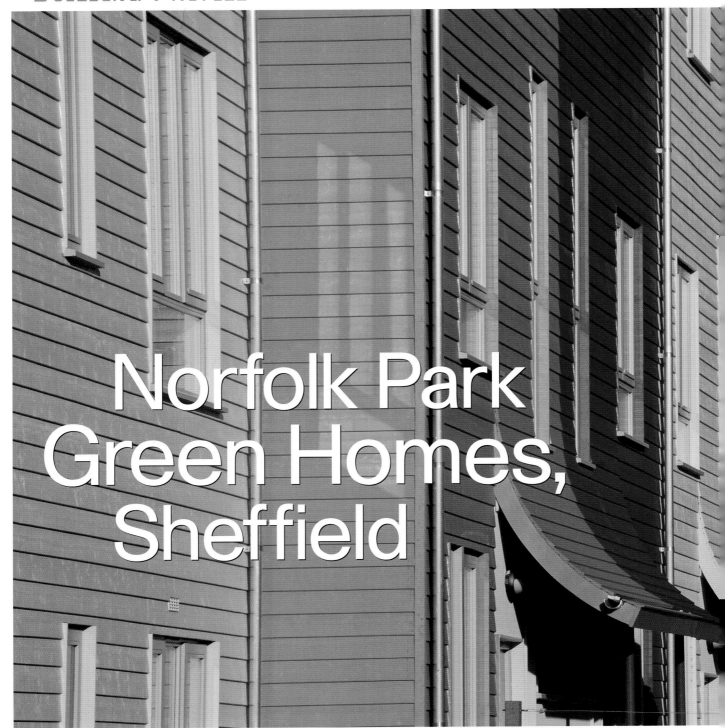

Norfolk Park Green Homes, Sheffield

In a neighbourhood of Sheffield that was once dominated by tower blocks, Matthew Lloyd Architects has created colourful timber-clad homes that resemble a community. **David Littlefield** describes how a determined architect and client, despite local scepticism, have been able to provide housing that is not only spacious, generous in size and sustainable, but also comparatively cheap.

The development of 47 homes in an increasingly pleasant district of Sheffield is a salutary example of two things: the fact that dogged determination can, eventually, overcome prejudice and scepticism; and that high standards do not necessarily cost the earth. Built on a site once occupied by 1960s tower blocks, the last of which was demolished in 2005, Matthew Lloyd Architects has delivered a distinctive, generous and well-detailed cluster of four buildings that appear to offer the right conditions (providing social and economic factors are also right) for a healthy community to establish itself. Homes are large, exceeding Parker Morris standards by around 10 per cent; ceiling heights are set at 2.7 metres (8.9 feet), which is more typically seen in office environments; and landscaping is varied and far from sterile, partly due to the Sustainable Urban Drainage System (SUDS) which slows and even prevents rainwater from running straight into the mains. A variety of sustainable measures keep energy costs down while warming communal areas, and the £5.2 million price tag for the entire development means that purchase prices can be kept low.

Matthew Lloyd's scheme is as much about politics as it is about design. Lloyd was originally commissioned to undertake the project by Jon Aldenton, Chief Executive of the Environment Trust, a body that worked (until the banking crisis caused a withdrawal of credit in 2008) in partnership with local authorities to develop low-cost, energy-efficient housing for difficult-to-develop inner-city sites. Both architect and client are motivated by a strong sense of social justice. 'Jon always said that if we could build it cheap, then we could sell it cheap,' remembers Lloyd, whose homes are being sold on a shared-ownership basis, part rent, part mortgage. 'And he said he wanted these houses to be big and spacious. He banged that drum every day.'

Matthew Lloyd Architects, Norfolk Park Green Homes, Sheffield, 2009
above: The houses in Matthew Lloyd Architects' Norfolk Park development are distinguished by their colourful timber cladding and porches created by peeling the cladding outwards.

below: Early sketch of the apartment block. Eventually, the development was to be built without balconies, effectively a cost-saving measure as the client wanted the homes to be built for as little as possible to maximise affordability.

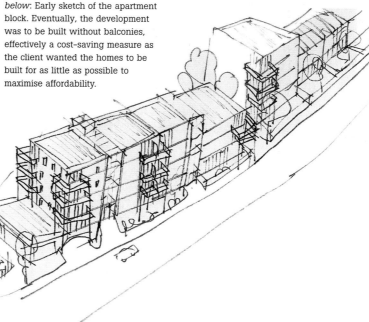

Rooftop photovoltaic panels provide power for heating communal spaces. Solar heat is also harvested to preheat water. Estimates for these well-insulated, airtight homes show fuel bills will be reduced to less than that of the average home.

Houses are picked out in individual colours. Architect Matthew Lloyd, who grew up in a yellow house, imagines residents identifying their home in terms of colour, as well as by number.

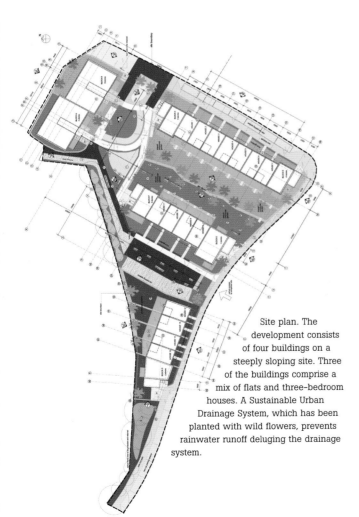

Site plan. The development consists of four buildings on a steeply sloping site. Three of the buildings comprise a mix of flats and three-bedroom houses. A Sustainable Urban Drainage System, which has been planted with wild flowers, prevents rainwater runoff deluging the drainage system.

Lloyd also bangs a drum of his own. In 2008 he co-curated the RIBA exhibition 'Evolving Norms of British Housing', where he outlined his own agenda for new homes. 'Good housing cannot be created by ticking off standards only to achieve low-maintenance, fortress flats,' he wrote in an accompanying catalogue. 'The responsibility for the designer of good streets and houses may only be to create good "blank canvas" homes. Bad architecture, after all, blights lives. The skill of the good housing architect is to be disciplined enough to create clarity and simplicity.' With the Norfolk Park development, Lloyd aimed for something that you might find in a typical German or Scandinavian town – decent, well mannered, well proportioned and well planned. The local planning authority did not quite see the scheme this way, however. The colourful timber facades of the houses, with their quirky 'peeled cladding' porches, were considered to be a little too radical for a neighbourhood that was quickly replacing tower blocks with conventional low-rise structures in brick. Lloyd's proposal smacked of experimentalism, and it took two years to secure planning approval.

By all accounts, the complex is still regarded a little sceptically by local residents, who call it 'Balamory' after the BBC children's programme in which people live in brightly coloured buildings. After the anonymity of the tower blocks, and many other developments nearby, these buildings do appear to be distinctive and even light-hearted, but Lloyd resists charges of whimsy. 'There is an element of fun, but everything has been designed,' he says. The colour and timber cladding could, if one is not careful, detract from the rigour of the overall design; there are a number of rules at work which provide a level of coherence which is not immediately apparent. For example, houses have pitched roofs, and the roofs of the apartment blocks, which 'book-end' the houses, are flat. Also, these buildings are hybrid structures – principal

Apartment blocks are typically more muted than the houses, employing olives and khakis. However, many local residents have dubbed the scheme 'Balamory'. The parapet on the right of the image has been artificially raised, as the right-hand block is three storeys high, compared with the four-storey block on the left.

Computer render of the scheme, illustrating the way houses are sandwiched between flat-roofed 'towers' of flats. The scheme sits on a site once occupied by 1960s tower blocks, the last of which was demolished in 2005.

external walls are of timber, while end and party walls (for reasons of acoustics and ease of securing bank loans) are of blockwork. Timber walls are clad in lodgepole pine, while walls of blockwork are, where visible, rendered.

This is a far from off-the-peg development. Matthew Lloyd Architects has laboured over these buildings to deliver energy efficiency, distinctiveness and a sense of 'home'. An exploration of thresholds is very much in evidence here, and houses are approached through a successive layer of gate, garden plot and porch; the communal areas of the apartments are double-glazed and heated via roof-mounted PV panels, offering a graduated entry from outside to inside that unheated circulation areas (which function more like airlocks than approaches to one's front door) lack. In fact, the entire development is highly sustainable, and a range of features including solar preheated water, large amounts of insulation and low-energy appliances could, it is predicted, lead to energy bills that will be considerably less than that of a typical home.

The danger with this scheme is that its colour and texture become too identified with its sustainable mission. But it was never Lloyd's intention to present low-energy housing as necessarily eye-catching or quaint. In fact, the cladding, supplied by Canadian firm Cape Cod Cladding, does not, in reality, resemble the fishing village aesthetic hinted at in photographs. These are not rustic weatherboards, but rather accurately cut, prepainted and expertly fitted timbers that achieve a far more machined aesthetic than one would imagine. Even the 5-millimetre

(0.2-inch) gap between the coloured timbers of adjacent houses is left uncovered, offering a subtle, dark shadow to add to the crispness of the facades. Lloyd recalls the maintenance manager of the housing association which now operates the development, tut-tutting to himself on first visiting the scheme. The problem, it seems, was the imagined expense and effort needed to maintain the facades – especially with regard to repainting. This irritates Lloyd, partly because the Canadian boards are guaranteed to retain their colour for 15 years, but more importantly because he believes maintenance should be part of the lives of buildings, not an inconvenience.

Underlying this scheme is a certain generosity of spirit. All the rooms and corridors in the buildings are no less than large, and second and even third bedrooms are big enough to accommodate a double bed, while windows are often full-height. Landscape architect Thom White has worked hard to avoid the monoculture that typifies the planting schemes in many similar developments, and each garden is being provided with fruit trees and vines to climb gabion walls. The irony with this development is that Matthew Lloyd has used considerable intelligence to deliver a scheme that does not seek to be particularly clever. What he has tried to do, really, is act humanely. △+

David Littlefield is an architectural writer. He has written and edited a number of books, including *Architectural Voices: Listening to Old Buildings* (2007) and *Liverpool One: Remaking a City Centre* (2009), both published by John Wiley & Sons Ltd. He was also the curator of the exhibition 'Unseen Hands: 100 Years of Structural Engineering', which ran at the Victoria & Albert Museum in 2008. He is a visiting lecturer at the University of the West of England.

Head Banging
Engineered Neutrality + the Parametric Ceiling

Through the work of Unit 15 at the Architectural Association in London, Francesca Hughes and Noam Andrews have been exploring the limits of parametric systems. Here **Francesca Hughes** questions whether parametricism has now hit a 'developmental ceiling'. What are the full cultural implications of the promised instantaneity of completed components in architectural production? Where does the 'strange engineered neutrality' of 'optimisation' take us? Is there a real danger that an ambivalence to context is returning us to the tabula rasa of Modernism?

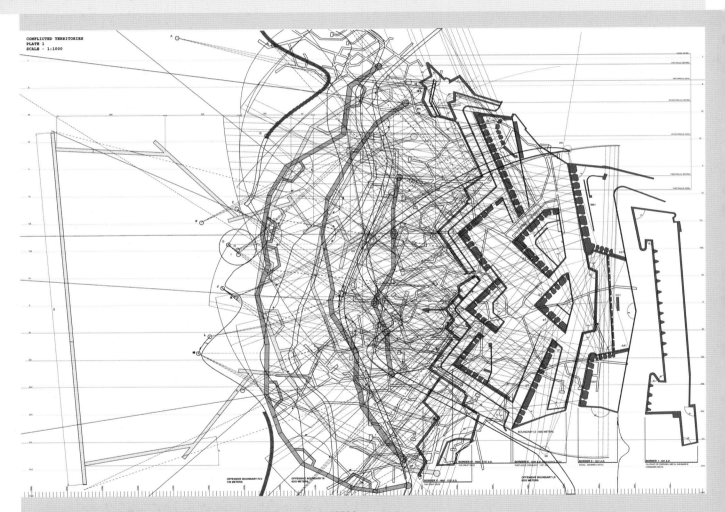

Noam Andrews, Optimal Conflict at the Murailles West, Ceuta, Spain, 2004
The boundary condition at the old city walls of Ceuta remains a form from which function has fled. This slow yet responsive architectural mechanism was precisely developed in order to repel invaders to the southernmost point in Europe, and each siege resulted in a further layer of concretised counterdefence. The mapping explicates a frozen landscape of modulated geometries responding to the developing capacities of ancient artillery technologies.

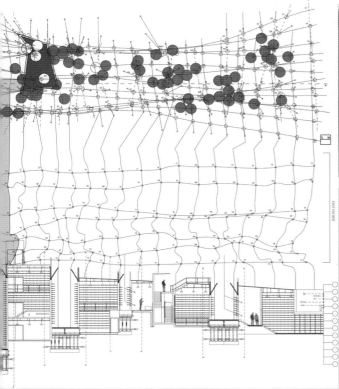

Giovanni Battista Piranesi, *Vedute di Roma*, Plate 58 – Veduta dell' Anfiteatro Flavio, detto il Colosseo, 1751
Piranesi's print of the Colosseum is unique in his oeuvre in that it combines the distortion of the *Carceri* (Prison) series and the realism of the *Vedute di Roma* (Views of Rome) series.

Noam Andrews, Hypertrophic Storage Facility, Ceuta, Spain, 2005
Conflicting datasets merge with a-functional parameters to create a low-tech architecture responsive to changes in local and global demand. Goods are buried internally for extended periods of time and excavated only after their value has increased due to their acquiring status as tax-free products of this Spanish tax haven. Tying together plan, elevation and section, time becomes a quantifiable commodity in a storage machine for the production of value.

Suffice to say, the use of parametric systems in architectural production is no longer in its infancy. Fifteen years or so on, and now common currency in many schools and the more technologically bent urban offices, is it not seriously time to ask how well this adolescent is growing up? Is it growing up? And if not, why do we seem to have hit a developmental ceiling?

As certain promised effects are still awaited, various unpleasant side effects of parametric systems are fast becoming entrenched. A crucially important, yet to be delivered promise of parametricised production is the transformation of the social, economic and labour culture of the construction site through the augmented component; a revolution almost unparalleled since the introduction of reinforced (that is, cast *in situ*) concrete a hundred or so years ago. Then, not only did the professional suddenly enter the labour realm (as lab coats first walked into the dust of the construction site to erect and enforce the concomitant crucial invention of standards and specifications to contain unruly slurry), but also the seamless flow of this new liquid medium eradicated overnight the block-by-block, rivet-by-rivet incrementality of all prior construction.[1]

In a perhaps less dramatic but no less important way, the information-heavy, augmented component has the potential to again further eclipse site construction: arriving on site with not only assembly sequence already embedded in its geometry, but also with zero finishing required. As soon as it is wired up, this new breed of component hits the ground running.[2] Instantaneously complete, it is the contemporary equivalent to the shockingly brief three days Le Corbusier's 1915 reinforced-concrete houses took to make.[3] But what does this new and relative instantaneity do to the culture of architectural production? To how we account for the generation of form? How we assess one form against another?

Le Corbusier well understood that the instantaneous, if properly marketed, has the authority of the immaculate. Indeed, his euphoria at his drawing being 'poured in from above' on to the site in many ways mirrors the rhetoric we find in the accounting of parametric production, where form 'is found', is 'self forming' (or 'emerges' from a system that is clearly not emergent in the true sense).[4] Be it the immaculate construction of form arriving 'from above' or the more secular construction of form 'finding itself' from within the matrix of technology, in both the net effect is the same: authorship is strategically abdicated.[5]

Simply put, parametric systems are being used to deliver the author from the minefield of formal accounting – this is a, if not the, crucial aspect of its successful currency. This is also its developmental ceiling, its failing.

The authority of parametric systems is predicated on their alignment to the instrumentalist premise – that technology is somehow outside of culture and therefore is both not answerable to culture and can arbitrate over culture's conflicts. This is the politics embedded in the thinking behind the term 'optimisation'. Form is delivered, conflict arbitrated, by the technical process itself. The parameters have spoken, so who are we to question the breathtaking computational power that has calculated their configuration?

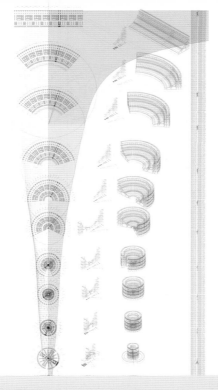

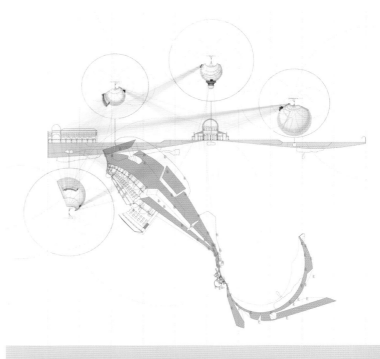

Gergely Kovács, Lessons from Piranesi, Rome, 2008
A digital forensic examination of the perspectival construction of Piranesi's famous fish-eye etching of the Colosseum revealed that the artist had notionally unrolled the Colosseum into a linear element and then projected it back upon a curved picture-plane. The line is thus found to be embedded in the circle. Here the process is extrapolated to its logical conclusion; as the Colosseum's radius tightens, it is turned inside out, and the result is a highly political inversion of an ancient engine of power.

Gergely Kovács, Inversion of the Temple Mount, Jerusalem, 2009
An impossible complex of overlapping cultural and political territories, the Temple Mount represents the ultimate site of conflict and the Holy Grail of constructed neutrality. Ex-President Clinton has proposed that a 1.5-metre (4.9-foot) underground neutral slab separate Muslim surface from Jewish underground. As a critique of the impossible simplicity of this, LI Magnus' 1831 inversion formula, which in mathematics is used as an alternative order or space for solving unsolvable conundrums, is here used to generate an inverted reflection of the most contentious zones in the temple, allowing spatial liberties and convolutions for joint occupation that are impossible both within normal space and under the current, and historic, political constraints.

Indeed, sadly, much of the current harnessing of the enormous potential of parametric systems is simply the latest version in the age-old denial of technology's own deep cultural inflection, and of the latent, undeclared indeterminacy in any 'technique' which itself institutes technology's weakness: its need for culture and qualitative judgement. Surely by now we know technology is a cultural production? So why, given this, do we insist on using the massive potential of parametric systems to carefully carry on skirting the indeterminate, the a-functional, the cultural?

Context in Parametricisation

The two side effects of parametricisation that most clearly manifest the consequences of this denial are the construction of 'context' in parametric models and the strange engineered neutrality that optimisation stands for. As with their liquid, Modernist predecessor the current applications of parametric systems do very strange things to the idea of context. No small matter, if we remember that Modernism (and thus the tabula rasa) could not have happened without reinforced concrete, and vice versa: construction technologies really affect relations to context.

Much has been written on how the dark, gravity-less space of digital production is a continuation of this project, the tabula rasa reincarnated. 'Context' in the culture of parametric production returns, or is reinstalled, already digitalised, and edited to the bone: typically as a set of three to five measurable, and thus necessarily quantitative, physical parameters (latitude, wind direction, and typical rush-hour capacity, say). Once optimised, these parameters effectively 'contextualise' the system or proposal, argue that it is in the right place at the right time. That is, context returns as a highly abstracted, carefully selected alibi.

Architects have always, necessarily, artfully reduced context to harness it as a generator and justifier of action. This is nothing new. What is new is that with parametric systems this reductive process from the outset excludes any indeterminate or qualitative content – ironically such parameters are usually the more site-specific ones.

The Politics of Optimisation

If we can accept to forgo all relations with that in our environment which cannot be directly measured, we are promised an ecology free of conflict. All conflict within this system is optimised; in a kind of engineered neutrality all parties are equally pleased (and equally displeased). But like other states of neutrality, do we dare ask: What does it actually deliver? Is it anything that anyone wants? And what is excluded in the engineering of neutrality? Difference and conflict:

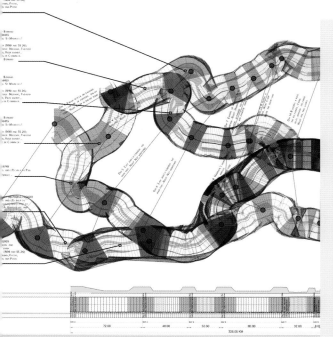

yes. But also everything that doesn't enter the parameter set in the first place: everything that is more difficult to measure – the qualitative, the key domain of the cultural, the incalculable.

Until parametric systems can be redesigned and redeployed to become both more porous (engaging with other systems) and more sophisticated (incorporating indeterminate factors as, say, weighting in statistics achieves), their incredible potential is capped. The Architectural Association Unit 15 projects featured here have been driven by a critique of (current) parametricisation in their active assertion and instrumentalisation of that which it excludes:

1 Hypercontextuality: hyperspecificity to extreme historic, economic and cultural contexts.
2 Incorporation of a-rational/a-functional parameters.
3 Managing indeterminacy: the co-negotiation between determinate and indeterminate physical conditions.
4 Conflict: the problematisation of the politics of neutrality and spatialisation of conflict.

That is, until the application of parametric systems can step outside of the (false) security of the instrumentalist premise and redesign its boundaries accordingly, it will continue to hit this developmental ceiling and fail to truly engage with architecture's ultimate 'client' and 'conflict': culture itself. 𝟄+

Karl Kjelstrup-Johnson, Hannibal's Indeterminacy, French Alps, 2008
The exact route of Hannibal's' seminal southbound crossing of the Alps en route to Rome with an entourage of 50,000 men and 37 elephants is still undetermined. Based upon conflicting historical accounts, the travel day becomes the marker of multiple potential routes connected by an indeterminate event network in which known instances such as setting frozen rocks on fire, losing yet another elephant, or skirmishes with enemy Alpine tribes negotiate against each other in order to establish the most likely 'optimised' route.

Having taught at the Bartlett for five years, Francesca Hughes started running Diploma Unit 15 at the Architectural Association in 2004, and was joined by Noam Andrews in 2007 alongside Matthew Wells as consulting engineer. She is author/editor of *The Architect: Reconstructing Her Practice* (MIT Press, 1996) and is currently completing a book entitled False Economies: The Architecture of Error. She is a partner of Hughes Meyer Studio, a multidisciplinary practice whose first built project, Artscope (in collaboration with Sanei Hopkins Architects) received an RIBA award in 2005.

'Unit Factor' is edited by Michael Weinstock, who is Academic Head and Master of Technical Studies at the Architectural Association School of Architecture in London. He is co-guest-editor with Michael Hensel and Achim Menges of the *Emergence: Morphogenetic Design Strategies* (May 2004) and *Techniques and Technologies in Morphogenetic Design* (March 2006) issues of *Architectural Design*. He is currently writing a book on the architecture of emergence for John Wiley & Sons Ltd.

Notes
1. See Amy E Slaton, *Reinforced Concrete and the Modernisation of American Building, 1900–1930*, John Hopkins University Press (Baltimore, MD and London), 2001 for a detailed account of the transformation the introduction of reinforced concrete brought about in construction culture, particularly via the institution of standards and specifications. The meeting of lab coat and labourer was most acute in the years preceding the invention of the mixing truck, when concrete batches needed to be mixed and, crucially, tested on site. How an augmented component 'revolution' might redistribute skill sets, resources and power in building production remains to be seen. I suspect that, like its early Modernist predecessor again, control will move back up the chain to the professional domain.
2. See Michael Weinstock, 'Can architectural design be research? Fabricating complexity', in Bob Sheil (ed), *AD Protarchitecture: Analogue and Digital Hybrids*, No 4, Vol 78, July/August 2008, pp 126–7.
3. See Le Corbusier, *Towards a New Architecture*, Architectural Press (London), 1989, p 230.
4. Ibid. See also Achim Menges' excellent article 'Pluripotent components and polymorphous systems', *AA File* 52, Summer 2005.
5. Though of course it is not. This is simply false modesty – as with most architectural accounts it is always clear exactly who the author is.

Karl Kjelstrup-Johnson,
Hypercontextual Urban Infrastructure, Naples, Italy, 2009
Mediating between virtual and geophysical data black holes, a subterranean superstructure utilises a 3-D temporal GIS system in order to insert space for aerobic waste processing and archaeological extraction in Naples. Navigating through the indeterminacy of toxic ground, Camorra activity, and a matrix of unsurveyed historic cavities in the volcanic tuffa, a responsive ground-penetrating and tunnelling system simultaneously constructs a virtual public database of subterranean Naples and a set of physical spaces hypercontextual to these complex local conditions.

Basking in a World of Your Own Making

As the credit crunch bites in, are pockets of young architects reviving a battle against commodified materialism? Neil Spiller describes how he has experienced this close to home with his own class of 2009 at the Bartlett which has reactivated its own brand of Surrealist cybernetic research, inspired by Dalí.

In a 1968 essay subtitled 'The Cylindrical Monarchy of Guimard', Salvador Dalí rallied against 'the total lack of eroticism of Le Corbusier and other mental weaklings of our most-sad modern architecture.'[1] Dalí offers us not the Corbusian 'machine for living in', but 'Houses for Erotomanes not to inhabit but to live in and even, with the permission of Monsieur Le Corbusier, to dream in, and even to rave in'.[2]

What is perhaps more significant is that with this particular essay Dalí manages to equate Art Nouveau styling and anamorphic techniques with the emerging sciences of genetics. He asks the reader to conduct an experiment by dropping a toothbrush into a shiny cylinder. The distortion of the reflection of the toothbrush imitates the geometry of the double helix of DNA and simultaneously the non-orthogonal geometries of Art Nouveau.

At this stage in his career, Dalí is interested in cybernetics, quantum physics, notions of hyperspace, genetics and holograms and much more, gleaned from an awareness of contemporary scientific advances. His art forever searched for the next lateral connection to enable him to expand the envelope of Modern art, and vicariously Modern architecture.

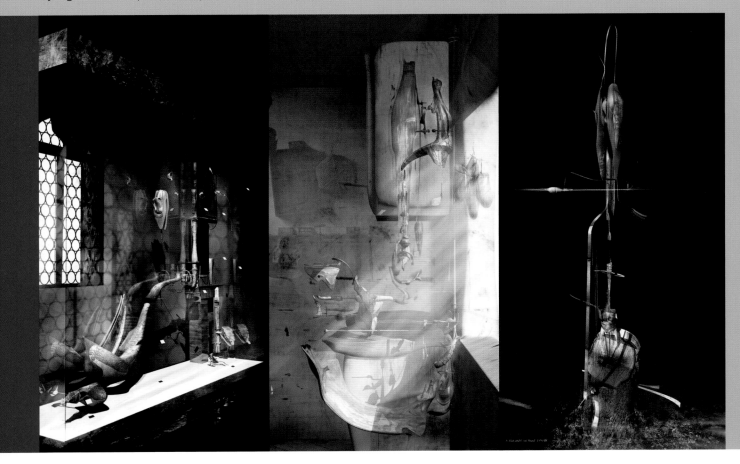

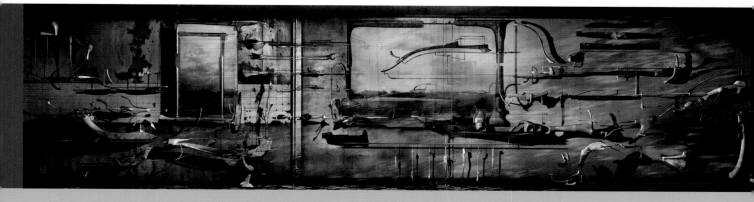

Tom Cartledge, Surrealist Auction House in the Woods, Unit 19, Bartlett School of Architecture, UCL, 2009
Tom Cartledge has created a self-contained world that references the fundamental notions of second-order cybernetics which believes we all create individual perceptions of the world and our place in it by 'building' within it. The work is also highly surreal as it posits a world that explores the psychic and phenomenal notions of its maker, but it is equally imbued by ideas of language and particularly its traces and poetics. On one level, it is also a language of love.

The activation of cybernetic research committees for the purpose of resurrecting and glorifying the great thoughts that fell victim to materialism. For example: the combinatory wheels of Lull(e), the natural theology of Raymond de Sebonde, the treatise of Paracelsus, the inspired architecture of the Gothic Mediterranean Gaudí, the hyperaxiology of Francesco Pujols, the anti-Jules Verne poetics of Raymond Roussel, the theoreticians of traditional mystical thought, all those who are truly inspired. Do not profane their unjust tombs. Exhume them and bury them again, but this time in the most sumptuous futuristic mausoleums ever imagined by Nicholas Ledoux.[3]

Just such a reactivation of Surrealist cybernetic research has occurred in my unit at the Bartlett this year. Tom Cartledge has developed an extraordinary concoction of ideas and forms that Dalí, while being jealous, would welcome into the Surrealist pantheon.

Cartledge's project is approached past a ring of Surrealist objects reminiscent of the unsettling parade that was part of the Exposition Internationale du Surréalisme at the Galerie Beaux-Arts in Paris in 1938:

Having circumnavigated Dalí's 'Rainy Taxi', visitors are led towards a corridor which featured a parade of sixteen mannequins. A different surrealist artist had 'dressed' each one, (only one woman artist was among these sixteen). Behind each mannequin was fixed a blue metal Parisian street sign, some real, some fictional, alluding to other Surrealist interests. With the exception of Arp's, the mannequin streetwalkers are engaged in sexual provocation, being in various states of undress and/or allure.[4]

But Cartledge's circles of associations are bizarre agglomerations of forms that set out the syntax of his architectural language. Their link to the mannequins of 1938 is through their allusions to movements and curvatures of the body, and the body's symbiotic relationship with the positing of architectural space and its trace within that making.

We next come across, in a clearing in a wood – always a wood – a small cottage with a simple door – a door with door furniture that a crazed Surrealist trapper might make, with furry sinews stretched into bloody mechanisms.

Once through the door, a world of breathtaking objects is displayed for the viewer's predilection. Each object says something about the owner's (Cartledge's) view of the world and its ordering. Every object is a juxtaposition of takes on the form/function dichotomy, its seasonal and diurnal calibrations and its implied history of its making and the body that made it. So, for example, some objects reach out to the horizon (through the cottage's windows) to accentuate differences in horizons on differing days and act, like Duchampian stoppages, as new ways to measure the interior of the cottage utilising light and shadow. The hand of their maker is also a register of bodily force and action. This is undoubtedly a house for an 'Erotomane', WHATEVER ONE IS.

So it seems there are still pockets of young architects up for the battle against commodified materialism. *Δ*+

Neil Spiller is Professor of Architecture and Digital Theory and Vice Dean at the Bartlett, University College London.

Notes
1. Salvador Dalí, 'Concerning the Terrifying and Edible Beauty of Art Nouveau Architecture', in *The Collected Writings of Salvador Dalí*, edited and translated by Haim Finkelstein, Cambridge University Press (London), 1998, p 373.
2. Ibid.
3. Ibid.
4. Lewis Kachur, *Displaying the Marvellous*, MIT Press (Cambridge, MA), 2001, p 38.

Designing for Disassembly (DfD)

The redundancy of existing buildings that leads to demolition and the unnecessary disposal of structures and their parts is one of the most challenging aspects of the current construction industry. This large-scale problem of obsolescence leads to the squandering of existing materials and resources on a massive scale. Here Elma Durmisevic and Ken Yeang advocate a means by which disassembly can be designed into buildings from the outset.

In nature, everything is recycled. The waste of one organism is the food for another. Designing eco-mimetically, we need to imitate ecosystems and reuse and recycle everything that we make and build as humans within our built environment, eventually reintegrating these back into the natural environment in a seamless and benign way. One way to address this is to design for disassembly at the outset.

A long-standing misconception is that buildings last longer when made of more durable materials. However, everyday demolition practice proves the opposite. Buildings are designed to last 70 to 100 years, yet today buildings with an age of only 15 years are demolished to give way to new construction. Developers and real-estate managers warn that there is a mismatch between the performance of existing building stock and dynamic and changing demands with respect to the use of buildings and their systems. Fifty per cent of investment in building construction in the Netherlands is spent on adaptation of existing structures, while only 42 per cent of new construction is due to the replacement of demolished buildings. In addition, the European building industry accounts for 40 per cent of waste production, 40 per cent of energy consumption and CO_2 emissions, and 50 per cent of material resources taken from nature.[1]

Currently, most buildings are demolished with little or no attempt to recover any of their constituent parts for reuse. Most are designed for an end-of-life scenario, for assembly but not for disassembly and reuse of their components. The different functions and materials of a building system are integrated (during construction) in one closed and dependent structure that does not allow alteration or disassembly. This inability to remove and exchange building systems and their components results

not only in significant energy and material consumption and increased waste production, but also in buildings that lack spatial adaptability and technical serviceability.

If the building sector is to respond to global environmental and economic challenges, it needs to adopt new construction methods. Rather than destroying structures and built systems to adapt them to new requirements, sections need to be disassembled and their components reassembled in new combinations. This requires consideration of how we access and replace parts of built systems, and how they are integrated so that they can be replaced later on.

Reconfigurable Building Structures with High Disassembly Potential

The moment when buildings start to transform is the moment when they can be reconfigured and reused, or simply demolished and sent to waste-disposal sites. Here, the technical composition of a building is crucial for the life cycle of the building and its materials. The debate concerning the durability of structures thus needs to focus not only on the type and durability of materials, but also on interfaces, arrangements of materials and technical composition.

Building components and systems have different degrees of durability. While the structure of a building may have a useful life of up to 75 years, its cladding may last only 20 years. Similarly, environmental service systems may only be adequate for 10 years, and interior fit-outs may change as frequently as every three years. Nevertheless, it is quite common for parts with short durabilities to be permanently fixed or chemically bonded, which prevents easy disassembly. Thus at the end of the components' or the environmental service systems' useful life, there is usually little option other than demolition, with its associated high levels of waste disposal.[2]

Recognising the potential of disassembly will mean that the flow of materials from disposal to reuse and recycling can be diverted to save not only the materials themselves, but also the energy they embody. One contention is that energy embodied in materials may have a greater negative impact on the environment than the operational energy used by buildings over their life cycle.

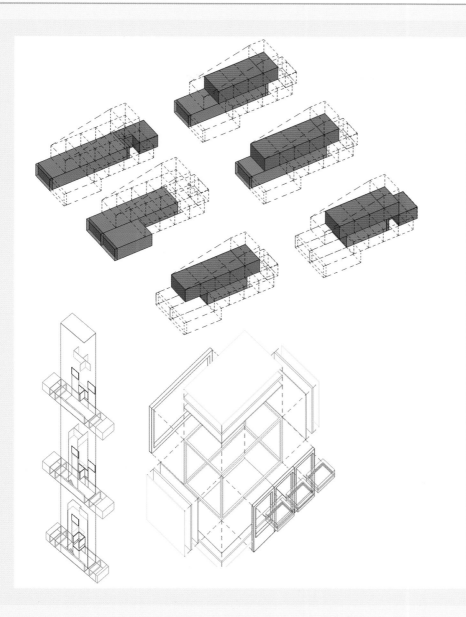

4D Architects, Transformation Study for a housing project, Enschede, The Netherlands, 2009
Different transformation scenarios correspond to different arrangements and hierarchies of subsystems and components.
top: Study of long-term transformation scenarios of the DfD housing project.
bottom: Matching of the scenarios with the hierarchy of independent and exchangeable technical systems.

Taking this into account, ecodesign could risk becoming ad hoc if designing for disassembly (DfD) does not become an integral part of the design process.

DfD aims at the design of transformable building structures made of components assembled in a systematic order suitable for maintenance and reconfiguration of their variable parts. Every scenario for transformable building results in a different technical composition and different hierarchy of parts. The DfD concept therefore affects the design of all material levels that are accounted for by the technical composition of buildings, and accentuates interdependent relations between the transformational process and disassembly techniques.

The concept introduces three dimensions of transformation for buildings: spatial, structural and material. The key to each dimension of transformation, which leads ultimately towards a three-dimensional transformable building, is disassembly. By adoption of the concept of DfD, spatial systems of a building become more amenable to modifications and change of use. New steps in the exploitation of structure by reuse and reconfiguration can be achieved, and conscious handling of raw materials through their reuse and recycling can be stimulated.[3]

The main characteristics of buildings designed for disassembly are:

• setting the boundary conditions for transformation and specification of long- and short-term use scenarios;

ALL ITEMS CONTAINED IN THE KIT APPEAR BELOW

REPLACEMENT BODY AND INTERIOR PARTS

1 × Replacement body shell
1 × Left hand light pod housing
1 × Right hand light pod housing
1 × Front bumper
1 × Rear bumper
1 × Bonnet
1 × Boot lid N.B. body and panels are unpainted
1 × Heater grill
1 × Front laminated windscreen
1 × Front windscreen rubber
1 × Front screen rubber chromed plastic filler strip
1 × Burr walnut veneered dashboard
1 × Pair of seat retrim cover assemblies
1 × Full interior black carpet set
1 × Full wiring loom (state alternator or dynamo preference)
1 × Interior centre console
1 × Pair interior screen pillar trims
1 × Pair underdash board wiring cover trims
1 × Pair door panel trims
1 × Pair door panel firmers

1 × Hood storage tray
1 × Hood frame
1 × Soft top hood P.V.C. (mohair optional)
1 × ¼ Tonneau cover (mohair optional)
30 × Female tanax fasteners
30 × Male tanax fasteners
1 × Packet hood buttons
1 × L/H door shell
1 × R/H door shell
1 × Crash pad on top of dash

REPLACEMENT MECHANICAL PARTS

1 × Lotus galvanised chassis
2 × Rear springs
2 × Rear shock absorber inserts
4 × Rotoflex drive couplings
24 × Rotoflex bolts
24 × Rotoflex nyloc nuts
1 × Engine mounting — left hand
1 × Engine mounting — right hand
1 × Gearbox mounting
2 × Bottom shock absorber bush kits
2 × Top shock absorber bush kits
2 × Anti-roll bar lower link bushes
2 × Top differential mount bushes
2 × Top rear suspension mountings
4 × Rear suspension large 'A' frame bushes
4 × Rear suspension small 'A' frame bushes
2 × Rear suspension 'A' frames
1 × Steering rack (rebuilt unit on exchange basis)
2 × Steering rack mounting bushes
2 × Front shock absorbers complete with springs

8 × Front suspension tubular wishbones 'with bushes fitted'
2 × Top front suspension ball joints
1 × Front suspension L/H bottom trunion
1 × Front suspension R/H bottom trunion
1 × Trunion bush kit for both trunions
Trunion and top ball joint nuts/bolts

£2,875 + Vat

LIMITED PERIOD ONLY

Open 7 days, kit on display at Northwich.
All goods are offered subject to availability, the Company reserve the right to alter or modify without notice, prices are subject to alteration without notice.

Christopher Neil Sportscars would like to point out that they have no association whatsoever with Lotus Cars Ltd., nor do they purchase parts directly from the Lotus factory. Now in our 10th year of business with literally thousands of satisfied customers worldwide the parts we sell are all Christopher Neil parts, proprietory parts or genuine Lotus parts.

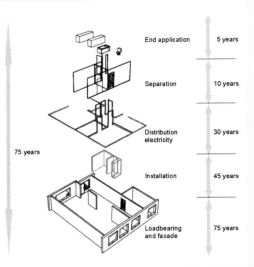

End application	5 years
Separation	10 years
Distribution electricity	30 years
Installation	45 years
Loadbearing and facade	75 years

75 years

4D Architects, Study of disssembly strategies, The Netherlands, 2004
Initial versions of the 1962 Lotus Elan car were available as a kit to be assembled by the customer. Like cars, buildings are made of components that have diferent life spans. The disassembly strategy here for a typical housing project in the Netherlands, proposes a hierarchy of independent systems (physical levels) that can increase the transformation capacity of existing and new housing.

- separation of material levels, which correspond to independent building functions;
- creation of an open hierarchy of distinct subassemblies;
- use of independent interfaces as the intermediary between individual components;
- application of parallel instead of sequential assembly/disassembly processes; and
- use of dry or mechanical connections in place of chemical connections.

To achieve this, a fundamental change in architects' perception of buildings is needed in terms of:

- conceiving buildings not as static structures but as dynamic and open ones that can easily adapt to changing requirements;
- extending the transformation capacity of buildings and systems by considering the whole life cycle of the building and building systems;
- treating building materials as long-term valuable assets through their whole life cycle by utilising reconfiguration, reuse and remanufacturing options at the building, system and material levels;
- considering waste and demolition as a design error;
- decoupling fixed function–material relationship in buildings via the design of reconfigurable systems; and
- involving the construction industry in the whole life cycle of the building and building systems.

Elma Durmisevic, Open building system designed for disassembly, 1999
The main interface of the Villa te Bilthoven building in Bilthoven, the Netherlands, is designed as an intermediary between six building components that accommodate different functions. Each component can be independently disassembled and replaced without disrupting the coherency of the structure. The building was designed in collaboration wth buro Evelein.

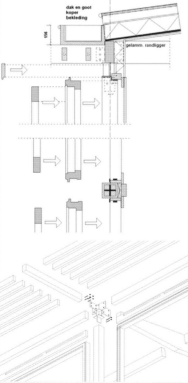

A building's technical configuration is an indicator of its sustainability. Green design and engineering therefore require a major shift away from closed building systems and assemblies and instead towards open and transformable systems with high disassembly potential, ie independent and exchangeable building components. DfD allows for future changes to external facades and to internal partitionings and configurations. It requires a building's services to be independent of its fabric and provide easy access for servicing and alterations. These are the prerequisites for future reuse and recycling that must be considered at the outset and will enable greater diversity in the design of our green buildings. ∆+

Dr Elma Durmisevic is the head of the 4D Architects office in Amsterdam, and is an associate professor at the Universities of Delft and Twente in the Netherlands. Her main focus is on new ways of bridging the current gap between demolition and disassembly, and her design portfolio includes urban planning, multifunctional sports facilities, offices, villas and flexible building systems.

Ken Yeang is a director of Llewelyn Davies Yeang in London and TR Hamzah & Yeang, its sister company, in Kuala Lumpur, Malaysia. He is the author of many articles and books on sustainable design, including *Ecodesign: A Manual for Ecological Design* (Wiley-Academy, 2006).

Notes
1. Center for Building Statistics in the Netherlands – Bouwvergunningen, huur-en koopwoningen, 2007.
2. E Durmisevic, 'Transformable building structures: Design for Disassembly as a way to introduce sustainable engineering to the building design and construction', PhD thesis, TU Delft, February 2006.
3. Ibid.

Futuristic Retail Spaces

Valentina Croci finds the entries to a competition organised by the Benetton Group, displayed at the 2009 Milan Triennale, a rich source for emerging retail design trends. Not only do the various schemes express new relationships between shops and the city, they also highlight the importance of interactivity and experience for the physical shopping environment.

1/3

Luís Pereira Miguel, Combispace, 2009
The focal point of the space is the double-height stair that becomes a foyer for visitors. The galleries on the various floors are sectioned off using movable curtains that allow for continuous changes. The surfaces of the first floor feature a pneumatic grid that can be used to raise or lower modules to create supports or seating. The display elements, such as the mirrors in the changing rooms, feature interactive devices that receive information about products or offer connections to the Internet. A 115-metre (377-foot) long conveyor belt of clothes runs the entire length of the store.

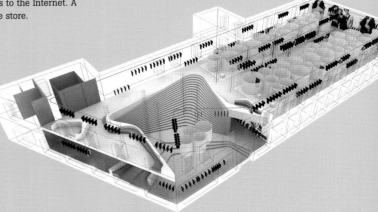

First Floor Imterior Organisation / End Side

FIRST FLOOR PLAN

Ground Floor Imterior Organisation / Approach Side

GROUND FLOOR PLAN

Ayako Kodera, Recyclescape, 2009
A continuous space is here divided by a sculptural element made from recycled clothes hangers. The latter functions as a spatial backdrop and support for the various display cases and stands. The architect took the idea of the stacked clothes hangers from falling flakes of snow.

The Colorsdesigner (International Retail Design Competition) is an initiative of the Benetton Group, promoted by POLI.design, the Milan Polytechnic's consortium created to offer university research to the business sector and foster creativity and innovation. The competition was launched in 2007 and concluded with an exhibition at the Milan Triennale in 2009. It received over 700 submissions from some 40 countries around the globe. The objective of the initiative was to stimulate innovative visions of retail spaces (for fashion stores like Benetton's). In fact, the brief contained few restrictions and no mention of a location, indicating only a maximum area of 500 square metres (5,382 square feet). The various projects submitted by young (mainly in their thirties) architects, notwithstanding a few naive and 'fashionable' trends, make it possible to identify important signals of change, above all in the role of retail spaces with respect to the city and the use of these spaces by those who visit them.

The winner of the competition, Portuguese architect Luís Pereira Miguel, presented an environment that reconnects with the theme of the famous Prada store in New York by OMA. The Combispace project fluidly combines the two levels of the store, focusing on an entry stair-foyer that is both a stage and theatre, turning visitors into actors on a stage. An elevated level of reconfigurability defines the display spaces: they can be easily and flexibly transformed by relocating mobile display units that can also be used to divide the store into different spaces. Surfaces, furnishings and equipment are integrated with interactive technologies, transforming the store from a simple retail outlet into a space for events or to relax in – there is also a cafeteria on the first floor.

The architect underlines the necessity of integrating digital technologies within the physical experience of retail, using not only interactive devices that facilitate the fruition of the products for sale, but also employing entertainment software that unites the real experience with its digital counterpart (for example, blogs or social networks). The retail experience is thus progressively more focused on personalisation and a sense of participating in the stories behind the products with which we identify. An increase in the user's direct and simultaneous participation in real and virtual branded spaces represents the new frontier of client loyalty, as well as the most effective method of communicating corporate values. This intuition, similar to the flexibility of space, unites the ostentatious store fittings – clothes-filled display cases that slide on tracks along the entire length of the store – and was one of the elements that sold the project to the jury.

A different approach was taken in Tokyo-born Ayako Kodera's Recyclescape project (special mention), which focuses on the reuse of clothes hangers to divide and fit out the store. The retail space thus becomes a sort of gallery of sculptural installations, where the goods on display are an integral part of the scenery. Finalist Milan architect Tommaso Bistacchi's Immensola proposal represented yet another play on the continuous redesign of the retail space. Using an approach more akin to that of a designer than an architect, Bistacchi proposed a transformable display module, leaving the architectural volume as a simple shell. The varying form of the interiors and the flow of visitors here render the space dynamic and constantly changing.

A similar concept is to be found in the Fabric Shop by Godefroy Meyer (special mention). This young Canadian architect presented a display system composed of a mobile structure made of steel cables and sheets of perforated steel that is used to compose the interior space. The transparency of the structure, reminiscent of a fabric, overcomes the visual barrier of traditional display systems.

More generally, the competition highlighted the need for retail spaces that function as points of social interaction, with a strong aesthetic character. Merchandise is no longer presented in the linear rows of a supermarket, but in structures that invite us to discover and experience spaces filled with elements in continuous transformation. The store is the physical outpost of the brand and must therefore respond to the evolution of the market and instruments of communication. It is not yet clear if the winning project – Combispace – will ever be built. However, the Colorsdesigner initiative represents, for Benetton, an important step in the investigation as to how to transform the retail outlet.

The Benetton Group has long been a pioneer in this field. Of the many important innovations implemented by the architects Afra and Tobia Scarpa in Benetton stores from the 1960s onwards, we can mention the elimination of the sales counter in favour of a simple table and cash register, thus removing the barrier between the seller and the buyer; the legibility of the store interior from the street-front shop window, without any backdrop; the use of diffuse lighting to underline the chromatic richness of the clothes on sale; the use of neutral, steel-framed shelving; and the removal of protective packaging giving buyers direct access to the merchandise – all of which are now standard practice in all stores.

The group has also focused on the capillary presence of stores in the world's city centres (5,500 stores in 120 countries) developing franchising chains that are united by a coherent and coordinated image. However, if the winning strategy to date was sought in standardised stores around the globe, Benetton is now developing unique megastores that propose a lifestyle in harmony with the culture and context of the country in which they are located. Ten new flagship stores are currently being completed by, among other well-known architects, Massimiliano and Doriana Fuksas, Alberto

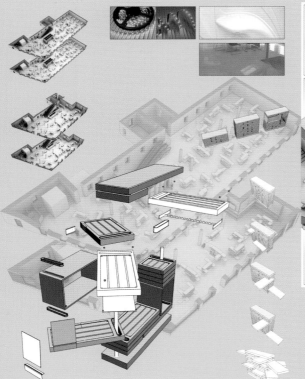

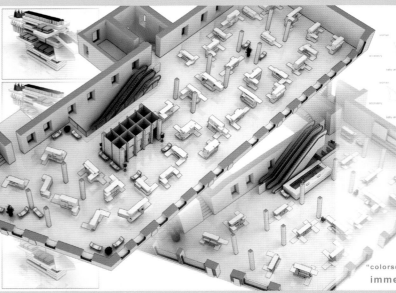

"colorsde
immer

Tommaso Bistacchi, Immensola, 2009
The interior design of the store uses a single display module that is kept free of the perimeter of the space. This element is composed of modular shelves that are fixed to one another and rendered self-supporting. Immensola's economic approach allows for the continuous transformation of the image of the store and variations in the flows of visitors inside its spaces.

Godefroy Meyer, Fabric Shop, 2009
The project finds its force in the structure and materials of the display cases. The perforated steel is reminiscent of fabric, rendering the display cases transparent. The modularity of the panels allows for the creation of different spatial configurations and houses the concealed lighting and wiring systems.

Campo Baeza and the less famous Arassociati and Laboratorio.Quattro. The stores will open in cities from Russian Samara to Pristina in Kosovo, Istanbul and the Kazak city of Aktyubinsk, underlining the importance of new markets.

The 700+ competition submissions revealed a number of important trends: on the one hand, the retail outlet as the extension of an experience of the city, recalling it with sounds, jumbo screens and images of urban contexts with the shop; on the other, retail outlets as isolated oases with lounge zones for cultural and recreational events. Kazuya Yamazaki of Tokyo proposed converting outlets into a series of temporary installations spread across the city, transforming these spaces into events and unique experiences.

The competition projects also highlighted the role of digital technology in the fruition of merchandise: digital and physical space penetrate one another in a personalised and direct approach, selected by the user. Indeed, a number of submissions proposed the development of software for self-picturing in the shop spaces and uploading directly to social networking sites.

The projects also demonstrated a concern for the sustainability and obsolescence of products. For instance, some entrants designed special containers for collecting old clothes, or systems of exchange between users for 'scrapping' old goods. Analogous to this, other submissions featured workshops and spaces within shops for remodelling clothes, highlighting a critical vision of product life-cycles and the mechanisms of consumerism.

Beyond the single solutions proposed, the competition ultimately pointed out the need to reconsider the user's experience in the retail space, and the rethinking of traditional shopping rituals. Δ+

Translated from the Italian version into English by Paul David Blackmore.

Valentina Croci is a freelance journalist of industrial design and architecture. She graduated from Venice University of Architecture (IUAV), and attained an MSc in architectural history from the Bartlett School of Architecture, London. She achieved a PhD in industrial design sciences at the IUAV with a theoretical thesis on wearable digital technologies.

McLean's Nuggets

Physical Models of Intangible Stuffs

With our increasing ability to digitally model the invisible physical phenomena of fluid-dynamic media such as wind or sound, it is too easy to forget the usefulness of trying to physically model such intangibility. In Fritz Winckel's exposition of physical acoustics he models the beginning of Beethoven's *Eighth Symphony* and creates a topological map of music, or at least a profile of frequency peaks and troughs with the added fourth dimension of time.[1] This attempt to model sound was also explored in the 1950s and early 1960s by Gunnar Fant, one of the pioneers of early vocal synthesis.[2] Developed at the Royal Institute of Technology in Stockholm, early experiments included what Fant and colleagues described as an 'Electric Line Analogy' of voice production – the vocal tract viewed as an acoustic tube of varying cross-sectional area, with vocal chords at one end and mouth at the other. Modelled electronically using a series of cascaded inductance/capacitance circuits, each circuit represented a length of vocal tract which could be adjusted to simulate a range of notional cross-sectional areas. By altering these various cross sections and by feeding a variable-source noise into the system, the tweaking of each circuit and combinations of these settings could reproduce English vowel sounds and some consonant sounds, creating an electronic circuit that analogised and manipulated physical space and, as a result, could speak. Solid-state electronics and, latterly, digital processing have replaced such self-illustrating audio techniques. More challenging again is the attempt by psychologist John H Clark to create a 'Map of Mental States',[3] or indeed a whole series of maps of mental states in his book of the same name. By defining a mental site or a map of the mind (not a mind-map) firstly in two dimensions and then in three, Clark diagrammatises a set of mental states in ordinary life, mental illness and mysticism. The maps start simply by ascribing intensity values to states of feeling such as pleasant or unpleasant, and then add specific events and levels of attention or concentration. Not only are these explorations interesting in that they explore the limits of such mind states augmented by meditation or chemical stimulant, but it is the various attempts to physicalise emotion and trace the oscillating mental state as a kind of reciprocating motion or trajectory that seem so remarkable. The foreword by cyberneticist Gordon Pask congratulates Clark for projecting his model (or 'nearly-a-theory' as Pask calls it) upon a geometrical three-dimensional space, and relates the almost reverse analogous process by which the human eye captures multi-dimensional space on to a two-dimensional retina.

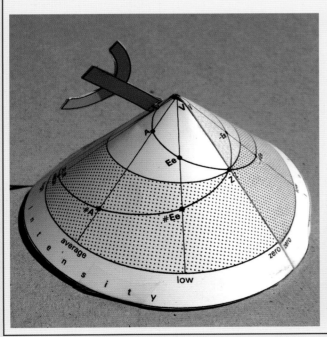

left: Physical model of Beethoven's *Eighth Symphony* from Fritz Winckel's *Music Sound and Sensation*.

far left: Paper model of a map from John H Clark's *A Map of Mental States*.

Time Gentlemen Please

Our ability to absorb and utilise a number of mobile electronic communication devices continues unabated, and while our patterns of social-communication behaviour are changing and possibly even evolving albeit in a technology driven one-dimensional symbiosis, we seem less able as human beings to comprehend, search out or indeed employ more innate means of information exchange. Biologist Rupert Sheldrake in his recent book *The Sense of Being Stared At* explores numerous serendipitous phenomena of the 'extended mind' that we all anecdotally understand and regularly experience, such as various human forebodings, *déjà vu* and the eponymous 'sense of being stared at'.[4] All these examples of what Sheldrake calls the 'Seventh Sense' relate to our potential abilities of precognition. In JW Dunne's remarkable book *An Experiment with Time* he describes his experiences of premonition, which he is eventually able to decipher through a process of recording and understanding (or at least interpreting) his dreams, a process which he sets out in some detail in a series of experiments for reader participation.[5] One crucial observation of Dunne's to which Sheldrake refers is that dreamt 'images which relate indisputably to the near-by future are about equal in number to those which pertain similarly indisputably to the near-by past',[6] and thus while sleeping we are divested of the unidirectional movement of time to which we are confined during our waking hours. Interestingly, a copy of Dunne's book was found in Richard Buckminster Fuller's 'core' library[7] and may explain Fuller's ability to be so continuously productive while constantly traversing spaceship earth. In 1981, Fuller calculated the total distance he had travelled by land, sea and air to date was more than 5.6 million kilometres (3.5 million miles) – equivalent to 440 times around the world. Fuller always carried three watches, one for each of three different time zones – past, present and future anybody?

Gum

In our continual search for new materials and material uses, we must be careful not to overlook the multipurpose utility of ancient concoctions such as gum arabic. This natural gum, harvested from the sap of acacia trees, is produced in Chad, Nigeria, Somalia and Senegal, with Sudan currently supplying two-thirds of global demand. Gum arabic is water soluble, adhesive, edible, and is used as a paint binder and stabiliser by artists, a non-toxic and lickable glue for stamps and cigarette papers, as an emulsion and binding agent in cosmetics, and is a key ingredient of many well-known confectionery products and branded carbonated soft drinks (it reduces the surface tension of liquids, thus enhancing the 'fizzing' effect). It is also used as a suspension medium and emulsifier of medicines to treat bronchitis, diarrhoea and upper respiratory tract infections. Gum arabic has an E Number of E414, which classifies it as a (thickener, stabiliser, emulsifier) food additive. It was used by the ancient Egyptians as part of the mummification process and, according to a recent statement by Anita Benech of German gum arabic importer Alfred L Wolff: 'The world still needs and requires gum arabic: No other product is able to cover as many functionalities.'[8] △+

Notes
1. F Winckel, *Music Sound and Sensation*, Dover Publications Inc (New York), 1967.
2. C Roads, A Piccialli and G De Poli, *Representations of Musical Signals*, MIT Press (Cambridge, MA), 1991, pp 300–01.
3. JH Clark, *A Map of Mental States*, Routledge & Kegan Paul (London),1983.
4. R Sheldrake, *The Sense of Being Stared At*, Arrow Books (London), 2004.
5. JW Dunne, *An Experiment with Time*, Faber & Faber (London), 1943.
6. Ibid, p 96.
7. Dunne's book is included in a list of 69 titles listed on the Buckminster Fuller Institute website as RB Fuller's Library. http://www.bfi.org/our_programs/who_is_buckminster_fuller/buckminster_fullers_archives/r_buckminster_fullers_library.
8. L Partos, 'Sudan scraps gum arabic monopoly to liberalize market', Food Navigator, 9 June 2009. Food Navigator provides daily news on one of the most technologically advanced global industries. See http://www.foodnavigator.com/Financial-Industry/Sudan-scraps-gum-arabic-monopoly-to-liberalise-market.

'McLean's Nuggets' is an ongoing technical series inspired by Will McLean and Samantha Hardingham's enthusiasm for back issues of *AD*, as explicitly explored in Hardingham's *AD* issue *The 1970s is Here and Now* (March/April 2005).

Will McLean is joint coordinator of technical studies (with Pete Silver) in the Department of Architecture at the University of Westminster. He recently co-authored, also with Pete Silver, the book *Introduction to Architectural Technology* (Laurence King, 2008).

Architectural Design **Architectures of the Near Future** September/October 2009

What is Architectural Design?

Launched in 1930, *Architectural Design* is an influential and prestigious architectural publication. With an almost unrivalled reputation worldwide, it is consistently at the forefront of cultural thought and design.

Architectural Design is published bimonthly. Features include:

Main section

The main section of every issue functions as a book and is guest-edited by a leading international expert in the field.

Δ+

The Δ+ magazine section at the back of every issue includes ongoing series and regular columns.

Truly international in terms of the subjects covered and its contributors, *Architectural Design*:

- focuses on cutting-edge design
- combines the currency and topicality of a newsstand journal with the rigour and production qualities of a book
- is provocative and inspirational, inspiring theoretical, creative and technological advances
- questions the outcomes of technical innovations as well as the far-reaching social, cultural and environmental challenges that present themselves today

How to Subscribe

With 6 issues a year, you can subscribe to Δ (either print or online), or buy titles individually.

Subscribe today to receive 6 issues delivered direct to your door!

£198 / US$369	institutional subscription (combined print and online)
£180 / US$335	institutional subscription (print or online)
£110 / US$170	personal rate subscription (print only)
£70 / US$110	student rate subscription (print only)

To subscribe: Tel: +44 (0) 843 828
Email: cs-journals@wiley.com

To purchase individual titles go to:
www.wiley.com